THE BEST OF FROM OUR OWN CORRESPONDENT
CORRESPONDENT
VOLUME 3

EDITED BY MIKE POPHAM
AND GEOFF SPINK

Broadside
BOOKS LIMITED

LONDON

Typeset by   BP Integraphics
              Bath
              UK

Printed by   Bath Press
              Bath
              UK

Cover photograph of the civil war in Yugoslavia courtesy of Magnum Photos Ltd,
London.

FOREWORD

"THANKS YOUR SIKKIM FOOC* JUST MADE SATURDAY MORN-
ING PROGRAMME REGARDS ROGER" the cable read.

By then I was back at base in New Delhi. Filing from Sikkim – this was
1959 – had presented communications problems unique even to the Indian subcontinent: no radio station, no radio circuits to London, not even a telex. But
the night clerk at the tiny, sleepy post office was equal to the challenge. "We
shall send your message to BBC London by Morse Code", he announced. Like
me he knew how to send the letters SOS (... --- ...) as well as the signal
for erase: .... (8 or more dots). But little else. Fortunately there was a book.
We learned as we went on. It was dawn before Calcutta acknowledged safe
reception of our dots and dashes, and promised to transcribe and telex our
effort to London.

The "Roger" in my cable is Roger Lazar, editor of *From Our Own Correspondent* for thirteen years, starting in 1955. None of us ever said No to Roger.
Partly because we all loved him dearly: no team of foreign correspondents could
have had a more considerate editor. But it was also that he stretched us, bringing
our reporting up to standards that some of us didn't know we could reach.
In my own case, I might dash off a two-minute news piece in twenty minutes
– and sometimes spend the whole of an agonising night, at the end of a tiring
week, writing and re-writing FOOC. It was an outlet that raised our self-respect.
Also, it was a programme that people listened to. And occasionally – this was
the ultimate reward – one's piece would be printed in *The Listener*.

When I had left televison production in 1958 to become a foreign correspondent, my chief at Lime Grove warned me that by joining News I'd be walking
into an editorial straight-jacket. Then in a bar I ran into Rene Cutforth, who
had returned, permanently embittered, from reporting the war in Korea and
had – so he claimed – punctured his resignation speech by throwing an ink
bottle at the Editor-in-Chief. "The bastards won't even allow you to say its
raining unless you quote a source," he growled.

But times were changing. Hugh Carleton Greene, who had been the *Daily
Telegraph*'s man in Berlin until he was expelled by Goebbels, vanquished the

---

* Fooc: the BBC correspondents' acronym for *From Our Own Correspondent*.

old *bête noire* of only quoting sources. "My advice", said Greene, "would be to sail as close to the wind as possible ... as long as you get it right."

FOOC, of course, was always the outlet for that kind of reporting, and happily it still is. As every schoolboy knows, the BBC has no editorial policy. Its correspondents are enjoined not to editorialise, in the sense of reporting from a fixed ideological position, and they show bias at their peril. What they do is interpret the news – "analyse" is the word favoured in high places – which I would translate like this:

say what you think as well as what you know, as a result of being where you are.

That is what I hope readers will find in this book.

Charles Wheeler,
London September 1992.

ACKNOWLEDGEMENTS

The editors would like to express their thanks to all of the correspondents and stringers who contributed to this book, and to Vanessa Whiteside, Ann Courtney and Catrina Popham who patiently helped prepare the manuscript. They are also grateful to the following for their advice and encouragement in compiling this volume: Catherine Bradley, Bob Jobbins, Alex Vincenti, Peter Brooks, Jenny Abramsky, Martin Cox, Brian Walker and Chris Wyld. Last, but by no means least, sincere thanks to Donna Eaton and the staff of the BBC's Foreign Traffic Department, without whose support no edition of the programme would ever be broadcast.

Mike Popham and Geoff Spink
BBC, London September 1992.

CONTRIBUTORS

Gordon Adam	Head of the BBC's Pashto Service
Paul Adams	Reported for the BBC from Israel
Janet Anderson	Senior Producer, BBC African Service
Chris Bowlby	Reports for the BBC from Czechoslovakia
Ben Bradshaw	Reporter with BBC Radio's *The World At One*
Mark Brayne	Deputy Head, BBC Central European Service
Alex Brodie	BBC Jerusalem Correspondent
Nick Caistor	Talks Writer, BBC Latin American Service
Tom Carver	Reports for the BBC from Southern Africa
Kevin Connolly	BBC Moscow Correspondent
Hugh Crosskill	Head of the BBC's Caribbean Service
Mark Doyle	Reported for the BBC from Ivory Coast
Leo Enright	BBC Dublin Correspondent
Matt Frei	BBC Southern Europe Correspondent
Misha Glenny	BBC Central Europe Correspondent
Carrie Gracie	Reports for the BBC from China
Brian Hanrahan	BBC Television Foreign Affairs Correspondent
Humphrey Hawksley	Reports for the BBC from Hong Kong
Jeremy Harris	BBC Washington Correspondent
Red Harrison	Reports for the BBC from Australia
Lindsey Hilsum	Senior Producer, BBC Current Affairs World Service
Jane Howard	Reports for the BBC from Yugoslavia
Dan Isaacs	Reports for the BBC from Mozambique
Stephen Jessel	BBC Paris Correspondent
Fergal Keane	BBC Southern African Correspondent
Bridget Kendall	BBC Moscow Correspondent
Andy Kershaw	BBC Radio One disc-jockey and freelance writer
Alex Kirby	BBC Environment Correspondent
Graham Leach	BBC Europe Correspondent
Alan Little	Reports for the BBC from Yugoslavia

Tim Llewellyn	Formerly BBC Middle East Correspondent
Simon Long	Reported for the BBC from China
Jonathan Marcus	Defence Correspondent, BBC World Service
Barnaby Mason	Formerly BBC Cairo Correspondent
Julian May	Senior Producer for BBC Radio's *Kaleidoscope*
David McNeil	BBC Washington Correspondent
Christopher Morris	Reported for the BBC from Sri Lanka
David Powers	Reported for the BBC from Japan
Hugh Prysor-Jones	Presenter with BBC World Service's *News Hour*
Adam Raphael	Freelance Broadcaster
Paul Reynolds	BBC News and Current Affairs Diplomatic Correspondent
Jonathan Rugman	Reported for the BBC from Turkey
Stephen Sackur	BBC Middle East Correspondent
Tony Samstag	Reports for the BBC from Norway
Charles Scanlon	Reports for the BBC from Mexico
Beppe Severgnini	Italian Journalist
Philip Short	BBC Tokyo and Far East Correspondent
Alex Shprintsen	Freelance Journalist and Broadcaster
Arthur Smith	Comedian and Playwright
Mark Tully	BBC Delhi Correspondent
Carole Walker	BBC Television News Reporter
Jenny Waters	Producer, BBC Current Affairs World Service
Tim Whewell	BBC Moscow Correspondent
Andrew Whitehead	Political Correspondent, BBC World Service
David Willey	BBC Rome Correspondent
Derek Wilson	Reports for the BBC from Italy
David Willis	Commentator on US Affairs, BBC World Service

CONTENTS

Page

THE AMERICAS

THE MIDDLE EAST

Page

Page

EUROPE: WEST

One thing common to several European countries, it seems, is the wave of racial intolerance borne out of a fear of mass immigration. Spain, France, Belgium, Germany and even Sweden all saw a dramatic rise in support for parties of the extreme right. The Austrian Freedom Party also became a beneficiary of that trend.

THE DWARF DEMAGOGUE

BEN BRADSHAW   VIENNA   5 DECEMBER 1991

You don't expect demagogues to be so small; but then historians would probably claim they often are, and anyway he would deny being one. Diminutive, but well proportioned, rather too trendily dressed and protected from the torrential rain by a group of umbrella wielding heavies, this was Jörg Haider – the latest darling of the European right, whose disingenuously named Freedom Party is celebrating a string of dramatic electoral advances. Mr Haider was in the market square in Klagenfurt, the capital of his regional power base of Carinthia in southern Austria, doing what he does best – working on the real and the latent fears and prejudices of ordinary Austrians, and showing off his all-year suntan. The weakness of the Austrian immigration law is not immediately apparent in Klagenfurt where there's not a foreign-looking person in sight, but with a suntan and row of teeth like Haider's, who cares. The local schoolgirls clearly didn't as they squealed for kisses and autographs, mobbing the 41-year-old lawyer as if he were a pop star.

In Austria, as in much of affluent Europe, the new buzz word is immigration. Mr Haider saw this coming some time ago and exploited his clairvoyance to devastating effect. When he won the governorship of Carinthia in 1989, it was the first time such a position in post-war Austria had not been filled by one of the two major parties. Since then, preaching a mixture of free market economics and immigration control, Mr Haider and his Freedom Party have gone from strength to strength. Campaigning on a blatantly anti-foreigner ticket in elections in Vienna last month, the Freedom Party trebled its vote and ousted the main centre-right People's Party from second place in the capital.

Austria, in contrast to Britain or the United States, could not be called a multi-racial society. Mr Haider and his friends want to keep it that way; putting an immediate stop to new immigration and the repatriation of foreign workers once their usefulness to the Austrian economy has been exhausted. That's not radically different from what Switzerland has done for years, but Austria doesn't have the same history. When an Austrian called Adolf Hitler annexed his native country in 1938, he was welcomed enthusiastically by many of his countrymen, who felt they were returning to the greater German fold where they belonged. In proportion to their population, there were four times as many Austrians in key position in the Nazi apparatus as there were Germans. After the war, the Austrians went through little of the soul-searching and denazification that characterised post-war West Germany; the Austrians were allowed, by and large, to sweep their past under the carpet. Little Austria, so the official version went, had been Hitler's first victim, not his most loyal henchman. So when Mr Haider gets steamed up about foreigners, eyebrows are bound to be raised. It's not just his size, his charisma and his skill at the visuals that Haider shares with demagogues. He's also much better at saying what he's against than what he's for. He's against immigration, of course, and against diluting Austria's Germanic culture. He's against more than one foreign child for every two Austrian ones in school classrooms. The implication – although many of the so- called 'foreign' children were born in Austria – is that they hold their Austrian classmates back.

He's also against high taxes, people he calls social security scroungers, and 'bureaucracy'. Here, he is cleverly striking a chord with Austria's economic liberals who might find the Freedom Party's xenophobic tendencies repugnant, but who feel their country is long overdue for a Thatcher-style social and economic revolution. Post-war Austria has been dominated by the consensus politics of the two main parties – the centre left socialists (now Social Democrats) and the centre right People's Party – recently so badly mauled by Mr Haider. While the system used to serve Austria well, it's degenerated badly in recent years into cosiness and complacency, job carve-ups between the two main parties, stagnation and a series of corruption scandals. To the frustrated and discontented,

Mr Haider can appear like a breath of fresh air. Add to them Austria's latent far-right vote, which some commentators put as high as twenty per cent, and the Haider potential becomes clear.

A few months ago it looked as if Mr Haider could be finished, politically, when he was forced to resign as governor of Carinthia after praising Hitler's employment policy. He has also saluted Austrians who did what he termed "their duty" under the Nazis, and has made no secret of the fact that both his parents were enthusiastic supporters of the Third Reich. He may have been forced to resign from the top job, but he's still deputy governor, leader of the Freedom Party and more popular than ever. Attempts to win himself and his party international respectability have eluded him: the Freedom Party has been forced to give up its voting rights at the Liberal International – the international grouping of liberal parties – because liberals from other countries feel Mr Haider is – well – not quite liberal enough.

Austria is a beautiful country whose friendly people bake delicious cakes. So it seems a bit unfair that it only hits the headlines when the world thinks it has something to feel embarrassed about. For the last six years that embarrassment has been President Kurt Waldheim, who symbolised his country's collective amnesia by not being able to remember exactly what he did in the Second World War. President Waldheim retires next year – but Jörg Haider could prove just as damaging to Austria's image. Whether or not he does will depend on whether or not the Austrian voters let him.

One of the results of the Maastricht Summit of December 1991 was that European Community leaders agreed to cooperate more fully on cross-border police matters. A new Europol police force was to be set up which, if some states had their way, could have turned into a body like America's FBI. But our Europe Correspondent, Graham Leach, found some Europeans only too keen to take matters into their own hands.

EUROPE'S NOSEY NEIGHBOURS

GRAHAM LEACH   BRUSSELS   19 DECEMBER 1991

"**D**addy, there are two policemen at the door." With these words, an Orwellian, Kafkaesque (or any other cliché you care to think of) nightmare began, with my family forced to witness my subjection to Europe's greatest miscarriage of justice since the Dreyfus Affair. It is a story of how Denis Healey and Sir Geoffrey Howe conspired to have me apprehended by the Belgian law enforcers. At its root was my frequent absence from home during the busy weeks prior to the Maastricht summit, and how, upon my eventual return to my own house, an over-zealous member of the neighbourhood watch reported me to the police as a suspicious stranger – a would-be burglar.

I have, with hindsight, pieced together the sequence of events. It began as I was driving home in my car last Saturday morning listening to *The Week in Westminster* on *Radio 4*. The aforementioned elder statesmen were engaged in a fascinating conversation about the results of Maastricht; it was, in fact, so absorbing that I stopped my car about two roads away from where I live to jot down a couple of points they were making. A woman drove by me in a white car, did a u-turn, and drove back past, administering a fierce glare in my direction in the process. With Sir Geoffrey and Mr Healey finished,

I completed my journey home but, by then, another interesting EC discussion had started; rather than lose the long-wave signal by driving into my garage, I stayed parked on the drive to hear out the programme. The white car reappeared; the driver again surveyed me closely. Half an hour later the police arrived: a full check of my identity card and car documentation ensued, my children observed, awe-struck.

Once the two officers had satisfied themselves that I was not an intruder, I asked them what it was all about. A lady two roads away had telephoned to say that I was not the person who lived at No.36. Indignant, I rang the lady in question, whose name suggested she was Flemish, Dutch or German, to ask what she was up to. "There have been several burglaries lately," she explained, "and I thought you might have been casing the house." "But that's my own house," I protested. "Did you not think to check with one of my neighbours?" "Yes, I realise now that's what I should have done," she replied apologetically.

Thus was the matter left. But there is a wider concern here. The Belgian police now have my name, address and identity number. I've no idea what kind of police computer I now appear on nor, given the growing ties between them, which other European police forces can now flash my name up onto their screens, even though I was innocent. And it's all down to the fact that one of my neighbours decided to extend her quite laudable fulfilment of civic duty to become a self-appointed policeman. But then, in these northern parts of Europe, the busy-body is a not unusual breed. There's always someone ready to report you to the police if you're not abiding by one or other petty law – like not mowing your lawn on a Sunday, nor on weekdays between twelve and two pm or after eight pm. Last summer, on a sweltering day, when lawn-mowing was possible only when the sun went down, a friend living nearby was confronted by a neighbour brandishing a copy of the communal regulations, simply because she was still mowing at ten past eight!

For me, the Germans are the worst. In the area around the Bundestag in Bonn, car spaces are so limited that there are provisions for leaving your vehicle half on, half off the pavement, on condition you allow a one metre gap for pedestrians to pass. I was once accosted by a crusty old man who actually measured out the distance, insisting I was five centimetres under the required limit. I'm not advocating disobedience of the law, you will understand, merely suggesting that in these parts the nosey parker and the police informant are more prevalent than in Britain. I'm also pointing to the protections that may have to be found as Europe's police forces increasingly harmonise their surveillance of Europe's citizens.

The latest nuclear-powered submarine to join Britain's Royal Navy – HMS Triumph – was completing its final trials before becoming fully operational at the beginning of 1992. Triumph is the seventh and last of the Trafalgar-class Fleet submarines to be built for the Royal Navy, and with the ending of the Cold War it may be quite some time before any more hunter-killer submarines are ordered.

GOING BELOW IN TRIUMPH

JONATHAN MARCUS   LONDON   22 JANUARY 1992

The sheltered waters of the Raasay Sound off the north-west coast of Scotland present an image of peace and tranquillity. Situated between the mainland and a chain of islands running northwards from the Isle of Skye, this is the typical picture postcard view of the Highlands.

As dawn broke, the fleet tender, no bigger than a fishing vessel, chugged out to sea and we could just make out the distant hills on each side of us sweeping down into the water. Up ahead a small red light glowed in the darkness, and slowly the brooding bulk of the stationary submarine became visible. For despite its apparent tranquillity, Raasay Sound is actually a high-technology naval training range. Hydrophones spread out on the sea-bed pick up acoustic signals from submarines and surface vessels enabling naval war games to be tracked in three dimensions. The British Underwater Test and Evaluation Centre is one of the most important training areas for Royal Navy submarines. And today the Trafalgar-class boats like *HMS Triumph* are among the most important vessels in the Navy – the true capital ship, having taken over from the battleships of old.

Once I had scrambled on board and descended into the belly of the beast, it quickly became clear that what I could see on the surface was only about one-fifth of the boat's total volume. There are three main decks housing the control room, weapons compartments, sonars, generators and of course the reactor that gives the nuclear submarine its extraordinary range and endurance. There are also the facilities for the crew – around one hundred officers and men – and in these boats nearly everyone has their own bunk. On smaller diesel-powered boats the watches or shifts still share bunks, each watch giving up its sleeping space as it goes on duty.

For anyone brought up on submarine films of the Second World War, one of the greatest surprises is actually the amount of space available. It is far from claustrophobic. But the differences with Second World War submarine operations don't end there. I suppose the greatest cliché from the movies is the episode when the submarine comes under air attack, the steely-eyed Captain and bridge-crew tumble down the hatch and the order is given to crash dive.

Well, those days are long gone. It takes *HMS Triumph* between eight and thirteen minutes to fully vent its tanks and disappear beneath the waves. But once down it tends to stay there until the end of its patrol. The essence of modern submarine warfare is to remain undetected. The pinging active sonar sending out sound waves to bounce off enemy contacts is carried, but active sensors tend to give the submarine away. And for the most part *Triumph* depends upon passive sensors which have no tell-tale signature of their own.

But with the Cold War over, what are boats like *Triumph* actually going to do? Their former task was to hunt Soviet submarines, either ballistic missile-carrying boats or hunter-killers like themselves that might have threatened the West's own nuclear deterrent. There is still a residual if perhaps less critical task in monitoring Russian submarine deployments. But naval commanders are stressing that the submarines' invisibility remains a major asset as a deterrent, to enforce internationally sponsored blockades or embargoes, or just to preserve an unseen presence in regions of possible tension.

As more and more countries obtain submarines for their navies, British commanders stress the need to maintain the sort of technical edge that boats like *Triumph* provide. But whatever the comforts of the modern submarine, I'm afraid that five hours underwater away from the daylight, was enough for me. Confinement gives you a rather different perspective on the world – when I boarded the night-sleeper train at Inverness for the journey back to London, my tiny cabin seemed almost palatial compared with what the crew of *Triumph* routinely put up with.

24

Early in 1992 David Willey published a book about Pope John Paul II called "God's Politician". How did he set about researching a volume about such a controversial world figure?

GOD'S POLITICIAN

DAVID WILLEY   ROME   22 JANUARY 1992

The Vatican is at once very tiny and very large. The Pope's temporal domain covers a few acres on the left bank of the Tiber but his influence extends worldwide. The difficulty in writing this book was one of scale, of access to the person of the Pope and also of language. Let me explain.

A pope, any pope, carries on his back the weight of almost two thousand years of European history and religious traditions. Suddenly, in 1978, the new Pope is a Slav, and, for the first time in four centuries, there is a non-Italian leading the Roman Catholic Church. Karol Wojtyla from Poland became leader of some 900 million Catholics around the world, half of them living in Latin America, the next largest group in Europe, then Africa, then Asia.

And instead of following the example of his predecessors and welcoming pilgrims to the shrine of Saint Peter in Rome, this Pope himself sets out on a series of unprecedented foreign travels. He has covered the globe, visiting more than eighty countries at the rate of four major foreign tours each year, interrupted only for a short period following the attempt on his life in 1981. It was during these exhausting journeys that I first began taking notes for an assessment of the political and religious power of the Vatican at the end of the twentieth century – or, as John Paul would put it, on the eve of the third Christian millennium.

On each flight, the Pope would come to the back of the plane, where the journalists accredited to the Vatican sat, to answer questions – any questions. It was the nearest that the Vatican has ever got to organising Papal press conferences which of course never happen in Rome. Very occasionally, a correspondent

25

would get invited into the Pope's private cabin for a short exchange of views, normally off the record.

There was also the chance to talk to Cardinal Casaroli, the architect of post-war Vatican policy in Eastern Europe, a courteous and charming man, and other members of the Pope's entourage: his top political advisers; his Swiss bodyguards (not wearing the dashing uniform they normally display at the Vatican, but dark suits bulging with shoulder holsters); his doctor; his baggage master and his valet.

So the travels provided an unexpected entry into the flying Vatican. Back in Rome, I tried - and must admit that I failed - to penetrate the tight barrier separating the Pope from the press. "The Pope does not give interviews," was the reply to my repeated written and verbal requests for an interview for my book, but it then occurred to me that this did not matter very much. There are so many papal utterances on record on every conceivable topic, all gathered together in a bulky volume at the end of each year, that there is no lack of detail about what the Pope thinks about any particular issue.

What I did have at my fingertips was a unique world view of the state of his church as seen by the Pontiff on every continent. From Alice Springs in the middle of the Australian desert to teeming and lawless Kinshasa in Africa, from turbulent central America to Hiroshima in Japan, I was able to see how the Pope dealt with the very diverse situations facing his bishops and priests in different parts of the world.

This contrast of scale - the worldwide activities and political influence of what is, in effect, a very small and tightly-run central bureaucracy of the church in Rome, working on the budget of a single small-to-medium-sized international business corporation - was very striking. So was the resentment I often heard expressed at the failure of the men in the Vatican to respond to the views of many members of the Pope's flock, including priests and even bishops, on birth control, for example; or the potential role permitted to the clergy in countries where great social and political injustices were being committed by governments against their citizens.

The complaint I often heard was that the Pope was applying different standards in his native Poland where his political influence over the transition from communism to democracy has been crucial, and in countries such as the Caribbean republic of Haiti whose elected president - a Catholic priest, Father Aristide, was sacked by his religious order for his political activities and ambitions, and who has received no support whatever from the Vatican, either before or after he was forced to flee his country in a military coup.

In writing about the Pope there is also a difficult linguistic problem. He thinks and writes in Polish, his daily working language is Italian, he is a talented linguist, but much papal talk is expressed in church jargon and needs explaining and clarifying for the uninitiated. 'Popespeak' is long-winded – when you have a political point to extract from a religious homily, you can find yourself wrestling with a serious semantic problem.

But the challenge of making this preliminary assessment of an historic papacy was well worthwhile, despite the inevitable inadequacies of my effort. I have also accumulated some papal travel souvenir kitsch which one day may have curiosity value, like that storeroom in the Vatican where the bric-a-brac of gifts accumulated during the Pope's travels is stored away for posterity. A beer can inscribed with the Vatican cross keys produced for the Papal mass picnic in Adelaide; a telephone and a hair-dryer stamped with his Holiness's name by one of the grateful airlines which provided the charter for his travels, and so many papal souvenir key-rings recording international travels which, if connected end to end, would stretch from the Vatican as far as the moon and most of the way back.

In Italy the campaign for the elections in April 1992 was just getting underway. It promised to be exciting and volatile because the established parties were being challenged by a plethora of new ones, representing a growing protest vote. In early February, one such party, the Partito dell'Amore – the Party of Love – launched its campaign.

ALL YOU NEED IS LOVE

MATT FREI   ROME   8 FEBRUARY 1992

As I sipped my glass of sparkling white wine, Marcella, the Love Party's Chief of Culture and Propaganda, explained to me why she had taken time off from teaching Italian literature to high school children to organise the party's campaign.

We were standing beneath a pink dome next to a gushing green fountain. There was flamenco music. The wall was festooned with election posters of the party's front-runners: Moana, Barbarella and Bambola. All three were stark-naked, although one of them was wearing what looked like a python around her neck. From their posters the candidates – all well-known Italian porn-queens – beckon the voter in poses which many a country would have deemed unconstitutional. The Love Party, Marcella explained, was founded to fill the vacuum created by the collapse of communism and the erosion of Catholic power in Italy. "These are historic times," she continued. "We are reaching the end of the century and an end of the century depression is looming. Many people are fed up and disillusioned; we, the Love Party, want to be an antidote to all this, and bring love back to Italian society."

This sounded surprisingly like the New Year's message of the Pope. "Universal love and complete sexual freedom," Marcella corrected. Ah, I see. "All the

28

candidates of this party," she said, "are heroes of our society." I was introduced to one of the heroes, Barbarella. She spoke about the need to defend gay rights in Italy and fight the continuing bigotry of the clergy on that subject. Barbarella who wore, amongst some other things, a huge pirate's hat and displayed a cleavage that looked as if it was about to combust, was being utterly earnest. Did her attire not detract from the seriousness of the message? "Not at all," she retorted, "it's an essential part of our appeal."

The party faithful were a mixed bunch: they ranged from giggling students who'd become familiar with the leading candidates in their other incarnation on the video screen, to earnest academics who intend to cast their protest vote through the Love Party. A porn queen in parliament is of course nothing new in Italy; in 1987 the bare-chested Cicciolina was elected and took her place with other independent deputies in the chamber. La Cicciolina has said she'll retire from politics, but in deference to her pioneer status, she's been made the Honorary President of the Love Party.

You may think the Love Party's a bit of a joke, but the people working for it certainly don't. They're merely following the well-trodden path of the protest vote, which has flourished in Italy for decades, thanks to the stifling continuity of party politics here.

Since 1948 Italy has had eleven general elections, but more than fifty governments. Most of them have fallen because the precarious majority of the ruling coalition has collapsed. It's made the process of government extremely difficult – not to say tiresome. But behind the chaos lies extraordinary continuity. With one interlude, the centre-right Christian Democrats have been the perpetual party of government. But the Italian political landscape is gradually changing, like a glacier thawing. Marcella was right: the collapse of communism in the former Soviet Union is having a profound impact on Italian politics. The left, which used to be dominated by the Communist Party – once the largest in Western Europe – is fragmenting and becoming weak, thus depriving the Christian Democrats of their justification for perpetual re-election. The end of the ideological divide in Italy has encouraged many Italians to focus on the inadequacies of their government, the deeply entrenched clientelism of the political parties, and the dead hand of a bureaucracy nurtured by party political patronage. As the glacier creaks into motion, the Love Party is merely one of the splinters thrown up by it. But there are others, equally bizarre.

Earlier this week another attractive young woman announced her candidacy for parliament; she'll be the front runner for the neo-fascist MSI Party in Naples, where she's almost certain to be elected. Her name is Alessandra Mussolini, and she's the granddaughter of the dictator who ruled Italy from 1922 to 1943. She told a newspaper earlier this week that Fascism was no longer a pejorative word, and that she was proud of her grandfather, whose example she would follow, once elected. But not to worry, Italy is not experiencing a resurgence of Fascism, nor for that matter will the Vatican have to defend the country from the temptations of free love. But who knows? In the new parliament, maybe the Love Party will hold the balance of power.

On 27th February, 1986, Sweden's prime minister, Olaf Palme, was murdered in Stockholm. Six years on, the murder remained unsolved and continued to arouse passions in Scandinavia. But this was by no means the first such assassination in the country's history.

THE JANTE LAW

TONY SAMSTAG   OSLO   27 FEBRUARY 1992

King Carl XII of Sweden was less than twelve years old when he killed his first bear, and by the time he was eighteen, he had moved on to people. According to one contemporary source, Carl's was "the name at which the world grew pale"; a modern Swedish historian describes him as "a classic figure in the gallery of world history . . . a man of his word and a spartan warrior-king." His incessant military campaigning won dominion for Sweden over the Baltic and much of central and eastern Europe during the early eighteenth century. His assassination in 1718 is still a mystery today, 274 years later.

The king was only thirty-five when he was shot fatally in the head by assailant or assailants unknown. He was fighting the Norwegians (among others) at the time, and modern Swedes have always been rather tickled at the thought that he might have been done in by one of their doltish country cousins. The assassination seemed to demoralise the Swedish forces even more than they were already; the various campaigns collapsed, and a fifty-year long 'Era of Liberty', as it is known, ensued.

Like the murder of Mr Olaf Palme in 1986, the aftermath of the 18th century regicide was pandemonium: Carl's body was spirited away, and there turned out to be far more holes in the official report on the assassination than in the king's head. One of the more persuasive and persistent theories is that he was shot by one of his own troops, most of whom were fed up with years of non-stop warfare and wanted to go home. One disaffected officer even confessed to the murder in delirium, during a fever from which he was not expected to recover;

31

he did, however, and promptly recanted.

As a journalist, I occasionally reflect ruefully that the assassinations of Carl and Palme, separated by almost three centuries, are possibly the only dramatic news stories of any international significance to have originated in this part of the world since the Vikings. That's my problem of course, and I do exaggerate. But the Scandinavians' problem is real enough: what to make of the Palme murder, which still looks most unlikely ever to be solved.

The Prime Minister, you may recall, was shot and killed as he walked home from the cinema late in the evening with his wife. He had dismissed his body-guards for the day, and apparently decided to go out on impulse at the last minute. Because the Nordic nations have long prided themselves on the open and egalitarian nature of their society, in which even leading statesmen are ill-advised to put on airs, the Palme tragedy is often described as 'the death of innocence' in Scandinavia. Moreover, as the bungled hunt for the Prime Minister's killer got nowhere, Sweden (and to a degree Scandinavia as a whole) was seen by a suddenly attentive world to be conducting its affairs with a naive incompetence, bordering on the farcical. So another image was badly tarnished: that of the orderly, efficient functioning of the Nordic social-democratic institutions.

Discussions of the Palme murder tend to peak, naturally enough, at this time of year. An English former colleague of mine (he recently left Stockholm to live in the south of France) has just published a book about Palme in which he proposes by far the most interesting theory I have come across for several years. The killer, according to this theory, was a very ordinary Swede – perhaps with some military training – but with no political axe to grind, and by Scandinavian standards, no personality disorder to speak of. He or she had reacted to Palme in a way typical of many Scandinavians – hating him simply because of his prominence and success: his brilliant performances in Parliament, his very public inability to suffer fools gladly, his high international profile as a man of peace and the first European statesman to take on the Americans over Vietnam; there was nothing average about Olaf Palme, and this, in Scandinavia, is an unforgivable sin. Many Swedes, perhaps even a majority, detested him for it.

There is a compelling logic to this theory, which few who have not lived in Scandinavia will appreciate. It is the poisonous logic of a very small society in which conformity is the supreme virtue. My former colleague explains it through the work of a Dane, named Axel Sandemos; a tormented soul, and one of modern Scandinavia's most influential writers, albeit virtually unknown outside the region. Sandemos wrote about a fictional community, Jante by name, based on the small Danish town where he was born in 1899, and subsequently hated. He emigrated as an adult to Norway which turned out, of course, to be much the same. The town lived by a set of rules, a parody of the Ten Commandments, known as *The Jante Law*. It is worth reciting in full – Scandinavians often do – and it goes something like this:

You shall not believe that you are anything.
You shall not believe that you are as good as us.
You shall not believe that you are wiser than us.
You shall not believe that you are better than us.
You shall not believe that you know more than us.
You shall not believe that you are superior to us.
You shall not believe that you are worth anything.
You shall not laugh at us.
You shall not believe that anyone cares about you.
You shall not believe that you can teach us anything.

Ironically, Denmark itself has come a very long way since Sandemos published his *Jante Law* in 1931; but the rest of Scandinavia has scarcely changed a bit. The *Jante Law* is still very much the law of the land, and more than capable of felling a giant. I would not be at all surprised if it was, in effect, the *Jante Law* that killed Olaf Palme – or, for that matter, King Carl XII, almost three centuries ago.

Amid millions of pounds worth of free publicity, the Euro Disney amusement park – just outside Paris – opened to the public in April 1992. As Euro Disney was the subject of some controversy in France, we asked Stephen Jessel to cast an eye over it.

GRUMPY GOES TO EURO DISNEY

STEPHEN JESSEL   PARIS   15 APRIL 1992

W hatever else Euro Disney may have done it has produced two good one-liners. From the Tricolour Corner, the claim that the park will be a cultural Chernobyl disseminating, insidiously and invisibly, lethal American cultural poison. From the Star-Spangled Corner, the observation that a nation with France's history and traditions should not be frightened by a mouse.

There are now four Disney kingdoms and I have been to three of them; all bar Tokyo, though it's 25 years since I went to the one in California and I remember nothing of it, but I was in Florida two years ago, and so in a position to compare. If I were a Frenchman, I would be immensely unworried by the arrival of this phenomenon in the sugarbeet fields of Marne la Vallée, but there are some things I might well dislike.

Disney's treatment of some of its subcontractors has not won it many friends here. Life for the people living nearby, treated to twice weekly firework displays late at night, plus all the traffic generated by the park, will be pretty miserable. As a citizen of the nation which did much to disseminate the idea of the rights of man, I would be offended by the insistence that Disney employees – I will refuse to call them cast members – should conform to a decreed type of physical appearance.

As a taxpayer, I might think that my money might have been better spent on projects other than new roads and railway links to service an American commercial enterprise. I would have been outraged that my left-leaning morning newspaper devoted its first 13 pages to the park one day last week... but a cultural Chernobyl? When the Champs Elysées are already lined with burger joints? When French intellectuals can argue that Jerry Lewis is funny and regard Woody Allen as a secular saint? Much of the comment here seems to me to have missed the point. If I had any money I would not invest it in Euro Disney, not for political or aesthetic reasons, but because I am not at all sure that it will work.

The day I went was warm and cloudless, better actually than any I had in Florida, but that was an exception. When the rain sweeps across the Ile de France, as it does quite often, the park won't be much fun. Euro Disney claim that more is enclosed here than in Florida but it's still a good trek from the Haunted House to Star Tours, excellent though they both are. The park is expensive, the entry price of about £23 – payable from 12 years old upward (childhood ends early *chez* Disney) – is perhaps justifiable; you do have the run of the park and its 29 attractions for 12 hours. But the merchandise inside, and the food, are far from generously priced and the adjoining hotels are no give-away either.

What it seems to me Disney's critics have failed to understand is that the park, while quite un-European in all important respects, is also quite un-American. I don't mean that the earnest efforts to present cheapened and coarsened versions of Peter Pan or Alice in Wonderland or the Swiss Family Robinson really reflect their European origin. Nor that Disney's comically valiant effort, to prove that the name originally comes from Isigny in Normandy, proves anything. And one thing at least is very American; the security men, products of a certain sinister school of charm, all blazers and sunglasses and earpieces and walkie-talkies; clones of the sort of experts who advise Central American police chiefs on the use of electrodes.

But overall Disneyland is just as unreal back in the United States as it is here. Take the passion for scooping up every trace of litter: have you ever walked, or rather, waded down Eighth Avenue in New York? Consider the pasted-on "have a nice day" smiles – notably absent, I may say, in Euro Disney where French moroseness is much in evidence, not without reason. For a really rapturous welcome, try changing a sterling traveller's cheque in Chicago; or the technical wizardry – why do you think the American car industry is on its knees? And the wild west rodeo with its celebration of physical skill and strength. I've been to American national parks where people never leave their cars.

Disneyland, wherever it is, is humour without wit, light without shadow, the present without a past, sound without echo. For good or evil, it has the cultural and philosophical resonance of a Tom and Jerry cartoon. If people rush to see Sleeping Beauty's castle, then refuse to take two hours to go down to the Loire Valley to see the real chateaux at Chenonceaux or Chambord or Amboise, that's because they wouldn't go there anyway, not because capering robots dressed as Caribbean pirates have used up all the cultural space available. Euro Disney, says President Mitterand, is not his *tasse de thé*; but he pointed out that it is providing a lot of work in an area that needs it, though he didn't add that the pay levels are not very high.

I went the day before it opened officially. An opinion poll conducted among 10-year-old children found some criticism of the organisation, or lack of it, at the pre-opening festivities; but also elicited the comment that the occasion had been one of the best days in the life of the sample (which was on the small side). But then again this was probably no less misleading than certain other opinion polls in recent living memory.

As for melancholy, misanthropic, middle-aged males, another sample of one found that he rather enjoyed it, though nothing on earth would persuade me to admit it publicly.

Ireland was gripped by an extraordinary scandal, in May 1992, following the admission, by one of the country's best known bishops, that he was the father of a seventeen-year-old boy. The bishop admitted that he had used more than £60,000 of church funds to pay maintenance for the child, but said that the money had since been repaid. According to Leo Enright in Dublin, only one scandal comes close to this in Irish history.

A FALL FROM GRACE

LEO ENRIGHT   DUBLIN   13 MAY 1992

"**P**ok! The tardy cork flew out of Mr. Crofton's bottle ... 'This is Parnell's anniversary,' said Mr. O'Connor, 'and don't let us stir up any bad blood. We all respect him now that he's dead and gone.'"

James Joyce captures Ireland's shame as we join his characters on Ivy Day in the Committee Room.

"THE DEATH OF PARNELL 6th October, 1891. Mr. Hynes cleared his throat once or twice and then began to recite:

'He is dead. Our Uncrowned King is dead.
O, Erin, mourn with grief and woe
For he lies dead whom the fell gang
Of modern hypocrites laid low.'"

The folk memory of Ireland will never forget what happened to Charles Stuart Parnell, the leader of the Home Rule Party, who died a broken man one hundred years ago last October. Somehow, sometime, perhaps, the Irish may forgive all that England did to them over the centuries. But can they ever forgive what they did to themselves?

Parnell was destroyed because he loved a married woman. The man who brought his country to the brink of nationhood, and who boasted that he could drive a coach and four through any English law, was cast out by his people because he broke the Sixth Commandment. The people were incited to this act of national suicide by their clergy. The parish priest of Roundwood in Co. Wicklow, put the Church's case quite succinctly: "Parnellism is a simple love of adultery and (I say to you as Parish Priest) their cause is not patriotism, it is adultery."

Memories came flooding back this week of Charles Stuart Parnell and the woman he loved, Mrs. Kitty O'Shea. A hundred years from now, they may still remember Bishop Eamonn Casey and his lover, Annie Murphy. It is the most sensational liaison in Ireland for an entire century. And the irony of all this has not been lost on most people. The Irish and their politicians still sometimes fear their bishops; but they don't necessarily like all of them. The fall of a bishop in such ironic circumstances – one hundred years and nine months after the death of Parnell – might appeal to the less charitable side of some, were it not for the fact that Eamonn Casey was the one bishop most people would prefer it not to have happened to. He was Ireland's ecclesiastical equivalent of the singing nun. Full of life and energy, and with a rebellious streak that outraged at least one superpower, and delighted the liberal-minded Catholics in Ireland who wanted a Church with a human face.

Casey devoted his early life to campaigning for the homeless in Britain. To the dismay of many, he was promoted as a result and taken away from the very work that he did so well. As Bishop of Kerry, and later of Galway, he was a constant thorn in the side of governments. First in Ireland, as he pressed for social spending, then abroad, as he stubbornly battled against American foreign policy in Central and South America. At a time when the Pope was decrying liberation theology, Eamonn Casey was exporting it from Ireland. When President Reagan visited Ireland, Eamonn Casey refused to meet him.

It now transpires, through the traumatic testimony we have heard this week, that when the bishop was refusing to meet the President of the United States he was also, time and again, refusing to meet his own son. Bishop Casey resigned last week as the scandal broke around him. He flew to the United States and remained silent for five days. Those five days of silence were more damaging than all the seventeen years of deception. For it gave Annie Murphy the time to tell her side of the story, and what the Irish people heard appalled many of them.

Casey's personal popularity with the public was based on a shared sense of fair play, of justice for the poor, for the homeless, for the dispossessed. Then

Annie Murphy told reporters of her struggle to save her son from adoption; of the rows over child support; of the bishop's claims that the boy wasn't his; of the years of denial and financial hardship. Bishop Casey was transformed from the status of Ireland's most liberal bishop to – in the eyes of some – a perfect simile for all that was reactionary and uncaring in the Church's attitude to women.

Bishop Casey has now publicly acknowledged the grievous wrong that he did to Annie Murphy and their son. It is the confession he had to make. It has restored some honour for him among his people. I feel certain that although this affair will be remembered for a long time, a hundred years from now the Irish will not weep for him, as some still do when they remember what the Church did to Parnell, and when they hear the anger in the words of William Butler Yeats:

"The Bishops and the party that tragic story made,
A husband that had loved his wife, and after that betrayed.
But stories that live longest are sung above the glass
And Parnell loved his country. And Parnell loved his lass."

On June 2nd 1992, the people of Denmark voted against the ratification of the Maastricht Treaty – thereby putting the brakes on closer European integration. The Danish result came as something of a shock, and was seen as a severe setback for supporters of a federal Europe.

A SPANNER IN THE WORKS

GRAHAM LEACH   COPENHAGEN   4 JUNE 1992

It's been a scorching week in Denmark, and I'm talking not just about the political temperature. Summer has announced itself across the entire Nordic region. In Copenhagen that's meant a boat trip along the city's canals, ducking one's head to avoid the low bridges, admiring the royal yacht moored in the harbour, skirting past the famous mermaid with her head restored following an act of desecration some years ago. And then, at a waterside restaurant, lunch of moist lemon sole, caught that morning by fishermen who are back in port before sunrise, downing their first six-pack of the day before breakfast.

As I sat at a pavement table watching the world go by, Denmark appeared a nation of beautiful people, apart from the hordes who spill off the ferry boats after an overnight trip from Sweden or Finland, merry on duty free booze. But then there are the flashing thighs of tanned, blond, healthy-looking Viking girls zipping by on their bicycles: all too much for a full-blooded Englishman. A taxing experience, too, at last weekend's final rally for the Maastricht referendum, at which the speeches were an interruption in an all day concert in the park – Woodstock revisited almost – where the vast majority of women present were topless and some of whom your correspondent was obliged to interview, purely in order to gauge the views of a broad cross-section of the crowd. Add to all this the boats bobbing on the gentle waves of the nearby fjords, the

Glen Miller sound rising from the orchestra at the bandstand in the illuminated Tivoli Gardens drowning out the screams of those on the big dipper, and, yes, without doubt this was summertime and, in Denmark, the living was easy.

So when the referendum came around this week, and the dawn heralded yet another day of glorious sunshine, Danes across the country must have woken up and thought: "my goodness, life is good." And perhaps the vast majority of them went to the polling stations in a mellow frame of mind. Some, as they entered the polling booth, may have thought to themselves: "I feel so good on this beautiful morning, I'm going to give the politicians the benefit of the doubt, forgive them for their unremitting propaganda, having to accept the Maastricht Treaty to save Denmark from international ignominy and agree to vote in favour of the Treaty."

But then, other Danes may have walked or driven to the polling stations, and thought: "ah, this is a wonderful country, why spoil it? Let the politicians go hang with all their nonsense about European integration. What have we got in common with the rest of the continent? As it is, we don't like the Germans very much and they're our closest neighbours. But what's worse, is the thought of being overrun by thousands of Spaniards and Greeks once frontier controls are lifted."

At the end of the day it was this latter group that won out, the 'No' camp; those opposing the Maastricht accord just outnumbering those in favour. What struck me most of all was how well informed was the debate prior to the referendum. Terms like 'subsidiarity', 'convergence criteria', and 'qualified majority voting', dropped with easy familiarity from the lips of the man or woman in the street. They weren't simply reserved for the politicians on TV.

It's not for me to give opinions on the value or otherwise of holding referendums, but what I've observed in Denmark has been a true exercise in democracy. The politicians have not been afraid to trust the public with the chapter and verse of what's in the Maastricht Treaty; and this in contrast to Britain where, thanks to a cosy conspiracy between the political parties and the media, the Maastricht accord, comprising as it does the most important changes facing Britain since the last war, was quietly forgotten in the recent election campaign.

It's at times like these that countries like Denmark, coalition government and all, seem to be thoroughly modern democracies. The politicians paid the price of course because the Danes spotted exactly what Mrs Thatcher had signalled in her speech in the Hague: that buried away within the clauses of the Maastricht accord are the seeds for the next harvest of federalism. Do the British know, for example, that come next year we will all be citizens of the European Union? Do many people know what that entails? Should we believe the government when it tells us that Maastricht marks the end of the road for a centralised Europe? The Danish Prime Minister relayed that same message to his people on the eve of the referendum. The majority of Danes didn't buy it, just like Mrs Thatcher.

The Danes have overturned the apple-cart because, somewhat presumptuously, they exercised their democratic right to acquaint themselves with the facts before voting. How many people back in Britain, I wonder, have such an intimate knowledge of the treaty or, if they wish to, would have the faintest notion of how to get hold of a copy?

In Britain, a new Parliament traditionally begins its work after the Queen has delivered what's known as her "gracious speech", outlining the government's proposed legislation for the next session. The Prime Minister and the Leader of the Opposition then resume their ritual exchanges across the floor of the House of Commons. But for new Members of Parliament the Palace of Westminster is a bewildering place in which to work.

HOUSE RULES AT WESTMINSTER

ANDREW WHITEHEAD   LONDON   5 JUNE 1992

"**M**edals may not be worn in the Chamber" – just one of the helpful hints for new Members prepared by the Clerk of the Commons. For those with a forceful debating style, he warns that "a Member ... must not ... advance on the 'enemy' across the red line in the carpet." And in case you've been wondering – and perhaps a few of the 140 new MPs have been: "a male Member must be hatless when addressing the Speaker." Except of course during a vote when, and I quote again: "a Member of either gender must be seated and wearing a hat. A proper hat must be worn" – the Clerk insists – "not an Order paper or other substitute"; and he adds "two opera hats, one for each side of the House, are available on demand for this purpose."

However, the rules of procedure are as nothing compared with the complexities of the building itself. The "New Members' Guide" lists seventeen restaurants, cafés and bars, all within the Palace of Westminster, all with their own opening hours and rules of admission. The Members' Smoking Room is strictly for MPs and those peers who were once MPs. Run-of-the-mill peers are allowed into the members' cafeteria, should they so wish; and MPs may invite up to three guests; indeed, officers are also allowed in, but only when Parliament is not sitting.

It's altogether more relaxed in the Strangers' Dining Room: where strangers – members of the public – are not allowed in unaccompanied, but members of the Commons staff with over seven years service can dine there – though only on Fridays, when it's not open for dinner, just for lunch. There is reform in the air: plans to scrap some of the absurdities of Commons procedure, to streamline siting hours, and – already well advanced – to build more parliamentary offices so that MPs can operate with a modicum of efficiency.

This new Parliament has already seen some changes. Betty Boothroyd is not only the first woman Speaker, she can be expected to bring a bit of joyful irreverence to the Chamber. Celebrated for her teenage career as a dancing girl, she is – in the words of one Parliamentary sketch-writer, which, as a Yorkshireman myself I am happy to endorse – blessed with a "Yorkshire-born cross of wit and practicality, blending discipline with jocularity." And just about her first act as Speaker was to dispense with the time-honoured horse-hair wig which gave some of her predecessors the air more of a pantomime dame than the chair of a modern parliament.

Once in place, Madam Speaker's first task was to swear in MPs, beginning with the longest-serving member, Sir Edward Heath, newly honoured with the Order of the Garter. This is the highest order of chivalry and surely one of the few British institutions which pre-dates Parliament itself. How he must delight in outlasting as an MP his successor as Conservative leader, Margaret Thatcher, on whom he continues to heap calumny and contempt.

This swearing-in, over several days, is part of the ceremonial, and it throws up a few surprises. The new Health Secretary took the oath as, and I must take a deep breath here, Virginia Hilda Brunette Maxwell Mrs Bottomley, while the new MP for Devizes swore allegiance as "Michael Andrew Foster Jude Kerr, esquire, commonly called Earl of Ancram and known as Michael Ancram." Not in the least common, by the sound of it.

But all the flummery of parliamentary life has failed to make amends for the sense of shock suffered by so many new MPs. Here they are, still preening themselves on their election success, on the advent of the Parliamentary career which they have sought for so long. And what do they find at Westminster? A dusty, dingy building, hidebound by its history; so short of space, that many newcomers – for the time being at least – are working out of a locker-room or in a corridor; and little to look forward to but long hours, late nights, and lots of letters from aggrieved constituents.

The Commons can be an unforgiving forum for the unaccomplished orator. The maiden speech, new MPs will be relieved to hear, is usually heard in polite silence. Not so subsequent contributions from the floor – greeted occasionally by displays of disagreement, or, more common and more dreadful, by the chatter of an uninterested chamber. The novice will find little solace for this in the Clerk's notes of welcome. He recalls the opinion of a predecessor two centuries ago who remarked that "the House were very seldom inattentive to a Member who says anything worth hearing."

In 1992 Italians celebrated the 500th anniversary of Christopher Columbus's first voyage of discovery to the Americas. Many of the festivities took place in the city of Genoa, the birthplace of Italy's favourite son, and the centrepiece was a spectacular waterfront exhibition.

GENOA REVITALISED

DEREK WILSON   GENOA   15 JUNE 1992

I was last in Genoa about a year ago – and a grim place it was, although as spectacular as ever. It was as if it had once been hurled by the hand of a giant against a sheer cliff-face and then left to tumble down to the sea. Or, seen from the motorway, strung out high above the city like a trapeze, Genoa looks like an amphitheatre, with the sea its apron stage.

I remember that in the late 1950s, all the action in Genoa was in bustling, medieval arcades and covered alleys running the length of the waterfront, crammed with stalls, shops, and bars, thronged until the early hours under a blaze of light by revellers, drunken sailors, and bargain and pleasure hunters. Returning there years later, I discovered only blackness. The arcades were deserted, risky too; shadowy figures darted about with knives in their fists; drug-pedlars haggled in chained-up doorways. The locals called it the Casbah because North Africans had moved in. The rest of the town at night was empty gloom as well.

It was a sad epilogue for a proud city that once held sway over most of the Mediterranean, after its crushing of Pisa, its nearest rival, in a thirteenth-century sea-battle. Later Genoa even came close to trouncing its arch-enemy, Venice, at sea, and once, English ships venturing into the Mediterranean sailed under the protective flag of Genoa, the flag of Saint George. One English visitor to Genoa in the fourteenth century, in the guise of a wool merchant, was none other than Geoffrey Chaucer, chronicler of *The 'Canterbury Tales'*.

Over the centuries, the Genoese have earned a reputation for tight-fistedness and extreme disruptiveness, and especially in the last twenty years, Genoa's slide into decline was partly due to its fractious left-wing dockers. Strikes kept the port more dead than alive; handling charges soared, and shipping companies deserted Genoa for Antwerp and elsewhere. A slump also hit Genoese ship-building, while output quotas imposed by the European Community all but crippled a local steel-industry. The Genoese decamped from the town centre to higher up the cliffs, and you can tell how long it has all been neglected: Second World War notices remain stencilled on walls 'off limits to Allied Forces' – and one forlorn sign on the water-front still reads in English: 'Sailors' Chapel and Reading Room'.

Now the rotting centre has been transformed, thanks to the Genoese architect, Renzo Piano, the man who turned the central market of Paris into a vast new pedestrian centre, the Beaubourg. He's turned Genoa's derelict old port into virtually a new quarter of the city. Until August the port is to house the Christopher Columbus exhibition, a fascinating essay by sixty nations on 'Ships and the Sea'. Britain shows off the world's first sea-worthy chronometer, and Germany one of the very first submarines. Most of the stands are in a long row of restored cotton warehouses but Signor Piano has also moored a huge floating new city square in the once stinking water. He's provided open-air theatres, a congress centre and a mammoth aquarium. The old high customs wall that once cut off the town from the port has been torn down. "I've given the Genoese their sea back," he says, and from the exhibition, people can now see their city properly for the first time.

The port area is already triggering off renewal in the rest of the old town. Miraculously, the arcades are coming back to life; fine seventeenth-century patrician dwellings have been rescued from ruin; so, stunningly, has the handsome Ducal Palace, the seat of the former Doges of Genoa, now to be a cultural centre, and nearby, the re-built opera house is now one of the most sophisticated in Europe.

This daring, if costly, face-lift for Genoa will be read as a message of hope by other old Italian cities with dying hearts. Venice is one, asphyxiated by tourism, as the population dwindles yearly. So now the city fathers of Venice are debating furiously whether to drive an underground railway beneath the Lagoon to revive the centre. But the sickest patient is once-fair Naples, not too long ago the pride of Italy, and now a desolate urban wasteland at night which is held in thrall by the local Mafia.

Mark Brayne was a foreign correspondent for nearly twenty years. Among the places he's reported from for the BBC are Berlin, Vienna and Peking. For the past four years he was the BBC World Service diplomatic correspondent. In mid-1992, however, he decided to hang up his microphone to become a BBC bureaucrat.

TOUR D'HORIZON

MARK BRAYNE   LONDON   26 JUNE 1992

In August 1988, in my early months as Diplomatic Correspondent for the World Service, I recall writing a report for this programme which I rather grandiosely titled "Whither the World?" The Soviet army was preparing to pull out of Afghanistan, peace was coming to Angola, the first Gulf War between Iran and Iraq was ending, and President Reagan had just been walkabout on Red Square in Moscow.

We suspected then that something pretty important was beginning, but who could have imagined just how dramatically the world was indeed about to change – a period of upheaval probably more fundamental than anything since the French Revolution 200 years ago. Overstating the case? I don't think so. The collapse of communism over the past four years doesn't necessarily mean the triumph of democracy. But it does signal the end of a hundred years of ideology and of many centuries of old-style imperialist expansion.

President Bush spoke at the end of the second Gulf War against Iraq of a New World Order – a vision met with predictable cynicism at the time by most commentators. With an eye to the Balkans, to South Africa and to the Caucasus that new order may indeed be more of a world disorder. But I believe that in essence Mr Bush was right. Information, television and satellite technology have revolutionised the way nations do business. It's more difficult than it has ever been to repress your people or devastate your environment without the world noticing. And for all its new uncertainties, the world is in my view a fundamentally better place today than it was even four years ago.

Those are the heavy thoughts as I prepare to move from front-line reporting to a bureaucrat's desk. But it's the personal memories of nearly 20 years on the road that I shall savour. Above all, there was the euphoria of Romanians in Bucharest at Christmas 1989, and of ordinary Chinese people on the streets of Peking earlier that year, when it appeared that people's revolutions were bringing down hated dictatorships.

In a messy sort of way, the Romanians won. Their story also landed the BBC with surely its biggest one-way taxi bill in history – one thousand eight hundred dollars for a Mercedes to get me overnight from Belgrade to Bucharest.

On the other hand, the Chinese on Tiananmen Square did not win – but as reform begins again to take hold in China, I remain confident that before too long many of the ideals of 1989 will be back on the Chinese agenda. The Peking massacre was for me possibly the low point of the last 20 years – as I watched and heard events unfold from leave in eastern England, where I'd gone to unwind after leaving an apparently peaceful Peking just five days earlier.

There've been moments over these years of high good humour. One of my favourite assignments was the coverage of Prince Charles and his then still fairly new wife Princess Diana to the Australian State of Victoria in 1985. We called it the Chuck and Di roadshow – and after the dour politics of China, it was a wonderful opportunity for some scurrilous, tongue-in-cheek radio reporting. Charlie, I remember, got his own back in some God-forsaken part of the outback by turning a water hose on the journalists following the royal couple.

There've also been many moments of exhilaration where I've had to pinch myself and ask, as on a journey along the Silk Road in 1986 or travelling with the Pope around India: "Am I really being paid to do this?" The Silk Road assignment produced incidentally my all-time favourite radio sign-off: Mark Brayne, BBC, Dunhuang, Gobi Desert.

It's not high politics that makes the biggest impact. As I hand the microphone over, at least temporarily, to other colleagues, I leave them with a chastening thought. Whatever the global upheavals I've covered, there are two pieces that most listeners appear to remember me by. A cycle trip along the Great Wall, and, after the birth of our baby daughter in 1987, how my wife and I smuggled 800 disposable nappies into China from Hong Kong. News and diplomacy are, after all, both about people. That's why radio reporting has been such fun.

EUROPE: EAST

One of the principal battlegrounds in the Soviet Union's propaganda war with the West has traditionally been its airport departure lounges where pamphlets on history and politics – in days of greater political certainty – were offered in their dozens to foreign travellers. But by autumn 1991 the supply of new titles had dwindled and our Moscow Correspondent, Kevin Connolly, considered this dying literary art.

CREATIVE WRITING

KEVIN CONNOLLY   MOSCOW   14 SEPTEMBER 1991

They are the Soviet Union's own airport paperbacks... but their relationship to the doorstep-sized thrillers you find in Western departure terminals is distant. You find them – small pamphlets with big titles – in neat rows on bookshelves in the special buildings where foreigners must wait, isolated from Soviet passengers, for internal flights.

They are easy to recognise. Their dust-jackets, often faded from long months of lying undisturbed under harsh artificial light, are always in those greens, browns and mustard yellows so beloved of communist designers – colours that don't occur in nature. They have about them, these days, an air of quiet melancholy, stockpiles of propaganda gathering dust, like ammunition from a war that has ended.

I can't remember now where I began to collect them. It must have been in some god-forsaken provincial city airport, probably late at night when I'd finished whatever book I'd brought with me for my journey. Aeroflot, the Soviet Union's much-abused national airline, has its faults but it's certainly driven me back to the reading of lengthy Victorian novels. That's proved to be the only way to make sure that I always have something with me to read on journeys in a country where departure announcements are sometime given in days of the week, rather than hours of the clock.

The first pamphlet I picked up was called *Economic Restructuring at the*

Crossroads and dealt with the perennial problem of the shortage of consumer goods and commodities. The state publishers were not, of course, afflicted by any such difficulties and there were thousands of copies in stock, most of them still in neatly-stacked boxes below the bookshelf. It is, I now recognise, something of a classic. It belongs to that uniquely Soviet school of analytical writing in which past mistakes were sorrowfully acknowledged, current problems deftly understated and future prospects optimistically trumpeted.

All such works were written in the same literary style; as though one figure of prodigious energy and omniscience had produced them all. For page after page the author posed wordy and complex rhetorical questions, which he then answered at enormous length – often quoting the writers of other pamphlets in the same series. I like to imagine them all, sitting at a row of neighbouring desks, loyally citing each other as authorities on everything from football to photosynthesis.

The economic essays could, of course, be a little on the dry side although occasionally enlivened by the imaginative use of English colloquialism, for example: "The problem of economic reconstruction is as long as a piece of string ..." It's the historical pamphlets which really fascinate – footnotes from a vanished world of insupportable fictions and spectacular distortions. In Siberia I found a copy of a guide to the Baltic states, written so vividly that if you closed your eyes you could almost hear the cheers of welcome as Stalin's tanks rolled in. From the far-east there is a biography of Patrice Lumumbe – "Scholar, Patriot and Humanist" – which attested to his long and now almost forgotten period as one of the Soviet Union's favourite foreigners.

In every airport there is at least one work about Lenin who, even now, is still being spared the final indignity of revisionism. My personal favourite is called simply *V.I. Lenin by his Foreign Contemporaries*. The front cover is a pencil sketch of the great man which, in striving to convey his wisdom and fatherly concern, contrived to make him look like a man who has just opened an unexpectedly large telephone bill. Portrait painters in the old days of Soviet power often faced the problem of attempting to produce images of warm, human figures from somewhat unpromising material. Attempts to give Stalin a fatherly twinkle in his eye often leant him the grotesque air of a bingo-caller or night-club comedian.

There was no uncertainty of literary tone, though, about the reminiscences of Lenin. Here was a paternal statesman by turns wise and witty, austere and approachable, unexpectedly compassionate, eternally right. Foreign diplomats, trade unionists, politicians, musicians, writers – all were allotted a few minutes alone with the great man, and all were careful to record that he was tireless in his efforts on behalf of the people. As a result, the cumulative effect of the book is unintentionally humorous ... after a while you can't help thinking that if he was indeed quite as busy as the contributors claim, he was able to spare a remarkable amount of time for his foreign admirers. The idea that Mr Lenin was in any way vain is not discussed in the book. The description of him proving that American democracy would collapse within a few years, that France was ripe for revolution or that sculpture was an intrinsically decadent for of art, share a tone of breathless enthusiasm which is a reminder of how much Moscow treasured the days when its system was provoking admiration rather than pity.

It's difficult to say now in what spirit such pamphlets were written; were they perhaps the work of cynical jobbing writers who jested at Lenin's expense even as they carefully tended his memory? I am inclined to hope not. For somehow, like lives of the saints written for children, they have about them an air of innocent sincerity. Here, you feel, are the authentic tones of writers who had the capacity to believe in what they were doing, even if this year's version of history might sometimes be wildly at variance with last year's.

Whatever their motives, they are out of work now. The cottage industry whose only function was to produce a safe, sanitised version of history is gone – a victim, like so much else, of communism's precipitate collapse. I flew back from the southern republic of Georgia last night and found myself at Tbilisi airport, instinctively heading for the familiar bookshelves which are now, of course, empty. Somehow, though, I like to think, the authors are out there somewhere, itching to produce one final pamphlet explaining how the coup, its collapse and the final crushing humiliation of the Communist Party, are somehow steps towards the distant but inevitable triumph of the old system they served so energetically.

I, for one, will miss them.

The former Soviet Union signed an agreement in October 1991 to give it associate membership of the International Monetary Fund. The country's leaders hoped that, by so doing, vital Western aid and investment would be channelled into the country before the onset of winter. But amid the gloomy economic forecasts, there were, superficially at least, some success stories.

LICENCE TO PRINT MONEY

KEVIN CONNOLLY   MOSCOW   5 OCTOBER 1991

A t the end of a week which has brought the usual news of food shortages, dwindling gold reserves and rising unemployment, here at last is a Soviet success story. It is a tale of two factories where tireless workers and indefatigable managers make and break new production targets with hypnotic regularity. Output in August was almost as great as that for the whole of last year. Where other Soviet managers ponder the prospect of reaching the point where chronic absenteeism starts to overcompensate for chronic overmanning, the men who run our two plants can contemplate a future of full order books and rising productivity.

But this is Moscow, where every silver lining is firmly enveloped in a cloud, and this silver lining is no exception. For the factories in question print bank-notes; every order successfully fulfilled serves notice of the growing danger of hyperinflation. It's become hard to describe the Soviet economy without reaching into the depressingly familiar lexicon of despair used by everyone who writes about it; it is teetering, tottering, crumbling, collapsing, or disintegrating; leading indicators are plunging, plummeting, nosediving or spiralling downwards. Safer, perhaps, to set aside the adjectives, and look at the figures.

The Soviet Union intended to print about 40 billion roubles this year – it has already issued 57.3 billion. A few years ago the largest banknote in circulation was the ten rouble; now there's a twenty-five, a fifty, and a hundred rouble note with a two hundred due out soon, a five hundred on the way before the end of the year, and a thousand already at the planning stage. It's not clear who will be on that yet, Karl Marx perhaps? Lenin is, or will be, on all the others, so the principle of illustrating the notes with the faces of the men who ruined the economy in which they circulate, is firmly established. But by the time the thousand note is with us, the hyperinflation it heralds may be well established.

The men who run the Soviet banking system are aware of the problem but they are reduced to speaking of it in the same tone of awed apprehension as the rest of us. There is, after all, a ruthless logic to the whole business: everything is in short supply so there's always upward pressure on prices; salaries are increased; as soon as they go up, there's enough money around to force prices up again. And so it goes on.

Attempts to tinker with the money supply have been marked by a predictable combination of foolishness and pointlessness, like the decision last year of the Prime Minister, Valentin Pavlov, to recall without warning all fifty and one hundred rouble notes. However many different denominations of banknote the country eventually comes up with, his chances of appearing on one of them disappeared forever in August, with the collapse of the coup he helped to mastermind – if that's the right word. Nevertheless he might yet claim – from the prison cell in which he now lives – to have had a lasting influence on the country's economy. He managed, more or less single-handedly, to destroy what little confidence remained in Soviet money. For a time it was impossible to persuade anyone to take high-denomination notes, so great was the fear of a further round of drastic and hamfisted monetary reform. It is possible to persuade people to take big bills again now, but they are regarded with the same hostility we reserve in the West for tax forms and telephone bills.

In an atmosphere where wealth is coveted but money is an object of suspicion, the smart thing to do, if you can, is to barter; to take something made by your factory and either swap it for something you want or sell it and cash in on the inflated prices attracted by anything which is in short supply. Sometimes goods are smuggled out of factories illegally, but increasingly they are given as part of a pay package. It is good for the workers because they have something to barter, good for the company because it doesn't have to worry about finding the huge amounts of cash needed to pay wage bills. This is fine if you work with things that other people want, like fur hats, furniture, food and so on; but it's not so good if you make something unmarketable like wing nuts, or non-portable like warplanes.

In the big cities the Soviet people are made streetwise from decades of surviving government economic mismanagement, but in many smaller towns it is a different story. Often they make things no-one wants or needs any more – like busts of Lenin – and they are in danger of being left out even of the crude barter market which is growing up. Every weekend enterprising Muscovites, their car suspensions groaning under the weight of sacks of sugar, salt or soap spirited away from state shops in shady back-door deals, head for the villages and towns around the capital. They are capitalism's outriders, bringing black market prices and much-needed goods to places which would otherwise have nothing; but often they charge as much as a day's wages for a kilo of meat.

Like many other sharp-witted young Muscovites, they have no incentive to worry about how things might be improved. They, after all, are making their fortunes working in the margins of the old collapsing system. So even in its death throes, the Soviet Union is still somehow misdirecting the energies of its people. No-one suffers any more from the delusion that a solution will quickly be found. Output, of course, has to be increased, but in this moribund economy, hopelessly locked into the endless production of tanks and missiles, that is easier said than done.

Few politicians have anything to suggest beyond appeals to the West for help. And as the country slides back, first into barter and then into God knows what scale of economic catastrophe, it's tempting to wonder if the workers at the Soviet banknote plant are among those who prefer to be paid with the goods their factory produces.

The break up of the Soviet Union into its constituent republics unleashed numerous ethnic tensions within the borders of the republics themselves. In the largest of them, the Russian Federation, minorities conquered under the Tsars began challenging Boris Yeltsin's claim that Russia was a single, indivisible state.

CHECHENS – BROTHERS IN ARMS

TIM WHEWELL   GROZNY   7 NOVEMBER 1991

"I t's a terrible how the price of arms has gone up," my guide Sultan complained, as we careered through the streets of Grozny in a sleek, black Volvo. "This revolver cost me 25,000 roubles. A few years ago it would have been only half that, but now everyone seems to want one." As he drove, he kept only one hand on the steering wheel, with the other he played with his gun. He loaded and unloaded it several times and then handed it to me, inviting me to take a few shots through the window to try it out. Just at that point we passed a policeman, but Sultan didn't seem too concerned. In Grozny the police don't even enforce traffic regulations. During the three days we spent in the town we never once stopped at a red light.

Sultan apologised for taking me in a Volvo. Most of his other cars, he said, were Mercedes: he had eighteen altogether. Was he a multi-millionaire? I asked incredulously. Sultan laughed at my naivety. To be exact, he had 270 million roubles, and several hundred thousand dollars salted away in a bank in Milan. I never quite worked out the source of Sultan's wealth. He was, he said, the president of a corporation which exported seeds from central Asia to western Europe. What kind of seeds? Well, some of them, he said, were used for medical purposes. He didn't really understand it himself. He also dealt in a kind of

57

poison extracted from snakes for which western laboratories paid 3,000 dollars a gram.

By this time I'd handed back the revolver, and further questioning seemed not only rude but also dangerous. Sultan preferred to talk about politics. A few years ago, he said, Soviet power had forced him to conduct all his business deals underground. He could have been imprisoned simply for driving a foreign car. Now he had come down from Moscow to help in the revolution that was sweeping the last vestiges of Communism from his Chechen homeland.

Mention Chechens to the average Muscovite, and he'll immediately think of the mafia. They're said to run a protection racket that extorts money from taxi-drivers, restaurant-owners, and market traders. Chechens themselves say they're hated because they're the one group of businessmen who refuse to pay protection money to the real mafia. Whichever way round it is, you can't move far in Grozny without meeting people who've been involved in late-night shoot-outs in Moscow cafés and markets.

Such 'businessmen', however, aren't the only people who carry guns. Virtually everyone seems to have some kind of firearm – a pistol, an old hunting rifle or a sub-machine gun. Even the press officer of the Chechen National Congress – an earnest language enthusiast who was exempted from army service because of his short-sightedness – turned out to have a revolver concealed inside his jacket. Chechens tell you it's a matter of honour for every man or boy to carry a weapon from the age of seven. It would be shameful, they say, for them to leave their dagger or gun behind even when going to the toilet. And they insist that in a society where the principle of blood for blood is strictly enforced, the easy availability of firearms is a stabilising factor: no-one risks picking a fight.

Among themselves that may be true. But the Chechens have certainly been ready to use their weapons to fight the Russians. In the nineteenth century it took the Tsarist army more than thirty years to establish control over the northern Caucasus. And after the Bolshevik revolution, the region again fought for its freedom. The Chechens believe it was their long history of insubordination that led to Stalin's decision, in 1944, to deport their entire nation to the steppes of central Asia. At dawn one February morning that year, whole villages were surrounded by troops and the inhabitants packed into cattle trucks. Hundreds of thousands died on the journey to Kazakhstan, and on the freezing wastelands where they were dumped with nowhere to stay except barns and stables.

The Chechens were allowed to return home only at the end of the 1950s. But among those who had avoided deportation there were some who'd kept up a constant partisan struggle against the Soviet forces. The last guerrilla fighter in the mountains died only in the mid 1970s, and now that Soviet power has finally crumbled, the Chechens are determined to resume the fight by winning independence from Russia. Their leader, General Dzhakhar Dudayev, looks like a 1920s American dandy in his fedora hat, striped suit and meticulously clipped moustache. He talks quietly and without emotion as befits a former Soviet air-force commander. But he's effectively allowed his supporters and their private army, the Chechen National Guard, to depose the legal authorities in Grozny. And when asked about the quantity of arms in the republic, he replies that although men and nations have various fortunes, the revolver makes everyone equal in the end.

General Dudayev's supporters believe they're spearheading a revolt against Russian imperialism which will be joined by other captive peoples of Boris Yeltsin's federation – the Tartars of the Volga, the Kabardinians and the Balkars and Daghestanis of the northern Caucasus. But some of the freedom fighters, who have Mercedes as well as pistols, hope the struggle won't last too long. "As soon as the revolution's over," Sultan told me, "we can get back to making money."

By the middle of November, 1991, the Croatian port city of Dubrovnik had been under siege from the Federal Army (JNA) for six weeks. A ferry carrying foreigners, pregnant women, children and wounded men left the port on November 14th, and hopes for a peaceful solution rested on the European Community's envoy, Lord Carrington. Our correspondent, Alan Little, spent a week in Dubrovnik – a city on the verge of collapse.

DUBROVNIK – A CITY BESIEGED

ALAN LITTLE   DUBROVNIK   14 NOVEMBER 1991

At sunset the sky above Dubrovnik's white stone walls glows smoky rose and salmon pink, and gives way slowly to encroaching night. The only sound is the lapping of the gentle Adriatic on the ancient fortified waterfront. The effect is bewitching. And that's when it starts.

You see the flash first, then, seconds later, hear the boom of the barrel as it sends another artillery shell, flying in a low arc, screaming over the ancient rust-coloured roofs of the old town. The Croats lob mortars and artillery of their own from positions around town, sometimes close to the old walls, bringing the might of the Federal response to within a whisker of the city's architectural treasures.

The Federal Army's presence is visible, inescapable, and menacing. They've taken commanding positions on the hills above the city. Offshore, their gunboats glide silently past. You cannot get away from this overpowering sense of being trapped. It's a presence that has worn down Dubrovnik's fifty thousand people to a state of depression, inertia and exhaustion. The town seems permanently on the verge of tears.

Take Andreo Ruso. He showed me into his son's bedroom. "Look through the hole in the wall," he said. If you refocus your eyes, they settle on Zarkovice hilltop where the Yugoslav national flag marks the spot from where they fired the shell that destroyed his second floor flat. I've seen this hilltop, framed in this way by broken bricks and mortar, in buildings across the city. The military rationale of much of the JNA's bombardment is bewildering. Why did they slam shell after shell into a complex of hotels housing three thousand refugees? They emerged from their underground shelter next morning bewildered, and, in some cases, clearly in shock. While I was there, raking through the physical and emotional aftermath, the siren struck up again. Instantly we were pushed underground by an official who knows only too well the cost of complacency. In the safest room in the complex, a group of young mothers were purging their own fear for the sake of their children, trying to distract attention from the pounding above by playing games, telling stories. I wondered what reserves of courage of energy they were drawing from. Some had endured this for five weeks.

Our hosts made a fuss of us, fetching candles so that we could see the faces of those we were interviewing, fetching clean plastic cups and flasks of hot coffee. We were their esteemed guests. Only afterwards did they raise, in a polite and embarrassed sort of way, the question of Europe. Why does Europe not care? I felt – I feel – humbled by the question, and by the way it is put by the ordinary, sad people here. I had no answer. My Croatian interpreter – a compassionate and courageous young woman – overheard a phone-in on Zagreb Radio. "You have to understand," said a caller from Hamburg, "that we live in the rich world. It sees its catastrophes on television. When it's seen enough, it presses the button."

I left Dubrovnik punch-drunk with tales of grief. The journey out was no relief. Ours was to be – though we didn't know it – the last refugee ship to be allowed to leave. Hours after we sailed, the Federal Navy imposed a total naval blockade on all Croatian ports. Even the single ferry a day, which held out the prospect of escape to a handful of people, is gone. On the quayside there was chaos. Two hundred and sixty people, mostly the elderly, pregnant women, or mothers with small children, had been selected. I watched one young man kiss his wife goodbye. He hugged his little girl, and held her head in his big hands, staring for a moment into her face. No-one spoke. Then he turned and left without a word.

We sailed at sunset, a new artillery exchange striking up on the hills above.

On board, Marko Rilovic was savouring his eightieth birthday slumped, exhausted and asleep, onto a black vinyl couch in the reception area where he and his wife had been dumped. Marko had lived all his life in the house in which he was born, keeping a small vineyard, some cattle and pigs. They'd fled ten days earlier. They had no idea where they would go. "I've put our names on the list in the purser's office. I think it's the Red Cross." She shrugged and tears dripped down her miserable face. It seemed that it was the indignity of it all that pained her most. "We are the Kurds of Europe." she said. Kate Boljan is twenty-two and eight months pregnant. Her husband, Ante, is still trapped in Dubrovnik. She had to choose, effectively, between him and her unborn child. "I don't know whether I will see him again, or whether he will see the child. My baby will need water and food and electricity. Of course it was a hard decision."

As we sailed in the dark past coastal villages in Montenegro, the refugees saw their first electric light in five weeks. One little girl, no more than five years old, screamed at her mother that all the houses were on fire, and asked whether the army was shooting here too. Children know the vocabulary of war – the difference between artillery and mortar, sniper and machine gun fire.

When I left Dubrovnik I thought I had seen the exercise of gratuitous cruelty by men who knew that they could do anything with impunity from the relative safety of their hill top bunkers. It seemed as though they were laughing at international public opinion, laughing at Europe's decision not to decide. I thought I was already witnessing an army inflicting its worst, day after day. I'd sat beneath a sturdy wooden desk, during a heavy artillery raid, on the telephone to London, and heard a Serbian politician tell *The World At One* that Dubrovnik was not – as he put it – perishing, that those claims were propaganda. There were mortars and shells dropping only two hundred yards away – the sound was deafening.

In fact I'd seen nothing at all compared with what has come since. Back in Zagreb, you can watch pictures from Zagreb television, shot from the very position on Zarkovice hill where the army has its closest artillery post. Now I can watch, every day, through my Zagreb television screen, the beautiful Adriatic port city from the other side of the lines; its familiar ancient alleyways, even that street from the old town to the Hotel Argentina, along which we strode quickly and nervously, hugging the wall and glancing anxiously at the Federal Flag flying on the crest of the hill. This has an unsettling through-the-looking-glass quality about it, especially when you see an artillery piece or a machine gun being fired, with what seems like cavalier abandon, into the very streets where the good, suffering people of Dubrovnik – the people who'd shown me so much kindness, and whom I left less than a week ago – are still cowering, in daily and increasing fear for their lives.

1991 witnessed the outbreak of the first war in Europe since 1948, fought between the republic of Croatia and the Yugoslav National Army, backed by armed Serb irregulars. The war's relentless brutality revived memories of the bloody three-way conflict, during the Second World War, between Croat fascists, fanatical Serb nationalists and the multi-national communist partisans. For the people of Yugoslavia, the prospect of Christmas looked bleak indeed.

EUROPE'S POISONOUS MIRE

MISHA GLENNY   KENTISH TOWN   21 DECEMBER 1991

In a recent attempt to purge my psyche of Yugoslavia for a few hours, I went to see the film *Robin Hood – Prince of Thieves*, starring Kevin Costner. I was thoroughly enjoying the escapism when, about half an hour into the movie, Kevin – a.k.a. Robin of Lockesley – delivered a rousing speech to the motley collection of outlaw peasants eking out a rather unfocussed existence in Sherwood Forest. In an effort to instil courage in Little John and friends, Robin tells them how he learned, during the Crusades, that a free man fighting for his home is worth ten others in battle. And the rest of the film goes on to prove that this is indeed the case and, consequently, good triumphs over evil.

My immediate mental response to the Costner oratory plunged me back into the hole of violence out of which I was trying to clamber. "Absolutely right Robin," I thought. "Someone fighting for his or her home is worth ten others, but what if the lines between good and evil are blurred, so that both sides believe they are fighting for their homes?" The question was of course rhetorical, because Yugoslavia provided me with the answer some time ago: the Serbs in Knin and the Croats from Osijek both believe they are defending their homes, and their brethren and the sestren form an uncontrollable leviathan that shall not rest until it has butchered the last Serb or the last Croat. Everyone believes they are Robin Hood, and the enemy is always the Sheriff of Nottingham.

The Croats are determined to regain all their territory, while the Serbs and their allies in the Federal Army are equally adamant that these areas will never again belong to Croatia. In a certain respect this makes the whole debate about whether Croatia should be recognised rather irrelevant. Germany, Italy and whoever else ends up granting recognition on January 15th, will be according diplomatic status to a country of which more than fifty per cent is under occupation. The Serbs and the army have made it clear that they will not budge. Indeed they have warned that they will respond to recognition by stepping up their military campaign. Now this may just be Serbian bluff, but given what we witnessed in Vukovar and Dubrovnik, it's a bit of bluff which is worth taking seriously.

The Croat government and people will of course receive an important psychological boost with recognition, but it will only be of practical value to them if the Germans then argue that the UN arms embargo, presently in effect against all Yugoslavia, no longer applies to a new, independent Croatia. Should new arms then flow into Croatia, this will even up the imbalance which currently exists between the massively armed military and the relatively weak Croat National Guard. It will not, however, stop the fighting.

I've been covering the story in Yugoslavia for six months, more or less non-stop; although I was able to predict the war before it happened, now that it has begun it's much more difficult to anticipate how events in the Balkans will develop. Society in both Croatia and Serbia (and to a lesser extent the other four republics in what was once Yugoslavia) has become traumatised and radicalised. Both Croatia and Serbia, for example, have a growing problem of extreme lawlessness; armed hooligans – maybe sponsored by some murky state organ, maybe not – are terrorising innocent civilians, sometimes for nationalist reasons, but often simply as straightforward muggers.

Old Balkan traditions of corruption – the blood feud and revenge – are now being writ large by men who find the deepest gratification in mutilating and torturing their enemy. Armed or unarmed, soldier or civilian, man, woman or child – it really doesn't matter. Many of us who have been involved in the war have been asking ourselves how these people, once happy and friendly neighbours, will be able to live together after it ends. How will a Croat, whose mother has been shot dead by a Serb in the next street, be able to sit down for a drink with him? How will the Serb, whose father was machine-gunned in cold blood by a Croat policeman, ever respect Croat law again?

After the Second World War, when the first episode of mass fratricidal killings between Serbs and Croats came to an end, the partisan leader, Marshal Tito, came up with a simple formula to end the mutual hatred: he denied everybody their human rights and all nationalist symbols were replaced by the internationalist paraphernalia of the Communist movement. For forty years Tito kept the peace in Yugoslavia, but he also exacerbated the fundamental problems by sweeping them under the carpet where they multiplied, preparing for the day when they would re-emerge. That day has now come. We now have to suppress the hatred and the violence; not, as Tito did, with totalitarian methods, but with democratic methods; that is, with the very processes which reactivated the problems in the first place.

I wish I could issue a happier Christmas message, but I would be lying. The Yugoslav republics are up to their waist in a poisonous mire, and the level is rising steadily all the time.

1991 began with Mr Gorbachev trying to reassert his authority over the Baltic republics, and ended with the Soviet President resigning on Christmas Day. Although he survived an attempted coup in August, Mr Gorbachev never fully regained his authority, and it was his one time adversary in the Communist Party, Boris Yeltsin, who ultimately emerged triumphant. But Boris Yeltin's problems were only beginning.

RINGING OUT THE OLD

BRIDGET KENDALL   MOSCOW   2 JANUARY 1992

T he other day the fine, upstanding Russian lady who helps keep our office clean asked me for the morning off. She's a mother of two, in her fifties, a fine cook and a former parachutist who can move a wardrobe single handed. In her youth she was one of those cheering and smiling sportswomen who strode across Red Square on May Day saluting their Communist leaders with red flags and slogans. Now she says she was an idiot to trust the authorities, and she takes a poor view of what has happened to her country in the last six years. Nothing makes her more angry than to go shopping at the private market down the road and watch the prices rise week by week. But nothing gives her greater pleasure than to squeeze a good bargain out of the Azerbaijani traders who control the prices of the fruit and veg.

Anyway she nearly bowled me over with her request for time off. She said she needed to pop down to the registry office to get married. "But Vera!" I said, "You've already got a husband who rings you nearly every day, and two daughters. How come you are getting married again?" It turned out she and her husband got divorced a few years back, not because their marriage had gone sour, but because their flat was on the small side. They still lived together as man and wife, and nothing had actually changed. But it was only if he got divorced, and told the authorities he had moved back to live with his mother, that he would have any right to inherit his mother's tiny flat when, in the end, she passed away. Otherwise it would revert to the state, because according to the old Soviet rules, he and his family would be occupying too many square metres – since, believe it or not, a rather mediocre-sized flat with two rooms, a kitchen and a balcony is all that's allowed for a family of four. But now the rules are being changed. It is all to do with one of the new bits of legislation being put in place by the non-Communist authorities as they try to work out how to privatize housing and create a new middle class.

So Vera could remarry, and her ex-husband could make an honest woman of his ex-wife without jeopardising his right to two more rooms. There was another reason for going through the formality of a second marriage ceremony – again an immensely practical reason – the chance to jump the shopping queue. Every new bride, it turned out, gets a coupon for a special shop. This store is in theory stacked with all sorts of things you won't find in a normal shop anymore – gold rings, curtains, bedlinen, crystal and china – and all the other prerequisites any bride needs for her trousseau.

At least that's the idea. In practice, this December, the gold ring counter was empty and there was no glass or cutlery worth buying either. Everywhere, even in special shops for brides, it seems, goods had been bought up, and shelves laid bare. Everyone knew the reform to abolish state subsidies on prices, which takes effect from January 2nd, meant prices would rocket, and that overnight everything would cost two, three even four times as much. You might think all those empty Soviet shops and the torturous lengths you had to go to under the old system to defend your interests – even to the extent of breaking up your own marriage to win the chance of a few more square metres to live in – would make people welcome reforms that promise to make life just a little bit simpler. Okay, from now on, young couples are going to have to save up a bit before they buy a gold wedding ring, but at least, if everyone is paying commercial prices, there will be rings in the shops to buy.

Some people accept that. "There's really no problem," one friend told me yesterday. "You can buy everything you need now in the new commercial shops. It's just a question of money." That is a logic acceptable to educated folk who watch foreign films, read foreign books and have the contacts and the language to make the odd trip abroad. They are now working out how to make a bit of foreign currency, by renting flats to foreigners, offering their services as translators, business consultants, drivers, babysitters, masseurs, dog walkers, car washers – anything at all. After all, the faster the rouble falls against the dollar, the fewer dollars you need to earn to make a killing in local currency and keep yourself well heeled.

They will be the new moneyed class here, the ones who will profit by the price reforms. But what about the rest? The Russians who can't earn foreign currency, and see their rouble salaries drop in value by the day? The typical image that comes to mind is of one of those elderly Russian ladies I often bump into in the bread shops here. She wears a drab coat, carefully mended, old gloves and a once stylish hat. And fumbling through her purse, she is causing a log jam in the queue at the cash desk, as she tries to work out what she can afford. You see old ladies like that every day in Moscow, a city with several million pensioners. They don't like these changes, and they are bitter that after working all their lives, their savings aren't worth anything any more.

Moscow's politicians and sociologists shake their heads and tell you it will take a generation or two to rid Russian society of those people who still firmly believe that it is the state's duty to provide. And already, they say, the next generation is breeding a new sort of Russian; young men and women who are very good at making money, and don't give socialism a second thought ... I wonder.

The other day I was invited to supper by a family who live on the outskirts of Moscow. The husband is in the police force, the wife has an office job, and their pretty 22 year-old daughter teaches French at a primary school. She showed me her bedroom – the dressing table stacked with cosmetics, posters of Sting and Abba above the bed. And then I noticed by the mirror, a clipping from a newspaper, tacked to the wall. It was a photo of the 'Putchisti', as they are called here: the eight men, led by Vice-President Yanayev and Soviet Prime Minister Pavlov, who led the attempted coup in August, and most of whom now sit in prison charged with high treason and awaiting trial. But underneath the photo, in careful big black letters, my young hostess had written 'They were only defending the motherland.'

At supper this well educated member of Russia's younger generation told me she didn't think they should be in prison at all. Their attempt to restore law and order had been justified and was still needed, and what was happening now was that black marketeers, thieving mafiosi, and unscrupulous foreigners were being given a free hand to rob Russia blind. This family didn't support Boris Yeltsin. They didn't like Mr Gorbachev much either.

And, as you might expect, they view this week's price reforms with a mixture of suspicion and trepidation. Decades of Kremlin governments had promised a bright new future, they argued, higher wages and lower prices. That had failed, and now a load of so-called democrats were handing the economy over to the mafia. There was not a glimmer of hope in this Russian household that life would improve because of Mr Yeltsin's reforms. And already there is a solid conviction that only a return to a strong leader and state control would make their lives better. If that's typical, then Boris Yeltsin may not have too many months to prove his reforms can work.

At the beginning of 1992, Georgia's President, Zviad Gamsakhurdia, was forced
to flee to neighbouring Armenia after being ousted by opposition forces in the capital,
Tbilisi. Mr Gamsakhurdia won a convincing victory in elections last May, and
has blamed what he calls a 'mafia' of former Communist Party officials for his
downfall. But his supporters continued to defy the orders of Georgia's interim
military government by demonstrating on the streets.

TBILISI TURNS ON
ITSELF

CAROLE WALKER   TBILISI   9 JANUARY 1992

Tbilisi used to be one of the pleasantest cities in the old Soviet Union: sunny, with abundant fruit and vegetables in summer, its people proud of their hospitality and of the Georgian food and wine they like to consume in great quantities. Here, the usual greeting amongst casual friends is an almost passionate embrace. But the violent battle for power has made it an apprehensive and rather frightening place under the rule of the gunmen, and these days almost every man is armed with a Kalashnikov.

On the morning I arrived, after an overnight drive over the mountains from Armenia, the Interior Ministry, next to the Parliament, was in flames. Machine-gun fire resounded around the almost deserted city. Rather naively, we dodged through backstreets to the Tbilisi Hotel – then the opposition headquarters. I stayed there a few months ago and had adored its crumbling grandeur and dusty chandeliers. This time, parked outside the front lobby was an armoured personnel carrier, mounted with a small cannon, blasting periodically in the direction of the Parliament. Dishevelled fighters were sleeping in the ornate restaurant. A couple of days later the hotel was set on fire during a counter-attack by troops loyal to the President. Today it is a blackened shell – the chandeliers a pile of broken glass.

During the conflict several people likened the network of narrow streets just above the Parliament to Beirut, under the control of a patchwork of different militia groups. But here at least the gunmen from whichever faction generally welcomed and helped us. Driving through this could still be a little scary; the nervous fighters, waiting around each corner, liked to point their machine-guns at your head. Six young men, bearing Kalashnikovs and the uniforms of the Georgian National Guard, danced in front of the car barring our way towards the rear of the Parliament, where President Gamsakhurdia was besieged. These were some of his troops, but it's often impossible to distinguish between the opposing forces. When I got out, rather gingerly, and explained that we wanted to see the President, we were whisked off towards his refuge rather faster than I would have liked. There was a fearsome wallop of artillery landing a block or so away, and endless outbursts of machine-gun fire apparently all around us. I felt terribly heavy and unbalanced in a navy blue BBC flak jacket, weighing something like 20 pounds, but I think I achieved a personal best on the one hundred metre sprint across open ground to a sandbagged window at the rear of the Parliament itself. All this to be told Mr Gamsakhurdia was too busy to talk to us. Within days he had fled.

It's still hard to understand how a split within the President's own government led to such conflict. Certainly a key figure was Tengiz Kitovani, the head of the Georgian National Guard, who took several of his men with him when he rounded on the President. The opposition lay the blame on Mr Gamsakhurdia himself. They say he became a dictator and failed to keep any of the promises he made in the run-up to his landslide victory in the presidential elections. He says it was down to bandits and criminals hungry for power. Both sides, variously, cite the involvement of the new imperialist Russia, the old Soviet KGB, Mr Gorbachev, the CIA and James Baker. There is evidence, though, that the disintegrating Soviet army may have played a part. Its soldiers did remain steadfastly in their barracks. The deputy commander of its forces in the Caucasus told me that this was a matter for the Georgian people to sort out amongst themselves – an attitude unthinkable a short while ago.

To some extent it is the bloody squabble that the hardliners long predicted would follow the erosion of central power, but there are strong indications, too, that what was the Soviet army may be responsible for the flood of weapons into this area – either directly or indirectly. One young fighter, leaning against a Russian T-55 tank outside the opposition headquarters, said it was obvious.

"Have you ever bought a Red Army watch?" he asked me – something almost every foreign visitor to the former Soviet Union is offered. I admitted these made good presents for friends at home. "Well," he said, "these are just a little more expensive." He patted the rusty tank and grinned. The huge Howitzer field guns almost certainly proved decisive in forcing President Gamsakhurdia to give up the fight. But the violence at demonstrations involving ordinary Georgian people may prove to be a more worrying indicator of things to come.

On Friday we were about to leave what seemed a rather low-key demonstration in support of President Gamsakhurdia, when a group of masked gunmen, dressed in black and straight from the pages of a cheap thriller, opened fire. At first the rapid crack of their machine-guns was over our heads; then I heard bullets whizzing past my ears. I tried to get behind a rather small pile of concrete construction blocks. My interpreter stood in a daze until I dragged her down beside me. A man in front of us just doubled up, a great flow of blood came from his stomach. Another man who'd been standing next to my cameraman was hit in the shoulder. With the attackers gone the crowd grabbed us and began dragging us from place to place, insisting we film the wounded and dying. One man had been shot in the head. But the image I cannot get out of my mind is the face of the gunman who got left behind – the one that was lynched by a hysterical mob. They had him in the back of a wrecked mini-bus, holding him by the scruff of the neck while they rubbed shattered glass into his face, and pointed a pistol at his throat. He turned his blood-streaked face and stared straight at the camera. Those eyes were, literally, blind with terror. Rather feebly, in English, I tried to tell the people to stop. The crowd turned on us, screaming that we must tell the truth, that we'd been telling lies; we just had to leave.

The animal violence that we saw there was somehow far worse than all the artillery and machine-gun fire: Georgian attacking Georgian with bare hands. It's hard to see how they can put that behind them now, how they will manage to bury their differences, and embrace one another in friendship again.

In Romania, numerous Western charities had been directing aid since the appalling conditions of life for many people there became known in 1989. One of these charities is the Comedy Store Fund for Sick Children. The comedian and playwright, Arthur Smith, went to Brasov in central Romania with his colleague, Jo Strand, where they visited one of the hospitals they had been working with.

COMIC RELIEF

ARTHUR SMITH   BRASOV   1 FEBRUARY 1992

W e made our way along the slushy road that weaved up the snowy mountainside. A thin slice of moon picked out the black silhouettes of towering fir trees and I imagined to myself that I was in Transylvania. And then I remembered that I was in Transylvania, although the taxi driver had shown no inclination to bite my neck. Like most Romanians he was more irritated than amused by British visitors' interest in this mythical story – although not so irritated that they don't organise excursions to Dracula's castle. Perhaps soon they will realise that, to market the castle in the true Western way, they should employ an actor with a cloak and some plastic fangs to frighten the tourists.

Until such heady times, Romanians remain in uncertain transition – or at least they hope it's transition because no-one wants things to stay the way they are. Conditions are as grim, if not grimmer, than they were under Ceausescu; there are shortages of virtually everything except stoic humour. Inflation now is such that the amount of money we were advised to take, by a knowledgeable friend, for four days was scarcely enough for an evening. Only foreigners, it seems, can afford to live in Romania.

We two foreigners were there for well-rehearsed reasons. Under the old government women had effectively been forced to have more children than they could afford to care for, and in the orphanages, where many of the unwanted children ended up, appalling conditions had been allowed to develop. It has subsequently become apparent that some of the aid sent out in response to these conditions has disappeared down a black hole of profiteering, pilfering and bureaucracy, and the compassion people showed was not always matched by their organisational abilities. I am pleased to report, however, that the project with which we are involved is a notable success. The charity trains and sponsors nine Romanian play therapists – called play specialists in Britain – who work in Brasov children's hospital. The children they look after, many from the local orphanage, have often led lives of such deprivation that they have retreated into their own private cocoons. The hospital might have treated their physical illnesses but could not cope with anything else. Colleagues from the charity who visited Brasov before the therapists were in place described dark, bare, dirty wards. Little or no attempt was made to stimulate children who were already traumatised by neglect. Some of them were tied to their cots to stop them moving about. There was an atmosphere of boredom and uncomprehending despair. A surprising number of children were infected with HIV or had developed Aids. This was because, under Ceausescu, doctors had tried to treat impoverished, underweight babies by giving them micro transfusions of blood – blood that was unscreened and contaminated. Many of these children had simply been left to die.

Given this background, the fact that the hospital is now alive with the sounds of children behaving normally is a huge step forward. It is not just a question of putting up pictures and playing with the children, although that is important. Taught by two British professionals sent to Brasov, the therapists have learnt a whole range of skills to help them cope with the sad state of some of the children. They have to understand various aspects of development and physiotherapy; they have to learn, for example, how to deal with a child who refuses to eat. One such little girl, Simone, I saw on a video that the therapists had shot. Simone had come from an orphanage and was eight, but looked like a horribly emaciated four year-old. She had never learned to walk or talk and initially screamed at the unfamiliar sensation of being cuddled. Cases like this require long hours of emotionally draining work. In Simone's case this was only four days before she had to return to the orphanage. Small successes though can be heartening: we also saw videos of previously sullen, defensive children giggling and dancing in the newly-created play areas. One boy I saw, I felt sure, could eventually be a Transylvanian Michael Jackson.

Jo and I spent our days at the hospital being useless but supportive and our evenings, as tourists, getting drunk with as many Romanians as we could drag out; they can't afford this so we paid as often as they let us. We also spoke in English since the only phrase we had managed to memorise in Romanian was *văd un om sub masa* – I see a man under the table. Over cans of German beer – the local brew being unavailable – we talked of Illiescu, the coming elections, King Michael and Vlad the Impaler, and on one night – I'm afraid to say – Jo was able to use our Romanian phrase in its correct context. On another, a man told us how, during the revolution, he had gone into the main square with a gun. "How did you know who to shoot at?" asked Jo. "I didn't," he said, and then added darkly, "I still don't." Romanians know best of all what many members of the new government used to be – members of the old government. You wonder if revolution is really an appropriate word for the change of government in December 1989.

There was no electricity at Bucharest airport on the morning of our departure, and even my thermal long-johns offered only partial protection from the bone-freezing cold. I was quite pleased to be leaving Romania for the luxury of Balham, south London, but my liberal conscience had, of course, been well pricked. We will keep the project going and hope its benefits might eventually be available in other hospitals in Romania; but what, I wondered, could I helpfully contribute from my glitzy show-biz world? Actually I knew. The therapists had told me how, at the end of a particularly difficult day, they raised their spirits by watching a wild Irish dancing song by Bob Geldof. They also enjoy the irony of the title – *The Great Song of Indifference*. Could I get him to send them a note? That, I reckoned I could manage.

Early in 1992 Alex Shprintsen returned to Kharkov, the Ukrainian city where
he was born. When he was 12 years old. his parents applied for permission to
emigrate to Israel, although they eventually settled in Canada. Alex decided to find
out what had become of some of his teachers and childhood friends, and in particular
his ex-classmate, Zhenya.

THE PRODIGAL
RETURNS

ALEX SHPRINTSEN   KHARKOV   19 FEBRUARY 1992

I desperately wanted to find Zhenya, especially since we'd never said goodbye to one another. Not only had he been one of my best friends, but also, as I had discovered, he too had become a journalist. Finding him wasn't very difficult since in Ukraine, for lack of choice, people tend to live their entire lives under the same roof – unless they emigrate, of course.

We met in Zhenya's large but run-down office on the outskirts of Kharkov late one afternoon. He greeted me with an emotional hug and to toast the reunion, he got out three bottles – one with pickled cucumbers as the appetizer, the other two with vodka. I knew we would be there for a while since tradition forbids throwing away unfinished vodka. Even before the first glass though, Zhenya's opening words caught me a bit off guard: he had decided to make a confession. "Before we go any further," he said, "I must get something off my chest. It's been bothering me for sixteen years, I feel very ashamed of it, and so please, please forgive me." I couldn't possibly imagine what he was talking about. After all, we were only twelve at the time. But I was curious to hear what he had to say and offered to forgive him in advance.

"If you recall," he began, "you left in the late summer of 1975. Well, on the first day of school in September, Marta Sergeyevna, our form teacher, gathered

77

our entire class for a special assembly. Angrily, she made an announcement: "Alex Shprintsen and his parents have betrayed the motherland and left for the terrorist state of Israel. Naturally, they are traitors, they are scum, they are worthless trash. Remember children, the good citizens stay."

"She then walked up to my desk," he continued. "Zhenya," she said, "of all the kids in this class, you and Alex were comrades. Now tell the rest of us – isn't he a traitor, isn't he worthless trash?" At this point, Zhenya's eyes reddened and his hands began to tremble. "What could I do?" he asked. "I didn't add to her diatribe, but I nodded. Of course I didn't mean it. Please, please forgive me." I wanted him to talk more about it, but he would only remind me about that old vodka tradition which, much to his displeasure, we ended up breaking: the second bottle was put back into the fridge unfinished, as my drinking just wasn't up to it.

The next morning I decided to go back to the school. I wanted to see how the place had changed along with all the other changes since Gorbachev. When I got to the entrance, I hesitated slightly, but since no-one challenged me, I just wandered in and walked around without saying who I was. The building hadn't really changed, although everything now seemed very primitive. Eventually I found the main office and introduced myself to the head teacher. When I told her that I was a former pupil and had come back to prepare a programme for the BBC, it became obvious that I was no longer considered a traitor. She told me how proud she was of me and asked if she could help in some way. I said that I'd love to see any of my old teachers who were still around, so she gave me a list of the staff. I only recognized two of the names.

Almost immediately, the two were summoned. Remembering me, they greeted me with hugs and tears. I felt like the prodigal son returning from some heroic adventure. For about forty minutes they peppered me with all sorts of questions, but I saved mine right until the end. As I was saying goodbye, I casually slipped in: "Remember my form teacher, Marta Sergeyevna. What's she up to these days?" One teacher then looked at the other, and after a slight pause said with a chuckle: "Funny you should ask. She left the school only recently. She's just emigrated to Israel."

In February 1992, a senior figure in the Russian government paid a visit to one of the coldest and most remote towns in the republic, Vorkuta, high inside Russia's Arctic Circle, to try to settle an industrial dispute in the coal mines. Lying thirteen hundred kilometres north of Moscow, Vorkuta was built in the thirties by Stalin to exploit the area's mineral wealth. It is a place so inhospitable that it is difficult to imagine how the people there survive.

VORKUTA - A CAPITAL FIT FOR HELL

KEVIN CONNOLLY   VORKUTA   22 FEBRUARY 1992

The runway lights stream up at you like burning coals out of the soft, inky darkness of the Arctic night. The small airport building glows unnaturally bright through the swirling currents of snow. At the gates, which lead from the edge of the airfield directly onto the car park – for flying here is a workman-like business – children are playing on makeshift slides in the ice.

It is an unseasonably warm minus twenty-nine. Clouds of exhaust gas hang in the air like unwanted special effects from a misconceived romantic film. The engines of a dozen or so waiting taxis throb dully in the sulphurous air, which is thick with the tang of cheap petrol. No one, not even the most parsimonious taxi driver, switches off the engine; re-starting it, or even unfreezing the catch which secures the bonnet, can take half an hour.

For this is Vorkuta, far inside the Russian Arctic; the second city in law of the Komi Peninsula, and in fact a capital fit for hell. Here and there in the centre there are touches of despondent gaiety, a neon hammer and sickle, an illuminated crest of crossed sledgehammers. But Vorkuta is, for the most part, grey – as grey as the freezing clouds which merge by day at the low horizon with the wintry wasteland on which it stands.

It was built in the 1930s by Stalin, a grim memorial to the fear and energy which lay at the heart of all Soviet achievements. The reasoning had the brutal simplicity which was the murderous hallmark of a bloody period: if there was coal, even coal buried half a mile beneath the Arctic tundra, then there must be men and women to mine it. They came at first, of course, to build where previously there had been nothing but ice. The first settlers were either political prisoners or young Communists, with fire in their hearts and red stars in their eyes. Legend has it that the statue of Stalin arrived long before the timber and slates they needed to put roofs on their homes.

But they came to build, and build they did. They left behind thirteen mines, countless apartment blocks and forests of white crosses marking the graves of those who fell to hunger and neglect, or to cold and overwork. The ringroad they constructed to link the settlement together is still there too, a dismal loop that runs from nowhere to nowhere, with the snow and ice packed ten feet high on either side, like some infernal bob-sleigh run. The camps of course have long been closed and their dead – six hundred thousand or more – buried beneath the frozen ground on which they laboured.

But Vorkuta labours on, peopled by the same mixture of the hopeful and the helpless which gave it life: much though has changed. The helpless are the families still trapped here, victims of a hated system which allows them to live only where they have legal permission to live. The hopeful are those who came here spurred by the desire of all parents to give their children a good start in life, better than the one they enjoyed themselves. The pay for a face-worker here is between ten and twenty times the national average, and there are two months of leave to spend in the sunshine of the south. There are American films on a cable channel, and food and drink too – if not perhaps as much as there was, then certainly more than there is in other towns elsewhere in Russia.

But if the rewards are high, then the price the miners pay is higher still; their life expectancy is, perhaps, forty-seven. Vorkuta is a ghostly town where no-one grows old, and no-one looks young. Their children are allowed to play outdoors until the temperature falls to minus thirty-six, a little colder and the schools are closed – a concession to the savage Arctic winds, begrudged by parents and children alike. They get more value here from the giant snow-figures all Russian children love to build in their parks and squares. Here it's cold and snowy enough to build them in late August, and early the following June, in most years, they are still there. In the intervening months Vorkuta is a town of unremitting cold and near perpetual darkness, which wakens only slowly to the latest spring in the world. When it comes in mid-June, they tell you, it has the flaring intensity of a match suddenly struck in a darkened room. But it soon gives way to a blazing summer, blighted by mosquitoes that never sleep.

This is a town built on hardship and sustained now by perverse pride, and by a sudden new hope for the future. If real economic freedom is to come, as it seems it must, then Vorkuta may be able to keep more of the hard currency its coal has always earned for the Soviet state. The leaders of the new Russian government tremble before the threat of a strike here, as surely did their Soviet predecessors.

Relations with other republics are fragile now in these uncertain days, even with Ukraine, even though almost half the town are descendants from Ukrainians exiled here during an unsuccessful struggle for independence in the fifties. The future won't be easy of course, but then nothing here ever has been. Vorkuta is remote, forbidding and largely ignorant of the ways of Western business it now must learn. But mixed in with the stubborn pride that life in such a place encourages, there is a touch, too, of unmistakably real optimism; perhaps it's not so difficult to understand. For these are a people who built where it should have been impossible to build, who endured what it should have been impossible to endure, and who now have only to make work what should be unworkable.

In a year which saw the all-powerful Soviet Communist Party toppled and the Soviet Union itself dissolved, Tim Whewell detected a mood which was anything but optimistic as people contemplated a future without communism.

REHABILITATING THE PAST

TIM WHEWELL   MOSCOW   3 MARCH 1992

It should have been a familiar scene. And yet, somehow, it belonged to a different world. In the courtyard of my block of flats, among the snow-covered children's swings and climbing-frames, a group of men in heavy overcoats and fur hats were sitting on a bench. They had their backs to us, but we could see that they were drinking in turn from a clear glass bottle and eating with their fingers from something wrapped in old greasy newspaper. At the sight of them my normally cheerful Russian companion lapsed into sudden wistfulness. A few years ago, he said, he and his friends had whiled away many weekend afternoons in similar fashion, sitting in the open air with a couple of bottles of vodka and some salami or dried fish. Now, no-one seemed to indulge in such simple pleasures, and the scene in my courtyard was becoming increasingly rare.

One reason for the change, he said, was practical. Vodka and salami, once plentiful and cheap, are now available only at vastly inflated prices or after waiting in a long queue. Dried fish – the traditional Russian accompaniment to beer or vodka – has not been seen in the shops for years. But more significantly, my friend said, there's been a change of mood in the country. Men are now expected to spend more time with their wives and children, and drinking in public is frowned on. In any case, everyone is so anxious about the future that a drinking session might be an occasion less for light-hearted banter than for morose analysis of Russia's plight.

My friend is an abstract artist in his late twenties. He's begun to sell his paintings to foreigners for hundreds of dollars apiece, and he's just been abroad for the first time in his life to take part in an exhibition. The reforms begun by Mr Gorbachev have given him opportunities he would never have dreamed of. And yet, as with most other Russians I know, his attitude to those reforms veers between ambivalence and bitterness. It's the bitterness that comes with lost innocence.

The Soviet Union that Mr Gorbachev gradually destroyed was a land where nothing ever happened. Its citizens could plan their whole lives without a thought for possible changes in political or economic conditions. Their standard of living and their careers depended on maintaining a complex web of personal contacts in shops, hospitals, schools and government offices. But the system of mutual favours worked well and was universally understood.

Now, everything is uncertain; goods must be bought with real money, at prices which change almost daily. Keeping a job can involve hard work and taking the right decisions. Fear of the future has now become so ingrained that few young people are prepared to have children. All over the country maternity wards stand empty. But even those who can cope with the new conditions feel they're pushed against their will into being ambitious. A highly energetic and successful journalist I know told me she and her friends used to laugh at the idea that, in America, people rang one another up and arranged to meet at a certain time a week on Friday, or two weeks on Thursday. Russians rarely had anything vital to do the same afternoon.

Now, however, to her horror my journalist friend is herself keeping an appointments diary, and thinking back, nostalgically, to the days when the sudden appearance of an old acquaintance at home or work would be the perfect excuse to drop whatever business was at hand and sit round a table for a few hours putting the world to rights. And those kinds of sessions were enjoyable, not just because there was no guilt at wasting time, but also because nearly everyone was on the same side.

You couldn't be for or against a government of shambling old men who talked in meaningless ideological clichés – you could only joke about it. But at the same time most people believed that communism had given them a basic, guaranteed standard of living, free education and health care and a degree of social harmony that never existed in the West. Moreover, Soviet citizens were proud of living in such a vast country, respected and feared throughout the world for its strength and achievements.

The sense of loss and betrayal at the destruction of the Soviet Union runs deep even among young people. My artist friend, for example, is typical in his belief that there were no serious inter-ethnic tensions in the country before the advent of *perestroika*. He's convinced that republics, such as Ukraine, have broken away only because self-serving politicians have deliberately set one people against another.

First-time visitors to the Soviet Union used to report how grey everything looked. Now they say capitalism is bringing a little colour to the streets. But all that's very much a foreigner's perception. Many Russians feel that what they've gained can't make up for what they've lost. One friend, a man without any sympathy for communists, told me the Revolution Day parades and the celebrations that followed at home had been a real holiday. Now, instead, there was Christmas, but what did that mean to him? Like most other Russians, he wasn't religious, and no-one in his family knew anything about the traditional customs once connected with the festival.

Three or four generations grew up under communism, and the attempt to revive pre-revolutionary ways is making them strangers in their own country. The ubiquitous slogans of the Soviet era bore little resemblance to reality but at least they were a familiar part of the landscape. Far more alienating are the new and seemingly endless advertisements for stock exchanges, brokerage places, and commercial banks, terms which mean nothing to most people but leave them with the uncomfortable feeling that they're missing out on something.

Now, for a sense of belonging, you have to return to the past. And even I, who once lived without any responsibilities in Brezhnev's Soviet Union, sometimes wish I could abandon my job, my car and my telephone, and join the drinkers in the courtyard.

After almost half a century of one party dictatorship there was a new party in power in Albania – the Democratic Party. A newcomer to the political scene, it went on to chalk up a sweeping victory, in March 1992, in the second elections since the collapse of communism. But while Albanians were trying to construct a pluralist democracy, their economy was being sucked down a black hole.

ALBANIA'S ECONOMIC MIRAGE

MISHA GLENNY   TIRANA   26 MARCH 1992

In the centre of Tirana there is a huge hole dug into the ground which, to give you an idea of its size, would happily accommodate a jumbo jet. Near the entrance to the hole is a board which sometimes stands and at other times cannot resist the force of Albania's wind. The board announces the construction, at some unspecified point in the future, of a dazzlingly modern Sheraton Hotel sponsored by the ubiquitous company, Illyiria Holdings. In order to dig the hole, Illyiria Holdings received permission last year, from the then Socialist-dominated government, to destroy a park, which had been completed but a year prior to this, after several years in the making. The man behind Illyiria, an Albanian who emigrated to Switzerland some years ago, still drives ostentatiously around Tirana in a yellow Rolls Royce, accompanied everywhere by two armed bodyguards. The hole, however, is resolutely unfilled and shows every sign of remaining so for a long time to come.

On the surface, the first snowdrops of a market economy are forcing their way through the barren soil of the Albanian economy. Little street stalls have sprung up around Tirana and other towns, selling soft drinks and cigarettes. One or two shops now offer electrical goods from the West; televisions, for example, which cost $365 each, and you have to pay in dollars. Perfectly reasonable, perhaps, until you discover that the average wage in Europe's poorest country is $11 per month, paid in the local currency, the lek. So, who can afford such a price?

There is a group of people who make it their business to steal car windscreens and then, two days later, to sell them back to their owners for $100. Then there are those people who generate wealth by appropriating livestock from state farms at gun point, before driving them over the border to Greece and selling them at what, for the Greeks, are dumping prices; but for the Albanian gangsters these represent handsome hard currency profits.

So do not be fooled by these harbingers of a free economy: they are nothing but parasitic flotsam whose main function is to ensure that the bottomless pit, that passes for an economy in Albania, remains resolutely unfilled. There is still food in Albania – true, ordinary people must sacrifice a lot of time trying to get their hands on it – but the recent food riots in several Albanian towns were caused not so much by the absence of comestibles as by poor distribution.

Other commodities are scarce or absent; this winter power cuts throughout a country that used to be a net exporter of electricity, lasted literally for months. Since the collapse of communism, the infrastructure has seized up and water is distributed now only to a minority of houses. The reservoirs are full but the antiquated pump and refinery equipment can no longer do its job and the engineers are no longer able, or can no longer be bothered, to fix it. It's almost beyond me to describe the squalor of Albanian hospitals: suffice to say that during a visit to the only operating theatre in Tirana, a friend turned to the accompanying surgeon and said: "This place looks like a butcher's." "If this were a butcher's," the surgeon replied, "they would have closed it down a long time ago."

Forty years of isolation, which initially brought the Albanian people many things in material terms, has now combined with a thoroughly Balkan indolence to seize up the economy completely. The newly victorious Democratic Party must cope with the most burdensome legacy of all in Eastern Europe. It is one which only the most resilient politicians will be able to overcome. The main task of the Democratic Party is to attract foreign investment from any country willing to risk it; and there is no doubt which is the Democrats' favourite foreign country: the United States of America.

It's hard for the Democrats not to be grateful; after all, American institutions provided them with Cherokee jeeps and computers for their election campaign and an unspecified, albeit not substantial, amount of dollars. William Rierson, the American ambassador in Tirana, and his diplomats openly endorsed the Democratic Party's campaign: in short, Albania may want to be part of Europe, but the most influential foreign power there is now America. Whether this is good or bad for its economy and its political stability is open to question, but just as Slovenia and Croatia may one day regret placing all their eggs in a German basket, the Albanians may be risking alienating some European partners by their excessive affection for Washington.

In the former Yugoslav republic of Bosnia-Hercegovina fighting broke out between the mixed communities of Muslims, Serbs and Croats. Tension rose to breaking point when the republic won international recognition as an independent state – a move that was fiercely opposed by the Serbs. Jane Howard was in the thick of it when clashes broke out in the capital, Sarajevo in the spring of 1992.

SHOOT-OUT IN SARAJEVO

JANE HOWARD   SARAJEVO   11 APRIL 1992

Tourists coming to Sarajevo to see the spot where Archduke Ferdinand was assassinated, the event which triggered the First World War, often used to stay at the Holiday Inn. When I checked in, I wasn't expecting a holiday. I was covering the civil war, and should have known it was a bad idea when I was met by two colleagues checking out. They reckoned that the hotel was becoming too dangerous. I knew it was the headquarters of the main Serb party which had fought against leaving Yugoslavia, and the last time I stayed there it was full of Serb bodyguards, concealing guns under their raincoats.

One night, Serb militants manned barricades and cut off the city for twenty-four hours. This time there was action within minutes of my arrival. I went upstairs to file my first despatch. I left a microphone on the windowsill to record the sound of a crowd outside, staging a peace protest in front of the parliament. Then, suddenly, all hell was let loose. Shots rang around the hotel and the crowd scattered in fear. As I spoke to my news-desk, two loud hand-grenade explosions rocked the hotel. I dived between the beds and hastily brought the conversation to an end. Only later did I realise that Muslim militiamen had stormed the building. They had come to search for Serb snipers, who they believed had opened fire on the crowd. The 'phone rang. It was a colleague from the Associated Press. "Something terrible has happened in the lobby," she said. "Come down, but be careful." I grabbed my tape recorder. On reflection, I put on my flak jacket. It's of a type worn by Norwegian policewomen, the only kind the BBC could find small enough for me.

The lift descended into the lobby and the doors opened. Three militiamen in battledress were pointing their guns at me. On the floor amid broken glass were four men lying face downwards with their hands tied. I thought they might be dead. Before I could think, the militiamen bundled me physically out of the lift and into the crowd outside. Then they hustled me back in, and I took cover beneath the reception desk. I stayed there, crouched down, for several hours. The police took the alleged snipers away. They were not dead, after all. In front of me was a row of 'phones, and after a while I plucked up the courage to ask a gunman if I could use them. I made several calls to the BBC describing the scene; it took my mind off things.

Meanwhile, gunfire and loud crashes could be heard inside the hotel as the militiamen broke down doors, looking for more Serbs. Later they allowed me to collect my belongings. There was a smell of gunsmoke in my room. I was lucky; just one flowery shirt was missing. Other colleagues lost computers and camera equipment. The correspondent from *The Times* lost his luggage, and wandered around like Father Christmas, with his things in a duvet cover.

But the ordeal was not over. The militiamen would not let us go. They said it was too dangerous. When they finally relented, they insisted on driving us to the hotel of their choice. Two tall militiamen climbed into my colleague's Audi saloon and stashed their guns on the seat beside me. The one who drove appeared drunk. When we lurched off in the opposite direction to the hotel they'd suggested, I became suspicious. As we drove past at least fifteen checkpoints manned by gunmen in green berets, I began to have visions of Beirut. But we finally arrived. The gunmen politely handed back my colleague's car keys.

Twenty minutes later, they asked if they could borrow it. They said it was too dangerous to walk back. She handed the keys over, wondering if she would ever see the car again. She did, the next day, in front of the Holiday Inn. As she ran towards the car, a gun battle broke out. She beat a hasty retreat. The Audi has been seen since; cruising round the streets of Sarajevo, the smartest battle wagon in town. Since then, I have come under sniper fire and artillery bombardment, but I have never been so frightened as during the shoot-out at the Holiday Inn.

Anyone arriving to live and work in a foreign country is bound to face various bureaucratic hurdles, which can reveal much about the nature of the country concerned. Chris Bowlby, who arrived to take up the post of BBC Prague correspondent in spring 1992, was struck by the local bureaucracy's obsession with the rubber stamp, reminding him of the work of Czechoslovakia's great literary son, Franz Kafka.

RUBBER STAMP IN PRAGUE

CHRIS BOWLBY   PRAGUE   17 APRIL 1992

It comes in all shapes and several sizes. It's applied either with loving precision or a vicious thump. If it's in the right place, life is suddenly easy. If it's in the wrong place, or not there at all, life falls apart. The rubber stamp is not, of course, unique to Czechoslovakia. I've seen it in use everywhere from Calcutta's banks to Colorado's youth hostels. But in other countries, in my experience, it's just a minor part of a wider bureaucratic process. Only here is the rubber stamping a process in itself.

On a seemingly endless tour of offices in Prague applying for residence permits, car registration and the like, it was always the rubber stamp or lack of it that caused me problems. The actual words on my application forms didn't seem to matter. As I apprehensively handed them over for official approval, I knew that, sooner or later, a sentence of doom would be spoken. "No stamp"; or "stamp in wrong place"; or even "sorry, right stamp, wrong form".

Sent back to ministries or lawyers for a second or third try, I'd find each institution baffled by the other's requirements. But all agreed that getting the stamps right was essential. As one official kindly explained: "I'd like to make it easier, but if I don't stamp it correctly nor will my superiors, and then where will we be?" Rubber may be flexible, but the rules of rubber stamping are as rigid as a bureaucrat's lunch break.

The rubber stamp, as I rapidly realised, is much more than a quick way to print information or register a document. It's a crucial assertion of power and place in the bureaucratic hierarchy. Junior officials carry their stamps in their pockets, next to house keys and identity documents. More senior figures display a box of different stamps prominently on their desks. Their ink pads, I noticed, are mostly manufactured by a huge state enterprise called Monopol. The most senior officials of all order their inferiors to apply the stamps, which they then approve with a superior signature.

The tyranny of the rubber stamp – *razitko* in Czech – was of course reinforced by Czechoslovakia's former Communist regime. Nothing suited that regime better than craven submission to strict hierarchy and monopolistic paperwork control. But in fact the tyranny has much deeper historical roots. Officials will also refer to the all-powerful stamp as the Stempel – a German word which betrays the lasting influence here of the Austro-Hungarian empire. Its bureaucracy was famously formidable, and Czechoslovakia's communists simply built on well established habits. These habits have, in turn, easily survived the fall of the Communist regime.

There is, however, another challenge on the horizon. The few really modern offices in Prague display the latest computer technology. As dedicated bureaucrats must be uncomfortably aware, the power of the rubber stamp will be seriously reduced in the world where computer screens replace sheets of paper. They'll do their best, no doubt, to ensure that deliveries of high technology never receive the proper authorisation.

It may in fact be years before Czechoslovakia can afford the technology as well as the training to make its administration truly modern. But there are already signs that two years after the velvet revolution, people are now taking rubber power into their own hands. Prague taxis have started to carry advertisements for do-it-yourself *razitko* shops, where the citizen can make his or her own mark of authority. I saw this used to striking effect in a queue at the traffic police headquarters. When one agitated motorist was told by a delighted official that he didn't have the correct stamps, he suddenly produced his own, and proceeded to self-authorise his form with immense satisfaction. His resistance probably didn't last long, but it cheered all those around him.

Yet I believe the best long-term solution does not lie in mass rubber stamp retaliation. I can't help thinking that a Czech friend's plea for all his country's rubber stamps is the best. In the best traditions of absurdist art, he wants to collect them together, melt them down and then produce one giant version as a memorial to all the years of bureaucratic futility. It would be placed on the platform high above Prague where a huge statue of Stalin used to stand. The necessary authorisation would, of course, be unavoidable. So he'd make a giant piece of paper too, and stamp on it an utterly conclusive end to the *razitko* rulers' power.

Communism may have fallen in Eastern Europe, but many of the people who ran the old system are still around. Some are keeping a low profile, fearful of retribution, others are visibly unrepentant. Julian Borger went along to a ball in Warsaw organized by former Communist Party members to investigate the lifestyles of the post-Communist rich and famous.

POLAND'S EX-COMMUNISTS HAVE A BALL

JULIAN BORGER   WARSAW   25 APRIL 1992

At first I didn't think we were going to get in. We had dressed up specially and gone along to Warsaw's Grand Hotel, only to find our way barred by a burly man in a dinner jacket standing in front of the lift doors. "And where's your invitation?" he asked, in the same tone of voice he must have used a few years ago to demand a totally different kind of Party card, a red one that was a sign of loyalty. The truth was that we didn't think we needed an invitation. We had heard that entrance to this Post-Communist Easter Ball was free for 'prostitutes, sinners and (to annoy the church as much as possible) Christian Nationalists'.

Everyone in our small group of party-goers felt that they qualified one way or another. The impasse at the lift doors was broken when two men in long raincoats turned up and strode past the bouncer into the lift pulling us in behind them as the doors closed. "Welcome to Neo-Communism, the New Poland," the taller and drunker of the two men bellowed jovially as the lift sped up to the tenth floor nightclub. His shorter, more reserved, companion, simply chuckled, a little embarrassed.

The lift doors opened on to a dingy hall already filled with people dancing to western hits from the seventies, the heyday of the Polish United Workers Party. Above the dance-floor a twenty-foot banner proclaimed: "No to Communism; No to Communism": this jubilantly negative tone was quite deliberate. The ball had been organised by a satirical magazine written by former Party hacks, which calls itself, quite simply, 'No'.

'No' specialises in offending Poland's powerful Catholic Church, and each issue strives to include articles and cartoons that are more obscene than the week before. Not surprisingly, it is doing extremely well, with a readership of 1. 4 million. The ball pursued the unholy theme. Sackcloth was obligatory and guests were invited to sprinkle themselves with ashes, in mock-penitence for the wrongs they had committed against the church as cogs in the Party machine. Some fairly big cogs had turned up for the extravaganza, and the dance-floor was bustling with the ex-nomenclatura – a former minister here, a deputy-prime minister there, all in high spirits. Even the General Secretary of the Social Democrats - the main post-Communist parliamentary group – was there, putting a succession of young women through their paces.

And then there was Jerzy Urban, the editor of 'No' who was chief government spokesman in the eighties. A short man dressed in dinner jacket and sackcloth, he stood looking on, rubbing his hands in impish glee. This was the ultimate revenge for the overthrow of the old system. Its former servants were celebrating – defiantly unrepentant and prosperous.

There is a widespread belief in Poland that the success of businessmen, under the country's experimental form of capitalism, is based on funds embezzled under the old system. The post-Communist Ball certainly provided much circumstantial evidence to confirm that suspicion. For the evening to be as decadent as possible, Mr Urban had planned some fun and games.

Three of the city's more elegant prostitutes took to the dance-floor and writhed seductively, to the disco-beat of an updated Gregorian Chant, in front of three kneeling men. Egged on by the master of ceremonies, the women slowly pulled themselves out of their party dresses to reveal colourful but flimsy underwear, which was then greedily devoured by the men. The crowd roared its approval, and the master of ceremonies announced the name of the local sex-shop which sold this particular brand of edible underwear. All this time, the two men we had met in the lift had been propping up the bar. "Don't think I approve of all this," the tall, talkative one said, pointing to the scene around him. "But

what I like about that Urban fellow is that he sticks to what he believes in."
He said his name was Wieslaw and that he used to run Polish military intelligence
in the Stockholm embassy.

Drawing me aside conspiratorially, he told me a British spy had once offered
him a secure future in the West in return for defection. Wieslaw had refused
on patriotic grounds but now, with what he called the 'feudal power' of the
church restored, he was beginning to wonder if he had done the right thing.
"So now you're surviving on a state pension, I suppose?" I said, rather naively.
"Of course not," he laughed, "I've got plenty of money set aside. We all have."

The vast, inhospitable wastes of northern Siberia contain the world's largest reserves of oil and gas. To the Russian government, the region offers a potential economic bonanza, but the territory once belonged to a group of small, nomadic peoples whose traditional culture has been engulfed by modern ¡civilisation and the dictates of communist ideology.

THE HAND THAT CARESSES

TIM WHEWELL   RADUZHNY   25 JUNE 1992

In northern Siberia the snow melts in late May; there's a brief flurry at the end of July, and by early September the countryside is, again, white. You might think the native peoples – the Khanty, the Mansi and the Nenets – would treasure their short fierce summer. In fact they talk about a sense of emotional release and spiritual cleansing that comes with the first autumn snowfall. At the height of the summer you can't speak out of doors without swallowing a mouthful of mosquitoes; the natives say they don't even notice insect bites – just as a child, slapped continuously about the face from birth, would soon begin to accept the treatment as a normal part of life.

Nevertheless, summer is inconvenient. Travel through the swampy forests is possible only by boat, or if you're well-connected, by helicopter; but neither boats nor helicopters are suitable for transporting large herds of reindeer – and the only reason for travelling is to move the deer from one grazing area to another. When the snow and ice return, the Khanty, the Mansi and the Nenets can harness the deer to their sledges and set off across the firm, frozen ground. The snow protects the fragile reindeer moss from destruction by hooves and feet, but leaves it accessible to a deer's foraging snout. Meanwhile the tracks of bears, foxes and sable, invisible in the summer months, are suddenly revealed for the hunter to follow.

Nowadays, there's also another, more sinister reason why native Siberians prefer the winter: when the ice melts a strange shiny film appears on the surface of rivers and lakes. Yuri Vella, the Nenets poet I went to visit, lives 40 km from the nearest oil field, but he's convinced that when the oilmen burn off excess gas from their wells the chemicals that fly up into the air eventually settle in the snow and are released, in spring, into the water supply. Yuri doesn't know what harm the chemicals are doing to him or his family but, year by year, he watches as the oilmen extend their operations at the expense of his people.

How many reindeer does a Nenets family need? Yuri encourages his guests to make the calculation themselves. An average family has perhaps a dozen members: a husband and wife, their parents, their three children (two of whom might already be married) and a couple of grandchildren. To lead a nomadic life, each person needs a sledge with three deer in harness. Then there have to be extra sledges to carry tents and food. Some deer are too young to be harnessed, some are too old or sick, others are kept for breeding or for meat. If you work it out, a Nenets family needs at least two hundred deer, and two hundred deer need a wide expanse of moss to feed on. Yuri can't decide whether it's fate, or the will of God, or a law of nature, but for some reason the places where oil has been struck also happen to be the places which offered the best grazing, fishing and hunting. The Nenets have been forced to move to areas they used to avoid, but even there much of the reindeer moss has been destroyed by fires or flattened by vehicles. The tiny brittle fronds don't grow back for five or ten years.

There's no direct equivalent in the Nenets language for the word rich. You can only say 'possessing many deer'. Without deer, the Nenets can't preserve their traditional way of life and Yuri fears their language will also die. If you're talking about special kinds of harnesses, parts of sledges, types of axes, arrows, lassoes and fish traps, you'll have to express yourself in Nenets. Sell your deer and buy a car, and you'll find that the words for road, carburettor, traffic lights and spark plug, exist only in Russian. Few of the young people in Yuri's village can speak Nenets. But even those who can have only a basic everyday vocabulary. Yuri says the rich language of songs and stories is already almost dead. That language contained, for example, many different words for hand – the hand that snatches, the hand that gives, the hand that caresses; and many words for fire – destroying fire, warming fire, cooking fire. But most of the traditional singers and story-tellers were shot by the secret police in the 1930s, accused by their neighbours of being shamans or witch doctors. None of what they knew was written down because the local dialect has no alphabet. Yuri Vella is fighting to preserve his people's tradition, but most other Nenets don't care; they want houses, cars and modern social facilities.

Down the road, in the oil town of Raduzhny, my Russian guide was angry that I'd spent so long with what she called 'the eskimos'. The oil men, she said, had built a new school and a kindergarten in the eskimo settlement: what else was there of interest? I didn't think it was worth trying to tell her about the hand that caresses.

THE AMERICAS

*Whenever George Bush finds the going tough with Congress in Washington, he
likes to compl Lthat the politicians on Capitol Hill have lost touch with the real
America. Our Washington Correspondent, Jeremy Harris, spent part of a week
far away – in every sense – from the politics of Washington, in the backwoods
of the southern state of Louisiana.*

DEEP SOUTH

JEREMY HARRIS   OLLA   17 OCTOBER 1991

They were still bolting together the toddlers' carousel when I arrived
at the fairground outside the small Louisiana town of Olla. A bare-backed
man in his twenties, with blond hair and a straggly moustache, was trying to
follow the instructions of his boss, hidden somewhere in the contraption's canvas
canopy. It was 4 pm on a warm early autumn afternoon; the fair, the man
told me in a drawl as slow as the Mississippi river, would start at six. His
boss, a black man in a red checked shirt, descended from the clouds of canvas
looking worried. There was no power supply yet, he said, to give the carousel
a trial run. He was the first and last black man I saw for several hours. The
fair was being set up on a dusty expanse of grass in front of the Olla Standard
Elementary School – a low, anonymous building enlivened only by a mural
of a large tiger stalking the front façade.

The school, like just about everything else in the community it served, was
built alongside the railway track. With a dwindling population of about fifteen
hundred, the line has survived not for the benefit of the inhabitants of Olla,
but for transporting the timber from which most make their living. The town
stands on the edge of dense woodlands stretching for miles towards the neighbouring states of Arkansas and Texas.

A few of the lumber-jacks, big stoop-shouldered men, mostly middle-aged,
in jeans, cowboy boots and hats – some with wads of tobacco swelling their
cheeks – were already arriving at the fairground in pick-up trucks and vans.

They'd been drawn, not by the annual chance to see how fast they could pitch a baseball, nor by the glazed apples or cotton candy. For them, everything the fair had to offer was a sideshow: the main attraction was political. Their favoured candidate in the imminent race for governor of Louisiana was due soon – one David Duke, former Grand Wizard of the Ku Klux Klan. A small wooden booth, draped in orange plastic and plastered with 'Duke for Governor' stickers, had been set up in front of the animal pens, populated by a noisy rabble of sheep, cows, and a beige-skinned bull. The men stood in small huddles, talking earnestly, their fingers jammed in leather belts slung beneath some ample bellies. Most of the women stood apart with their children, some of whom sported sweatshirts championing both David Duke and assorted Teenage Mutant Ninja Turtles. One small boy had already seen Mr Duke the previous evening, and pronounced him 'cool'.

The combined drawing power of David Duke, and the annual visit of the travelling fair to Olla had not been wasted on the town's own politicians. The Mayor, Mr Hill, was there early to press the flesh. A rotund, bespectacled figure, he confided he was weary of the burdens of office and was planning to step down as soon as his pet project, an old folk's home, got off the ground. Also working the gathering crowd of locals was Mr David Patton, campaigning for election to the Louisiana State Senate more than a hundred miles away in the capital, Baton Rouge. Undaunted by my admission that I was unable to vote for him, or anybody else for that matter, he handed me a copy of his election manifesto. The spelling wasn't all that good, but the message was clear enough: Mr Patton was hoping to ride to office on the coat-tails of Mr Duke; the blacks were taking over, he explained, the whites were becoming a minority. Someone had to stand up and speak out for the white man.

His manifesto made no mention of the subject, but Mr Patton was keen to demonstrate his grasp of international affairs: Britain was a great ally – now and in the past – especially during the Second World War when he'd served as a lowly corporal; but one, by his own account, with a modest place in history. He claimed to have loaded personally the bombs that were dropped on Hiroshima and Nagasaki. Mr Patton told his story with pride; he was not a man to cry over spilt milk. At a nearby refreshment stall set up by the local Baptist Church, root beer, hot dogs, iced teas and pecan pie were being dispensed. There I encountered another local politician with a more recent war on his mind: Mr Steve Gunn. Election slogan: 'Don't grieve, vote for Steve'. Mr Gunn described himself as the people's candidate for the lower chamber of the Louisiana parliament. His manifesto took up the issue of tax increases and Operation Desert Storm. Mr Gunn's line was forthright: the only reason for raising taxes would be if Saddam Hussein personally invaded Olla and stole Mr Gunn's deer hunting equipment. Not surprisingly perhaps, Mr Gunn was a firm advocate of the right to bear arms.

Hunting is about the only thing the majority of white voters in Olla seem to prefer to David Duke. When he finally arrived to address the faithful, Mr Duke recognised as much. He appealed to his supporters to cast an absentee ballot before they went shooting. Mr Duke's main message was a familiar one: too many people were living on welfare at the taxpayer's expense. He didn't need to spell it out; the racial sub-text was obvious to every listener; welfare recipients were black, taxpayers white. As I looked round at the rapt faces of his supporters, I couldn't help wondering how many – like David Duke himself – had once been members of the Ku Klux Klan. After Mr Duke had left, in a swirl of autograph-signing and hand-shaking, I chatted with a few. By no means all were blue-collar: there was a doctor, a nurse and several school teachers. They were polite, soft-spoken people who regarded themselves not as racist, but as defenders of a way of life being eroded by an uncomprehending and hostile America. Backwoodsmen maybe, they argued, but not bigots.

By now, dusk was falling and the 'Duke for Governor' stickers – white on black – were fading into the lights of the fairground. The black owner of the carousel – conspicuously absent during the Duke Rally – re-emerged with his white assistant to put the finishing touches. Soon other black faces were in evidence, working the attractions, and riding them. Disco music began to blare out, drowning the strains of country and western from a folk dancing display. More cars arrived; a few had bumper stickers extolling other candidates in the governor's race. The atmosphere felt relaxed and festive; shouts of excitement mingling in the evening air with the aroma of barbecued chicken. Suddenly, Olla seemed less isolated, less at odds with the received wisdom about mainstream America in the nineties.

But within a few days the funfair would move on for another year, and Olla would be thrown back on its habitual introspection. As I drove across the railway track again and headed for the main highway south, it seemed a faintly chilling prospect.

By the beginning of 1992, President Bush's hopes for a second term in the White House were looking less certain than in the aftermath of the Gulf War. He was facing the challenge of a depressed economy at home as he embarked on a tour of south-east Asia to try to drum up some support for struggling US corporations. While in Japan, he contracted stomach 'flu.

THE INDEFATIGABLE GEORGE BUSH

DAVID MCNEIL   WASHINGTON   16 JANUARY 1992

I f you find yourself suffering from jetlag there really isn't much point asking someone with medical knowledge to explain its causes to you: you won't be able to make sense of the explanation, because your brain will be stuck in neutral. Many of us who accompanied the President on his eleven day, twenty-six thousand mile odyssey through numerous time zones and climate changes, had trouble with the most basic pieces of information – like what day it was, or the time of day at any given moment in some other part of the world. As a foreign correspondent of long-standing, I've become used to thinking in hours ahead or hours behind London. But in a state of jetlag, it became necessary to write the information down in the form of a simple sum to make sure I had it right each time it changed. The experts say it takes at least a week to adjust the body clock after flying half way round the world.

But for some reason, George Bush doesn't seem to take the effects of jetlag into account when he travels. Admittedly he flies in some comfort: his state-of-the-art jumbo is equipped with a bedroom. But when he made his first stop – for refuelling in Hawaii – the President went for a jog around the military base. Now that may make sense to Mr Bush – physical fitness experts and jetlag know-it-alls might even recommend it. But to those of us who'd been trying to grab what sleep we could, sitting in our seats in the press charter, the President's action seemed to be taking to ridiculous extremes the concept of stretching the legs after a long flight.

George Bush doesn't just exercise, he's addicted to it. He can't keep still for long, has to be doing something – running, playing tennis or golf. When he had spare time on this trip – and there wasn't much of it – he would head for the exercise room in the hotel where he was staying to ride an exercise bike. When he reached Tokyo, he insisted on playing tennis with the Emperor even though he wasn't feeling very well. And when he and his partner were beaten in the first set, the highly competitive President insisted on a second. That evening he left the receiving line at a state reception in his honour to be sick in the bathroom. But still he wouldn't give in; against his doctor's advice he stayed on for the dinner, in the middle of which he treated viewers around the world to the extraordinary sight of the President of the United States vomiting all over the Prime Minister of Japan. I have known some moments of journalistic pandemonium in my time, but it would be hard to beat the chaos in the press centre of the Oikura Hotel when word spread that the President had collapsed at dinner.

The American correspondents, who had been doing their best to ignore those Japanese colleagues who'd travelled with them all the way from Washington, suddenly found they needed them to translate from Japanese television – for a time the only source of information. The room was a seething cauldron of reporters shouting into telephones and at one another, and jostling for position in front of the television sets. Until then, the most widely-used pictures of the whole trip had been those of Mr Bush happily joining in an ancient Japanese ball game he was meant to be observing. Many of the Americans I was travelling with thought it was an embarrassing lapse of protocol on the part of a man who simply cannot resist hitting, kicking or throwing a ball if he gets anywhere near one. The Japanese didn't seem to mind.

The way Mr Bush likes to travel is in sharp contrast to the style of his predecessor, Ronald Reagan, who once took a week to get to Tokyo: he stopped at restful places like Honolulu and Bali for a few days at a time to adjust his body clock, a gentle approach to travel deemed necessary after he fell asleep during an audience with the Pope. President Bush says he has no plans to slow down, and it has to be said that criticism of his frenetic lifestyle has been greatly overshadowed by criticism from those who said he should never have made the trip in the first place; or at least he should have stuck to the original purpose which was to visit a number of countries, wearing his foreign policy hat, and seeking a new global partnership with Japan. Unfortunately for the President, he turned it into a cheap and somewhat tawdry exercise in salesmanship, playing the role of the super-salesman for the superpower. Startled by a stunning Democratic victory in a Senate by-election in Pennsylvania, he first postponed the trip, then rescheduled it, announcing that he was going to try to crack open Asian markets and provide jobs for the American workforce. Critics said he was taking the wrong people with him – heads of the big three American car companies who complain that the Japanese won't allow them access to their market – when the real problem with the American car industry is that it can't sell cars to Americans because it is offering a vastly inferior product. The avalanche of agreements that descended on us following the talks in Tokyo failed to impress economists here in the United States. Most of them seem to have concluded that the President's efforts won't have much effect on the huge imbalance of bilateral trade in Japan's favour.

Mr Bush's popularity rating continues to plummet: the Asian trip seems to have done him more harm than good, his advisers don't seem to know how to reverse the tide that's now running against him. This year's Presidential election is a one-issue campaign: the state of the economy and the speed of recovery from recession. If there's a marked improvement in economic prospects between now and November, and the American people recognise it as more than a short-term wonder, they will probably send Mr Bush back to the White House for another term, largely on the strength of his handling of the Gulf War. But if economic conditions worsen in the months ahead, Mr Bush will need all his skills as a political street-fighter to pull through. He still has the odds in his favour: the power of incumbency should never be under-estimated in an American presidential election. And so far no one Democrat, of the five seeking their party's nomination, has managed to set the country alight. But there is a mood of bitterness and disillusion in the land. The optimistic days of Ronald Reagan's 'morning in America' have been replaced by long lines of unemployed, by increasing numbers of homeless people sleeping rough in the streets, and by an anger directed not for the first time, but now with what looks like real venom, at the country's political leaders.

These days, no incumbent can take voter apathy for granted. The electorate will respond to the recession in one of two ways: voters will either stay away from the polls in even greater numbers than they do now, or they will seize the moment to express their frustration and disappointment. Given the mood of the nation as reflected by the opinion polls, Mr Bush will have to work at least as hard on his campaign this time as he did in 1988. And if the Democrats can unite behind a credible challenger, the result will be much closer than anyone could have predicted when the troops came rolling home from Kuwait in triumph.

In 1979 Greenland won home rule from Denmark, and in 1985 it became the first part of the European Community to secede from Brussels. Since the end of the Cold War, Greenland has also lost much of its strategic significance. Julian May found a country struggling between an old and a new identity.

MODERNITY AND ANCIENT WAYS

JULIAN MAY   NUUK   21 JANUARY 1992

T he sea was like molten lead taken from the heat, thickening into a crust of ice clogging the fjords, great gashes in the coast. Craggy black rocks jutted through the snow, then the inland ice, like white felt and empty as far as the eye could see, and much further.

When I caught my first glimpse of Greenland I was astonished, not just by its austere beauty, but by the inappropriateness of its name. This was bestowed in the late tenth century by the first European to live there, Eirik the Red, and the Norse Saga of the Greenlanders makes it clear the name had little to do with the nature of the place, but a great deal to do with taking possession of it. Eirik argued that people would be drawn to settle there if the land had an attractive name. So he called the country he had discovered Greenland.

Eirik's Viking sales pitch worked and there were Norse settlements in Greenland at the turn of the sixteenth century, when they faded into mysterious oblivion. But Greenland has another name, given by the Inuit people who now make up most of its population. They call their country Kalaallit Nunaat, 'the land of the people'. At first I thought this as much a misnomer as Greenland because although it's the second largest island in the world, there aren't many people – only about 55,000. But Greenlanders are straightforward people, particularly when it comes to names and Kalaallit Nunaat captures their relation with their country exactly. It's *their* land, and they love it.

The names they gave to places are descriptive. Their capital, now a city of 15,000 people, is Nuuk, the peninsula. Further north of the town beside a glacier which calves huge floating mountains of ice, is Illulissat, the place of the icebergs. When the Danes came in the fifteenth century, with Lutheran Christianity and economic ambitions, their naming criteria were somewhat different. Nuuk they called *Gothab* – Good Hope, Illulissat (the Place of the Icebergs) was christened *Jakobshavn* after Jakob Severin, a merchant who controlled trade over a huge area of west Greenland. In Qaqortoq (The White Places) they built a little town square boasting the only fountain in the country and called it *Julianehab*, after the Danish queen. Almost everywhere in Greenland has two names, arising from two very different cultures, so it's not surprising that by the time I left I felt the major issue in Greenland is not economic or political so much as one of identity.

Illulissat, high in the Arctic circle, has a population of 4,000, which makes it a major conurbation. Even so people are outnumbered two to one by sled dogs, who live outside, chained to rocks. There are streets of brightly painted modern houses, cars – even though there isn't a single road connecting one town to another in Greenland – a fleet of seventy fishing boats and big shrimp and halibut processing factories. People have faxes, CDs, central heating. But all this modernity dissolves at dusk into the ancient blues of dogs howling.

In the winter, when the boats are icebound, the fishermen take to their dog sleds and go ice fishing on the frozen fjord. Each can bring back up to three hundred kilos of halibut, enough, just about, to keep the high-tech processing factories ticking over. So, modernity is underpinned in Greenland by the ancient ways. But only to an extent. On one of the sleds I saw coming home was a seal. The hunter was very pleased and proud – that would feed his family and dogs. He'd make a little money selling the skin to the tannery in Qaqortoq. But few people will wear a sealskin coat these days; the manager of the tannery told me he hadn't sold a single one to Britain for more than a decade. The price of skins has fallen and is subsidised by Greenland's Home Rule government. In the far north Greenlanders do still depend on hunting; none of the species they take are in danger, but misplaced environmental concern has threatened their way of life. I would argue that every conservationist in the south should go and buy a sealskin coat, to save the Greenlandic hunter from extinction.

In the past the Greenlanders' survival, social status, and self-respect depended on hunting skills, and how well they could handle a dog sled or *qayak*. Now a job in the halibut factory is more important. So it's no wonder I saw men lying in the snow, stone drunk behind the supermarket in Illulissat. They might have been great hunters – but the factory wasn't taking anyone on. There's a very high incidence of suicide in Greenland, particularly among young men. Ole Kristiansen – Greenland's most popular rock singer – gave me some idea why they are so alienated. "Climb a hill and look at this town," he said. "Everything's been brought from Denmark – the houses, the cars, everything except the people. You have to find a balance between these new things and your own roots. But it's hard. Our roots are in great hunters, great qayakmen. And they are so far away from where we are now."

There's no doubt about that. The *qayak*, the very image of Greenland, is scarcely used for hunting now. Down by Nuuk's old harbour there's a club where young people are learning to build them for sport. And Jonas, the old *qayak* maker, thinks that without their function the boats themselves have declined: "They're not so beautiful as when we had to use them."

But Ole Kristiansen and other Greenlandic artists are striking a balance and forming an identity. He uses ancient Inuit drumming techniques with up-to-date digital recording equipment to create a modern but specifically Greenlandic rock music. Polar Reggae, he calls it. It's surprisingly difficult to find though. The thawing of the Cold War has penetrated even Greenland's icy vastness, and local musicians have been ousted by bands from Bulgaria playing Euro-rock for little more than board and lodging. But the only professional theatre company in the Arctic, Silamuit (the People from Outside), are doing something similar to Kristiansen, using traditional myths to speak about contemporary life. Their most recent production is *Tupliak*. The *Tupliak* was a small carving which had power to kill an enemy, but power which might also turn to destroy its creator. It's a ready made metaphor for nuclear weapons.

"In Europe and the East there's always conflict," the director Simon Lovstrom says. "We're using this myth to discuss that. I think the rest of the world could really learn something from the way the Inuit thinks." He's right, and some communities are looking carefully at Greenland's experience, especially those of the 'fourth world' – the native peoples of America, New Zealand, Australia.

Greenland won Home Rule from Denmark in 1979 and the nationalist politician and poet, Aqqaluk Lynge, reminded me of the significance of this. "It's the 500th anniversary of Columbus," he said, "and we've found a way of living with the past, while shaping our own future. That's unique among colonized indigenous peoples." The Greenlanders' pride in their self-determination is an expression of their love of their land. Despite all trappings of modernity, that unforgiving environment reasserts itself in surprising ways. On my way to the airport at Narsarsuuaq the helicopter broke down. I had to take a boat down one fjord and up another. The ice closed in, and one engine failed. It was worrying, but the Northern Lights were exhilarating.

In some ways Greenland is still undiscovered by the rest of the world, or forgotten by it. As I flew out of Narsarsuuaq I looked down on the rubble and twisted iron of the old American base there. It's known as the 'hospital', another misnomer as really it was a dumping ground. During the Second World War and the Korean War American servicemen, so maimed that they might affect public morale, were sent there. Not one ever went home.

There's still a huge U.S. base in the far north, at Thule, and an Inuit settlement was shifted unceremoniously to make way for it. Now that there's no danger of the Red Army invading America across the ice of Greenland, the future of the base must be in doubt. Perhaps soon Kalaallit Nunaat, (the land of the people), might be completely returned to them.

Early in 1992, President Bush's hopes for a second term in the White House were being threatened by the continuing economic recession. The Italian journalist Beppe Severgnini toured the country extensively and found that in some respects, the recession had hardly begun to bite.

KING-SIZE RECESSION

BEPPE SEVERGNINI   CHICAGO   29 FEBRUARY 1992

T hey don't stop even when they're up against a snarling King Kong, a Miami Vice shoot-out or a squeaky ET, who still wants to go home but has not yet apparently managed to do so. Even at Universal Studios in Hollywood, where tourists from all over the world are herded about like unruly sheep, Americans stand out from the crowd. Nobody eats the way they do.

No other nation in the world has quite the same bored, methodical, relentless appetite. In no other country apart from America can people walk and at the same time chomp, nibble, snack on or sink their teeth into giant-sized hotdogs, extra-large packs of crisps, hamburgers, cheeseburgers, fishburgers, fried scampi, apple pies and waffles with syrup. Many of these people are on diets, or at least it is reasonable to suppose that this is the case, as they are drinking Diet Pepsi. But they drink it in cups the size of small buckets, with the innocent look of schoolchildren on holiday in their eyes.

In the United States, I soon realised, when you talk about food, the key adverb is not 'how', but 'how much'. The motto to go on the flag, along with the stars and stripes, is just three words long: 'large', 'extra-large' and 'king-size'. Not even in these difficult times – and it doesn't really matter whether the Americans are in the grip of economic recession, or whether they merely think they are – has the situation changed. America is ready to do without a host of little luxuries, but she doesn't intend to accept smaller portions.

Stroll around any supermarket, from San Diego to Milwaukee, and you'll see that the packets of potato crisps are as tall as five year-olds. Slip into a cinema in Miami. You will notice that the audience isn't particularly interested in the film, partly because they can only glimpse it from behind their astonishing helpings of popcorn. Talk to your friends in San Francisco. You'll see that they are prepared to examine the moral justification of artificial cream, but not to give up sweets. Professor Rathjie, a leading American authority on waste (he's been rummaging through rubbish for sixteen years) maintains that in the waste tips he regularly finds chocolate biscuits and cream cake leftovers along with wholemeal bread wrappers. This shows that Americans are being economical with the truth, as I had suspected all along.

However, although they are naughty in the privacy of their own kitchens, Americans are paragons of virtue in public. Everybody, from the President down, seems obsessed with the topic of 'food'. Exhibiting a passion matched only by the superficiality of its acquaintance with the subject, the nation argues about it, watches TV programmes about it, reads about it. A book called *The American Gourmet* was a bestseller. Written by a husband-and-wife team, Jane and Michael Stern, it tells the story of American gastronomy, beginning with the fifties, when people only had to put the contents of three different tins on a plate to feel creative, and set on fire anything that came to hand in the name of flambé.

California, which imposes on America the fashions which America then imposes on the world, is particularly keen on this game. One of the latest fads is to disown French cuisine, after a love-affair which had lasted for more than a century. Today, eating *à la Parisienne* is considered disastrous for one's figure, dangerous for one's heart and catastrophic for a wallet that has already been hard-hit by the recession. The anti-French mood is producing its first casualties. L'Ermitage and La Serre restaurants in Los Angeles have closed, while the reputation of L'Orangerie is rapidly disintegrating. Today's fashionable cuisine, explains Richard Rayner – the British author of *Los Angeles Without a Map* – is a mixture of Italian, American and Japanese: Italian because it's good, American because it's familiar, and Japanese because the restaurants' owners are from Japan.

Anyone who isn't too busy boycotting restaurants can have fun reading the papers. The press has long understood the power of the word 'food'. Newspaper columns which sing the praises of goat's milk cheese or bewail the demise of quiche lorraine are legion. The *Los Angeles Times* included the following in its New Year's Resolutions: "Look after your health. Look after your friends.

Watch what you eat". The suggestion was pointless because, as we have seen, Americans do nothing else. The only problem is that, after watching what they eat, they put the whole thing in their mouths.

Knowing this, the American Dietetic Association came up with the following tip for housewives: "Stop yourself nibbling. Before going into the kitchen, place a surgical mask over your mouth." It didn't help; between Christmas and the New Year, the average American put on six pounds. In his most recent book, Professor Robert Bellah of Berkeley University reports the fascinating outcome of an opinion poll. Asked about 'the object in their lives they couldn't do without', most people answered: 'my microwave'.

The American obsession with food is such that one third of the products on sale last year bore some sort of promise regarding health. Words like 'lite' and expressions along the lines of '20 per cent less fat' are now held to be *de rigueur* by manufacturers, but they have lost all meaning. For example, it is not clear what 'lite' margarine is lighter than, nor what the basis for the calculations of 20 per cent less fat in a hamburger is. Even the Federal Government has had to admit that 'supermarkets have become Towers of Babel'. Last November, the Food and Drug Administration laid down that expressions like 'low fat' or 'lite' should in future mean the same thing and that all products should bear a label, which will indicate the total number of calories, the fat-derived calorie content, saturated fats, cholesterol, the total carbohydrate content, sugars, dietary fibres, protein, sodium, vitamins, calcium, iron.

All the details will be given 'per serving' and it is here, without doubt, that the fur will begin to fly; for it will be necessary to decide how big these serving sizes should be. This will be a red-letter day in the history of America. For someone, somewhere, is bound to realise that Coke can be served in cups which contain less than a gallon, and that the English language provides other adjectives apart from large, extra-large and king-size.

In the spring of 1992, preparations were underway to mark the anniversary of the recapture of the Falkland Islands. But the deadlock between Argentina and Britain over the disputed islands continued. However, other aspects of life in the Falklands have changed – not least the attitudes of the islanders themselves – as Brian Hanrahan discovered – almost ten years after he first sailed the eight thousand miles to the Falkland Islands.

FALKLANDS REVISITED

BRIAN HANRAHAN   PORT STANLEY   5 MARCH 1992

Stanley Town Hall comes from the blockhouse school of architecture – a cement lump of no distinction built cheaply by a poor colony. It was put up between the wars – that is between the Second World War, and the Argentine invasion; a period, which in retrospect, might be termed the Falklands' era of stagnation. And if the Task Force had been successful in its attempt to blow it up, with the Argentine High Command inside, nobody would have grieved for the building. Instead it survived, a smudge on the Stanley waterfront, amid the speckled blue, green and red roofs, but the only decent-sized hall for public entertainments.

So it was there on Saturday evening that a local schoolgirl watched, saucer-eyed, as a magician blew up a condom and tried to burst it. He was part of a travelling show to entertain the British garrison, and as the evening went on, and the barely dressed dancers mooned at the audience, one wondered if the culture of the British forces wasn't as alien to the islanders as the Argentinians they were keeping at bay. What the 1982 war did was to flood the islands with new people and new ideas, and quite apart from the military campaign, it was an extraordinary shock to those who lived there. They had largely let the world slip by them, and suddenly it was there – insisting they should catch up. It wasn't a very pleasant experience; the couple of trips I made back after the war showed that, physically, the islands were recovering. The rags and the rubbish were cleared up, the roads and the roofs repaired. But there was still a sense of bitterness, and a kind of listlessness about what to do next. Now that's changed and there are signs, everywhere, of a community that's put itself back together. Fresh paint and flowers brighten up the town; there are new lamp posts, and litter bins with the Falklands crest replacing the rusty old oil drums; gardens full of vegetables – one with a vividly-coloured collection of gnomes; books on local history which hark back to the early years of the century when there was more reliance on the pioneering spirit, and less on the company store. The Falkland Islands Company, which had come to dominate life, is selling up. One of the new businessmen who is moving into the vacuum it is leaving said the hardest thing was to look the old company managers in the eye. When he was growing up you had to keep your eyes turned down.

But I thought the most telling change was that trees were being planted again, in an attempt to break the eternal wind that tugs constantly at everybody and everything. When the island was a company fief, nobody seemed to care. The islanders talk of these changes with the frankness of people who've been very sick and run through the course of their illness. They say the recovery was quite recent: until about two years ago none of these little flourishes of the spirit were happening. And most of them will tell you it's just as well the Islands were shaken up. Without the war they would have slipped into economic oblivion. The farms were becoming unprofitable, and there was no other indus-try. Now there's fishing, which is generating enough money to subsidise the sheep stations, build the rough, gravelled roads which are only now linking the settlements together, and buy time for the islanders to try out some enterprise of their own.

Of course it's all rather tenuous. The fish might swim off as magically as they seemed to appear after the war, and the oil that so many hopes are pinned on may never be discovered. And there's Argentina: the land the islanders hate bitterly, prefer not to talk about, and refuse to have any links with, even though it's the nearest thing to a neighbour they've got. There are a few voices which say this cannot go on forever, but even they are talking about change coming with another generation; perhaps the blow-up condoms and spangled dancers will help the schoolchildren develop a more open-minded approach.

It may not take that long. Before the Falklands can come to terms with Argentina, it's got to come to terms with itself. The islanders have to sort out how they feel about themselves and how many of the changes they've had to accept are the sort they want to stick with. And the signs are that process is now under way. On my last evening there I ran into a friend of mine, driving a battered and gaily coloured amalgam of parts cannibalised from old Land Rovers and captured Argentine vehicles. "Tomorrow," she said, "we're getting a new car." Her husband had boarded a Russian merchantman sailing home from Japan. The Captain had some new cars which he doubted would be very saleable in the turbulent conditions he was returning to. Her husband had bought them at a knock-down price. He had the money, the opportunity and a sense of enterprise; all factors which are only just coming back to the islands. They'll need them all.

The city of Atlanta, Georgia, business capital of the American South, is also known for other things. It will host the 1996 Olympic Games, and is home base for two world-wide corporations. One is Mr Ted Turner's Cable News Network, CNN. The other makes a soft drink. David Willis discovered on a visit to Atlanta that the drink now has its own museum. He says he approached it with caution.

HOMAGE TO A SOFT DRINK

DAVID WILLIS   ATLANTA   24 MARCH 1992

A drink is a drink, isn't it? I mean, nothing more, nothing less. How could a drink have its own museum? A pretentious form of advertising, surely. Well it was part of Atlanta, so I'd go. I certainly would not be impressed, even if the drink was Coca-Cola, and even if it was one of the most cleverly marketed and advertised products in the history of capitalism and the free market. So I walked down Peachtree Street, turned left and began to cross an open square towards a rather unprepossessing three-storey building with a giant globe suspended in front of it. As I drew closer, the monument to a drink began to block from view a monument to the law: the Georgia State Legislature building, surmounted by a golden dome.

The drink, according to a brochure in my hand, was now sold in more than 160 countries, and drunk more than 448 million times every day. Well, it was still only a drink. No, said a guide in a red uniform on the top floor, it's an American phenomenon, a way of thinking. Surely not? Well, a phenomenon perhaps.

A video film told the story of a product which has gone from a syrup with a secret formula, invented by an Atlanta chemist, Dr Joseph Pemberton, in 1866, to one with what the company claims is the largest production and distribution network in the world, from Belgium to Burma.

I wasn't too impressed by the futuristic bottling machine on display nor by another video film which struck me as advertising unadorned. And yet display after display of advertising signs and slogans from the 1920s onwards began to awaken all kinds of memories. I began thinking how old I'd been, and where I'd been, when I first saw the familiar red and white signs proclaiming: 'Pure As Sunlight', 'The Pause That Refreshes', 'An Arm's Length From Desire'. Yes, the images were commercial. They did associate the drink with sexual attraction, with family life, with masculinity, with femininity, with childhood, with sport. But they were undeniably nostalgic as well – even though I knew that the company knew that the exhibits would have this effect, both on me and on the one and a half million people who have been through the museum since it opened almost two years ago.

Surely I wasn't actually beginning to enjoy the visit? There was the first tin ever to contain Coke, dated 1941. It looked like a tin of motor-oil. You had to use a tin-opener to get into it. There was a 1940s Coke dispenser. During the Second World War the company rushed sixty-four portable bottling plants to Europe and the Pacific so that no American serviceman would have to fight without his Coke. Patriotic? Shrewd, too: the portable plants were the basis of many a permanent plant when peace returned.

Here was the first non-returnable bottle of Coke, designed for cruise ships to Europe and South America. Green, with gold foil, like a champagne bottle. Were they thrown overboard? A cheerful young guide thought there could be a big underwater reef of Coca-Cola bottles somewhere in the Atlantic Ocean; and here was the first Coke tin ever to fly into space in 1985 with a special pressure top to prevent the tin exploding and squirting astronauts with weightless black liquid.

Next stop: a space-age room where you could drink all the products the Coca-Cola company makes, free. Well, not exactly free: you've already paid two dollars and fifty cents to get into the museum. But children love it. Parents feel cosmopolitan as they sample some of the eighteen drinks the company makes but sells only abroad – including a sour cherry drink tailored for Czechoslovakia, and a mixture of bitters and tonic water called Beverley and said to be popular in Italy and Switzerland.

The final stop: a Coca-Cola shop downstairs, a supermarket of Coke-mania, the Seven Ages of Coke, a monument to the inventiveness of the free market.

People were snapping up watches with 1930s cowboys or bathing beauties advertising Coke on the dials, wall-clocks, cassette tapes, thermometers, key-rings, toys, portable telephones, and dozens more items with a Coke motif. Well, I could resist those. Wait a minute, though. My son might like that watch.

One of the most eloquent and charismatic figures in the Caribbean, Michael Manley,
stepped down at the end of March as Prime Minister of Jamaica, after 40 years
in politics, due to poor health. Hugh Crosskill, head of the BBC's Caribbean Service
(and a fellow Jamaican) reflected on Michael Manley's varied political career.

MANLEY DEPARTS THE STAGE

HUGH CROSSKILL   LONDON   28 MARCH 1992

I was a blissfully ignorant teenager living in Jamaica when my interest in politics was first awakened by Michael Norman Manley. The 1960s were drawing to a close and, despite five years of independence, the country was still being governed by a colonial mentality. I remember when tanks were sent to the University campus to crush protests after Guyanese-born lecturer Dr Walter Rodney was declared persona non-grata by a government worried at the rise of black consciousness.

Jamaica was crying out for social change, and Michael Manley and his People's National Party managed to encapsulate that desire under the campaign slogan "Power for the People". They were swept into office in 1972 with a landslide electoral victory over the Jamaica Labour Party.

Mr Manley set about his task of reforming the social order. No longer would household employees be known as 'maids', instead they would be called household helpers; the jacket and tie was replaced with the bush-jacket in keeping with the tropical climate rather than a European notion of proper dress; the Rastafarian was no longer to be treated as a pariah but instead was drawn in to take a rightful and colourful place in the social fabric. Michael Manley promised change and in many ways he delivered. But it carried a heavy price tag. While middle-class Jamaica could accept change in the social structure, it became very nervous when that was extended to matters economic and ideological. Manley and his party entered office aiming to guide Jamaica towards the sort of social democracy practised in Scandinavian countries. But halfway through their first term in office it was the Cuban model that was being promoted as the way forward.

As the PNP romped to victory in the 1976 election, it became clear that Michael Manley was undergoing a sea-change. Increasingly he put a leftist slant on the Fabian socialist principles he had been taught by his father, Norman Manley, founder of the PNP and one of Jamaica's national heroes. By the time Michael Manley got around to bear-hugging Fidel Castro and promising to march with him to the mountain top, key areas of his support were beginning to evaporate.

As middle-class criticism of his relations with Cuba began to intensify, Manley became increasingly adversarial. In a now famous outburst, he advised those unhappy with his government's policy to "catch one of the five flights a day to Miami". Thousands did, taking with them a massive chunk of Jamaica's fast diminishing foreign exchange reserves. As economic pressures increased, Michael Manley turned his guns on Washington and the IMF. The U.S. administration was accused of destabilization and the IMF of administering a medicine that threatened to kill the patient. Opposition-inspired graffiti started appearing, saying that IMF really meant 'It's Manley's Fault'. The island's major daily newspaper, *The Gleaner*, started to turn up the heat, and hardly a day passed without most of its columnists engaging in Manley-bashing.

Manley strongly denied claims that he was turning Jamaica into a communist state, but it was hard to square that against the large number of Cuban workers invited into the country, the bloated levels of staffing at the Cuban and Soviet embassies and the strident rhetoric of party apparatchiks. Towards the end of the 1970s, I believe Michael Manley began to realise that the ideological war being waged with the opposition was destroying the country. The bottom had fallen out of the economy, the brain drain had gathered pace and political violence was rampant. He was being put under immense pressure by his party's Executive Council to break with the IMF, and I believe it was at this point that Manley made up his mind that the flirtation with socialism had gone too far. He rejected the demand and soon after plunged the country into its most violent election ever. When the dust had settled, over 800 people had been killed and Manley and his party had been unceremoniously swept from office. I could have sworn

I heard him breathe a sigh of relief as the Jamaica Labour Party, preaching the gospel of pro-U.S. free-market policies, took over the reins.

Three years later Maurice Bishop, the Grenadian prime minister, was murdered by his Marxist colleagues and Michael Manley may well have thought: "there but for the grace of God go I." In 1983 Manley and his party boycotted the snap election because it was called in breach of a promise to complete electoral reforms. This I felt was another major mistake, as it effectively turned Jamaica into a one-party state, although a *de facto* opposition was maintained through a series of People's Forums staged by the PNP.

Mr Manley turned his attention to writing and produced *Global Challenge; From Crisis to Cooperation: Breaking the North-South Stalemate, Up the Down Escalator* and a *History of West Indies Cricket*. He also joined the U.S. university lecture circuit.

Meanwhile, the U.S. administration which had helped to hound Manley out of office was becoming increasingly frustrated with the man who succeeded him, Edward Seaga. Rather than being the Caribbean version of Ronald Reagan, Seaga showed that he was more of a statist than Manley ever was, and he resisted pressure to privatise national entities willy-nilly. By then Michael Manley was completing the circle of his political beliefs and was re-emerging as a strong advocate of the free-market. Initially Washington and many Jamaicans were sceptical. Could a leopard really change its spots? Manley showed that it could and in 1989 he returned to office with a political outlook that put him to the right of the leadership of the British Labour Party.

But by now ill-health had begun to dog a man who has always placed great emphasis on physical fitness. Prostate cancer and diverticulitis forced him into five strength-sapping operations. But it was a bout of pneumonia that took the greatest toll. Manley lost one third of his lung capacity and found it impossible to keep up his normally hectic schedule. When he announced his decision to retire he told the nation: "The will is there, undiminished by the passage of years. But quite honestly, my friends, I can no longer give it those 16-hour days."

Manley went at a time when his government's popularity had been waning because of cutbacks in state spending and a series of scandals involving party officials. While Manley himself remained broadly popular, his policies failed to excite the imagination, and the gap between rich and poor had widened considerably. The policies of his successor will determine which of the Manley legacies will take root – the populist, socialist oriented policies of the seventies or the free-market, deregulated policies of the nineties. I cannot help feeling that what Jamaica really needs is something in between, something that Mr Manley promised during his first incarnation but failed to deliver.

So how will history judge Manley? With mixed feelings, I suspect, as a man who engineered change and then took his hand off the wheel allowing the vehicle to career out of control. And by the time his hands regained control, the direction had changed and the country was travelling down a new road, still unsure of the final destination. Like great oak trees, Caribbean leaders such as Michael Manley have tended to overshadow all who served under them. Now the oak trees have all but fallen and an anxious region waits to see just what has grown in their shadow. And while we wait, I'll miss Michael Manley, probably the most eloquent spokesman the Third World has ever had.

While acknowledging the many mistakes he made during his political career, my enduring memory will be of a leader committed to the democratic process when many around him wanted to abandon it for a shallow and eventually discredited ideology. In the end Michael Manley remained true to his father's principles, and for that reason his place in history is assured.

In March 1992 Mexico City suffered its worst-ever environmental emergency. Pollution levels reached four times the international safety limit. Schools were closed down, traffic was restricted and industrial activity was curtailed. Charles Scanlon reported on life in what's long been regarded as the world's most polluted city.

BREATHING IN MEXICO CITY

CHARLES SCANLON   MEXICO CITY   28 MARCH 1992

I had been in Mexico City for some months before I saw them for the first time. Walking a familiar route outside the presidential palace, I looked up and there they were – Popacatapetl and Ixtaccihuatl. Two magnificent, snow-capped volcanoes towering above the city from the East. I had been told they were somewhere out there. I had even seen maps proving it, but sometimes it was hard to believe. Then for a few weeks in January, strong northerly winds blew the grey blanket of smog away from Mexico City and the transparency of the cool mountain air was breathtaking.

That's what Mexico City used to be like, said the old timers, before the 1960s and 1970s when the population exploded into the mega-city of today. Twenty million people in a mountain valley choking on petrol fumes and industrial particles. The reappearance of the two volcanoes after so long caused a sensation. Newspapers ran front page colour pictures of them, radio presenters talked excitedly about the unexpected apparition, and amateur photographers flocked to vantage points in the city.

We haven't seen the volcanoes for a while now. The pollution is back with a vengeance. Mexico City is suffering its worst-ever environmental emergency. If you look to the spot where the mountains were, a grey mist partially obscures the tall buildings just a few kilometres away. The sky is still blue, the colours still vivid in the bright sun, but the horizon has dissolved into a grey haze. It's not much comfort to know that the largest component of the pollution is ozone, which is invisible. When the pollution gets this bad the only solution is to stay inside as much as possible.

I can tell immediately when ozone levels are high; first I get a tingling sensation in my nose, which gets steadily more uncomfortable. Next come stinging eyes and finally, after half an hour or so, a feeling of nausea and even a headache. Fuels burn badly at this altitude, more than two thousand metres above sea level, and the stench of petrol fumes is sometimes overpowering. Many residents complain of being tired and listless when the pollution is bad. As people haven't been exposed to such high levels of pollution for long enough, they suspect that cases of respiratory diseases and cancer will increase.

It's a bit like being in a huge laboratory. Just how bad can the air pollution get before people start falling over? Ozone is created by the reaction of sunlight on exhaust emissions. In March ozone levels reached their highest-ever level, three hundred and ninety-eight points. The World Health Organisation says it is unhealthy to be exposed to more than a hundred points of ozone for more than an hour a year. The government reacted by closing down schools the following day, restricting factory emissions and ordering forty per cent of private cars off the road. Light winds and low humidity mean the bad conditions could prevail for weeks.

Mexico's leading environmental campaigner, Homero Aridjis, says government emergency measures can't be expected to solve the crisis. Only the wind can do that. But the government does seem to be trying, if rather belatedly. Amongst other proposals, it is considering building huge ventilators across the city. The idea is that they will heat up the polluted air, causing it to rise and then get whisked away by the winds which hopefully will be passing above the valley.

Earlier ideas included slicing large holes through the surrounding mountains to allow the pollutants to escape. Mexico City people don't laugh at these schemes. They know that something dramatic has to be done, as long as it doesn't involve them personally. The middle classes love their cars and they don't like the idea of squeezing on the crowded metro or into sweaty buses. When the 'day without a car' programme was first introduced many went straight out and bought second cars so they wouldn't be inconvenienced. There is a tendency for everyone to blame everyone else for the problem. The most frequent target is the government for only waking up to the problem after it was too late. Its efforts are still too often hampered by corrupt officials who see a ready source of income in environmental control.

Finally though, the city may have been given the shock therapy it needs. People now talk about pollution constantly, the way Londoners talk about the weather, with a mixture of disgust and awe. Certainly the pollution is becoming as unpredictable as the British weather. It's supposed to be at its worst during the winter months, but January saw some of the clearest air that anyone could remember. Instead it's the hot weather that is causing the problems. There is precious little wind and the sun is cooking the gasses into a swirling poisonous soup. The doom merchants are having a field day. What do you expect, they say, when you take a highland valley with a fragile environment, and pack in twenty million people and the greatest concentration of industry in Latin America?

Most of the world's great cities were founded because of some specific geographic or economic advantage, a river perhaps, or a harbour. Mexico City is different. It was chosen as a capital because Aztec chieftains saw an eagle eating a snake on the site. Not very scientific. Perhaps in this five hundredth anniversary year of the discovery of the Americas, the Aztecs are finally having the last laugh over their Spanish conquerors.

*A dispute was developing between Canada and the European Community in the
spring of 1992, over the level of fish stocks. The problem was centred around
Newfoundland on Canada's Eastern fringe.*

THE SECOND COD
WAR?

ALEX KIRBY   ST JOHN'S   2 APRIL 1992

Sir Humphrey Gilbert, a Devon man, landed in Newfoundland in 1583
and claimed the island for Britain. Under grey skies, with drifts of dirty
snow cluttering the sidewalks, often blanketed in the fogs which swirl in from
the Grand Banks where the Arctic waters of the Labrador Current meet the
Gulf Stream, I've tried several times to imagine the relief he must have felt
– even on this inhospitable shore – to have put two thousand miles of the
Atlantic safely behind him.

At times you can almost suppose that Sir Humphrey's descendants had decided
it wasn't worth the effort to push any further west. St John's, and the nearby
coast of Eastern Newfoundland, feel in some ways like a transplant from the
other side of the Atlantic that has still to come to terms with its host. It isn't
just the familiar red telephone boxes or the street names – Cavendish Place,
Water Street, Kings Bridge Road – or even coastal villages like Torbay, still
betraying the influence of Devon. It isn't even the way people speak. Many
Newfoundland fishermen I've talked to have an unmistakable Irish accent, and
sound as if they'd be more at home in Cork than in St John's. More than
anything it's the apparent unwillingness, or inability, of many of Newfoundland's people to see themselves as thoroughgoing Canadians that gives you pause
for thought.

Although St John's is more than two thousand miles from London, there's still another thousand or more to go before you come to Montreal. And the sense of distance owes at least as much to history as to geography. It was only on March 31st 1949 that Newfoundland voted, by the slimmest of majorities, to give up its status as an independent dominion, to become a Canadian province. There are people in St John's today who will tell you that if the vote were taken again it might well go the other way. One reason for the persistence of this aloofness, this lukewarm trust that Ottawa even knows where Newfoundland is, let alone what it wants is distance. Newfoundland, or at least the Eastern part of it, is fish, or it is nothing.

You can sit at the bar of one the biggest hotels in St John's in May and June, overlooking the narrows where the harbour gives straight onto the sea, and watch the icebergs floating serenely past on their way down from Greenland. Newfoundland is on the same latitude as France, but its climate is that of Northern Norway. You can't grow wheat here, or apples, in fact you can't grow very much at all. What you can do is fish, and that's what generations of Newfoundlanders have done; but they doubt their ability to do so for much longer. A combination of modern technology, ruthlessly applied, and a willingness to catch almost anything that swims, have cut such a swathe through the schools of cod, flounder and other species on the Grand Banks, that whole communities here believe they are on the brink of becoming welfare ghettos. What especially irks people is what they see as foreign over-fishing. Some years ago Canada imposed a 200 mile economic zone around its coast from which foreign boats are banned. The snag is that the zone doesn't quite include the whole of the Grand Banks and the Continental Shelf on which they sit. Crucially, three areas lie outside the limit, the Nose and the Tail of the Bank and the Flemish Cap – a relatively shallow underwater hillock, a little farther out before the Shelf plunges down into the Atlantic deeps.

The Canadians say foreign boats, chiefly from the European Community, and especially from Spain and Portugal, lie just beyond the 200 mile line and catch everything they can. Worst of all, they say, the foreign boats are taking the spawning stock on which the very future of the fishery depends. While Canada has brought its catches down in recent years to try to protect the stocks, the European nets have grown steadily fuller, often with fish no bigger than a man's hand. The Canadians say they are near the limits of their patience. But not all Canadians are convinced that the foreign boats bear all the blame. Some point to the burgeoning seal population and say that something must be done, whatever the protesters may think. Others say that a significant climate change may be occurring in the North Atlantic, sending down a stream of water so icy that the cod have simply swum off to find somewhere warmer.

Most Newfoundlanders seem stolid and amiable; people not likely to take to the barricades, but few think things can go on as they are. Some say that Canada should extend its jurisdiction beyond the 200 mile line, even as far out as the Flemish Cap. Others say the Europeans should be told that they have three months to mend their ways and that after that the Navy should be sent in.

What appears to unite most of the Newfoundlanders is a belief that in the end they will have to work out their own salvation without any help from Ottawa. Some of the most talked about visitors to St John's in recent weeks have been the Icelandic fishermen who came here to recount their exploits in the seventies; cutting the nets of their enemies and ramming and boarding them in the last Cod War. Britain's earliest overseas possession looks set, if the fishermen's patience does run out, to emulate one of Britain's most recent antagonists.

*Since Argentina's defeat by Britain in the Falklands War in 1982, the country
has turned from a military dictatorship to a democracy, and survived a peaceful
change of power from Raul Alfonsin to the Peronist government of President Carlos
Menem. Nick Caistor lived in Argentina during the 1970s, and reported from
Buenos Aires during the Falklands war. He went back recently and noticed that
although on the surface Argentina now appeared to be economically and politically
stable, underneath things were a bit more shaky.*

THE CASE OF THE FALSE GNOCCHI

NICK CAISTOR   BUENOS AIRES   2 MAY 1992

L ast Wednesday I went to my favourite restaurant in downtown Buenos
Aires. As it was the 29th of the month, I chose the special dish of the
day, *gnocchi*, an Italian meal of potato pasta. In Argentina, where about half
the population is of Italian origin, *gnocchi* are served on the 29th of each month
not just because they are delicious, but because they are supposed to bring good
luck and money for the month to come.

The friend I was sharing the meal with told me the story of the *gnocchi
trucho*, or the story of the fake *gnocchi*. The Argentines are very inventive with
their slang, and as an extension of the original meaning of the word *gnocchi*,
it is also used to refer to people whom political bosses have rewarded for favours
with non-jobs. All they have to do is to appear – like the *gnocchi* – on the
29th of each month and collect their wages.

In recent weeks in Argentina though there has been a further twist to the
story. A Buenos Aires man was sent notification that he had been dismissed
from a post, in the provincial senate, that he was supposed to have held for
several months. But the man claimed he never even knew he had the job, and

had neither worked at it nor received any money for it. Apparently the wage paid to him on the 29th of each month was going straight to the senator on whose payroll his name appeared: and so for the newspapers, he became famous as 'the case of the fake *gnocchi*'.

This kind of abuse of the system is rife in Argentina. In another recent incident, press photographers snapped a picture of a member of the national parliament apparently fast asleep during a debate. This became a much more serious matter when it was discovered that the person asleep wasn't even a member of parliament, and had no right to be there. Once again, it came out that this man was a fake – in this case a *diputado trucho*, or "fake MP", allegedly brought in by the ruling Peronist party to make sure there was a quorum for an important piece of legislation that they wanted to push through, even though the opposition parties were boycotting the debate.

My friend showed me yet another fake. He got out his wallet, and produced what was apparently a new banknote, in the new pesos that Argentina introduced in January. But this note, instead of showing the head of one of the past heroes of Argentina, had on it a caricature of the current president, Carlos Menem. The banknote was meant as a joke, but during the recent holidays it seems it was not uncommon for Argentines to use these fake notes on unsuspecting shopkeepers in the neighbouring countries of Uruguay and Brazil, who were not amused at these Menem-*truchos*, or 'fake Menems'.

On one level, these stories make a good tale for the lunch table. But on another, they point to a deeper worry that many Argentines share. The country has enjoyed civilian rule for almost a decade now. But representative parliamentary governments are never entirely secure in Latin America, as recent events in Haiti, Venezuela and most recently Peru have demonstrated. Politicians have to keep on proving they are more honest and responsible than an authoritarian military regime or a dictatorship would be.

At the moment Argentina is booming – the lunch in Buenos Aires cost me more than it would have done in London – but if the old days of inflation and economic chaos were to return, the jokes could easily turn into something much more serious. The politicians, public employees and others in responsible positions have to show clearly that they are building something worthwhile, and not just a *democracia trucha* – a fake democracy.

For centuries the tiny, landlocked Latin American state of Paraguay has been alternately isolated from the outside world or dominated by its more powerful neighbours. Three years after the end of the longest-running dictatorship in the Western Hemisphere, Paraguayans are working their way towards democracy.

FORGETTING STROESSNER

JENNY WATERS   ASUNCION   20 MAY 1992

Making the flight from Brazil to Paraguay, the feeling of having arrived comes even before take-off from Rio de Janeiro. The bus ferrying passengers from the terminal to the plane might just be on a short journey down the street. Everyone seems to know each other. If not friends, they're at least nodding acquaintances. Paraguay is a small country by Latin American standards. And the privileged few among its four million people who make regular air journeys must bump into each other quite often.

The feeling of unity increased when the hapless Brazilian air stewardess announced that we were about to arrive in Asunción and would soon be landing at President Stroessner Airport. Her blunder was greeted with hoots of derision. Paraguay may not be famous for much but the end of Stroessner's record thirty-five year dictatorship in 1989 briefly catapulted it into the international headlines. Since then his name has been removed from cities, roads and the airport alike. But even if the Brazilians are no longer keeping a close eye on events just over the border, who is taking any notice of what's happening in Paraguay? Internationally its profile is low. Outsiders will probably have heard of General Stroessner, rumoured nazi war criminal hide-outs, and Paraguayan beef, but that's just about where the list ends.

In fact it's a state that boasts a collection of bizarre national statistics. It buys in more Scotch whisky than any other country in Latin America – puzzling considering the tiny population – until you realise that the whisky is part of Paraguay's economic lifeline. The country specialises in importing goods, legally and illegally, from as far away as Europe and Japan, and selling them on at a profit to neighbours with more rigorous trade tariffs. Brazilians make the trip across the border to buy their own coffee which, thanks to the strange logic of international trade, is cheaper in Paraguay.

In my hotel I stumbled across Paraguay's latest lucrative export industry – babies. Most of the other guests were young North American women with prams. The shortage of children available for adoption in the United States has long been bringing couples in search of Paraguayan sons and daughters. The legal process here used to be quick and comparatively simple. Prospective mothers could be in and out of the country in three weeks, leaving with a full carry-cot. But as local unease over the outflow of babies increased, the workings of the courts grew slower and more erratic. Now some women wait up to a year in the hotel, living with their chosen child and waiting from day to day for the judge's verdict.

Paraguay has always been a country of ethnic diversity. I set off on a Sunday in search of a Lutheran pastor, to talk to him about his years of campaigning for political prisoners. My guide, of Japanese origin, helpfully pointed me in the direction of St Andrew's Church which, like almost anywhere you'd want to reach in Asunción, was a short walk down the road. Before I found Father Ihle, preaching powerfully in German, I'd mistakenly called in at two other St Andrews's, and taken part briefly in an evangelical service in Spanish and a sedate matins in English.

Later in the evening, I went on to see how the Paraguayan theatre revival was faring. *Romeo and Juliet*, as staged by Asunción's newly appointed municipal theatre director, is not attracting large audiences. Jose Luis Ardissone is at a loss to know what will draw the crowds these days, though he'd thought Shakespeare would be a safe bet. He believes that after years of revelling in theatre that obliquely criticised the dictatorship, Paraguayans don't want to be taxed too much – they just want to have a good time.

So have Paraguayans really succeeded in forgetting Stroessner? The country is certainly taking substantial steps towards democracy. Two hundred politicians meet every day to decide on the new constitution and argue with each other with unprecedented freedom. But among most people cynicism remains. Aren't they excited about the prospect of elections in a climate of openness unknown in the country's history? The answer as often as not will be: "They're usually rigged – I expect they will be again."

In May 1992 a spate of armed uprisings in Nicaragua led to a state of virtual anarchy in the countryside. Faced with the growing disorder, the government of Violetta Chamorro has become increasingly dependent on support from the still powerful Sandinistas who were voted out of office in 1990. But even this failed to stop the waves of protest against poverty and massive unemployment.

DEMOCRACY AND DISILLUSIONMENT IN NICARAGUA

CHARLES SCANLON   MANAGUA   27 MAY 1992

The question that first came to mind on arriving in Managua was, "what happened?" Clearly something pretty disastrous. The answer could run as follows – a devastating earthquake, followed by a revolution, followed by a civil war and a United States economic blockade. Managua has still not recovered from the first of those disasters, the earthquake of 1972. What used to be the central plaza is now virtually deserted except for the occasional hawker and a few parked cars. It's still fronted by the old cathedral, but that was gutted in the earthquake, and is still in a state of dilapidation. A few blocks away on the lake front, there are no buildings left standing and the road is made of gravel.

It's easy to get lost in Managua. The city sprawls over the hillsides to the south of the lake, there are no street names in evidence and precious few signposts. Directions are by land marks. You might be told something like 'University traffic lights, three up two and half south'. Confusing for out-of-towners.

Just over two years since the Sandinistas lost office in a surprise election defeat, Nicaragua remains one of the poorest countries on the continent. Unem-

136

ployment is estimated at sixty per cent. Crowds of vendors swarming across major roads are testimony to the hardship. Young boys sell chewing gum and newspapers – common enough in Latin America, but at one traffic light a woman offered a large parrot to motorists, others sold what looked like small deer and one young boy tried to interest me in a cub *tigrillo* – an ocelot or Central American wild cat, as I found out later.

One business leader told me Nicaragua was heaven compared with what it was under the Sandinistas; then he said you had to queue for soap, toilet paper, a piece of chicken. People in the street don't agree with him. Few are nostalgic about the civil war and the state of emergency, but at least then, I was told, there was work, and education and health care were free. Now the so-called peoples' pharmacies have been privatised and medical treatment is costly.

Not that the health service is much to boast about. A doctor at Managua's leading maternity hospital told me there was a shortage of even the most basic supplies. Often there were no needles and no anaesthetic gas. Sometimes he had to delay crucial operations for months. There was also no bed linen, none had been delivered for two years. Women who had just given birth lay on makeshift beds in corridors, often still in soiled clothing. Maternal deaths during childbirth are now double what they were three years ago.

In the countryside conditions are even harsher. The rains are late and the land is brown and dry. The approach of the growing season has led to an explosion of land disputes. Former Sandinista soldiers have joined with ex-Contras to demand land and loans which they say were promised by the government. In recent weeks armed bands have taken over whole towns to press their claims. There were persistent stories in Managua that even a women's group had taken up arms in the north of the country.

I found them in the town of Ocotal near the border with Honduras. At least I think I did. They called themselves the Nora Astorga Movement after a Sandinista heroine. Many were elderly, others carried babies in their arms or had small children trailing behind. I talked to one of the members, Martha Mendez, who was in the Sandinista army for ten years before being demobilised. She said the women had allied themselves with a farmers' group and a band of ex-combatants. The previous week they had held the town for three days, she said, occupying the bank, the mayor's office and the pharmacy, and blocking the Pan American Highway. But Martha insisted the women were not armed, this was strictly a civic protest. Their demands include sewing machines to set up a co-operative, material for building houses, and food. Most of the women are single and had lost their jobs when thousands of demobilised Sandinista soldiers returned home.

There is a bewildering variety of militant groups across Nicaragua, all demanding that the government fulfil its promises of help. The administration of Violetta Chamorro appears overwhelmed, and is increasingly dependent on support from the Sandinistas who retain control of the army and the police. The universal hope is that Washington will make good its promises of aid – a hundred million dollars is pending at the moment. But there are now fears that the U.S. Congress will object to the growing Sandinista role in government and cut back on the desperately needed funds.

The Earth Summit in Rio, which ended in mid June 1992, drew the world's attention to the thousands of children forced to eke out an existence on the streets of Brazil. Many of them are killed by death squads hired to control the appallingly high crime rate. Our Environment Correspondent, Alex Kirby came to regard the killers as simply performing a function which, elsewhere, happens by default.

THE NEIGHBOURHOOD GRIM REAPERS

ALEX KIRBY   RIO   25 JUNE 1992

The very name Brazil is evocative. Flying down to Rio, my mind was full of the exotic associations learnt in childhood, of parrots, mahogany and anacondas, overlaid with more recent imagery – of a uniquely rich environment facing unprecedented threat. But behind all of these was another picture. Brazil is a country where they kill children. And if the same thing happens in other parts of Latin America, it happens often enough in Brazil to suggest it has the consent of a number of influential people.

Figures tell part of the story. In Pernambuco, in north-east Brazil, an average of three children a week were being killed by the death squads in early 1988. And a campaigner I met, Ivanir dos Santos, who lived on the streets himself till the age of four, says the number of children killed in the state of Rio de Janeiro alone last year was 442 – more than one a day.

Rio is a violent city: two friends of mine were robbed at knifepoint during the Earth Summit. Most of the children who die are killed on suspicion of involvement in crime. If they are criminals, it's not too surprising. Brazil has perhaps the greatest disparity of any country between rich and poor. More than half the national income goes to the richest 10% of Brazilians. The poorest 10% eke out among themselves 0.6% of the country's wealth. With the economy rocking on its heels – savage inflation and an immense foreign debt – the poor in Brazil are very poor, which helps to explain why seven million children have to fend for themselves on the streets.

The street children are the prime targets for the death squads – though not the only ones. I met two poor but upright mothers whose children were in a group abducted by the police almost two years ago. None of the children has been seen again: to be young, poor and black in Brazil is to ask for trouble. Most of the killing is thought to be the work of serving or former police officers, and of private security guards, usually paid by shopkeepers, to deter crime by eliminating those thought to be either actual or potential criminals.

I wanted to meet some of the killers. Not surprisingly, I wasn't able to. But the distinguished Brazilian film-maker, Octavio Bezerra, had interviewed some of them and he let me listen to his tapes. My abiding memory is of men who not only show no trace of remorse for what they do – one remarked that he felt not a drop of pity – but who are convinced that they are doing society a favour. They see themselves, quite simply, as pest control officers. Several believe they are in fact doing their victims a favour, too. Better die now in childhood, they argue, almost in so many words, than live to be an adult criminal ten years hence. Had I not been in Brazil for the Earth Summit, I might have found it easier to write off the killers as the psychopathic products of a horribly warped society. In fact I find it hard to condemn them. They, at least, are straightforward about what they do. And they care enough about their society to do something, even if the thing they do plumbs depths we thought were behind us.

The Summit was about environment and development. But more and more it seemed to me that I was watching two Summits. The one that discussed the environment, although it could have done much more, did carve out some essential toeholds for future progress. But the Development Summit, so far as I could see, did very little. It failed to agree on a more rapid increase in overseas aid, the most elementary step possible for reducing poverty. It certainly didn't agree to reduce the poorest countries' debts, or to change the rules of international trade in a way that would give them a better chance of earning their own living. And it did not agree that the rich countries should limit their own over-consumption.

The industrialised world has learnt to worry about the environment, and it's also learnt to live with poverty; the wretched of the earth are part of the familiar backdrop of life. They're wallpaper. They won't go away; they don't need to, because nothing they can do or be could ever threaten us. Statistics can often simply numb the mind. But every now and then you come across a formula which will not leave you, some set of digits which casts a new light on the scene. The reality of poverty is summed up, for me, in the recollection that every day 40,000 children aged under five die of preventable causes – hunger, or easily treated diseases like measles. A friend puts it a different way: the daily 40,000 he visualises as a jumbo jet crashing every fifteen minutes, with the loss of everybody on board.

This isn't news, it's the way things are – reality. And the Earth Summit failed, in any way I could discern, to decide to change reality. Perhaps it's unreasonable to have hoped otherwise. Perhaps it would be reasonable, instead, to accept the Summit's promises that some time – after the recession, after we've sorted out eastern Europe, when things pick up – we *will* get around to tackling poverty. George Bernard Shaw thought there was a place for unreason. He wrote: "The reasonable man adapts himself to the world. The unreasonable man persists in trying to adapt the world to himself. Therefore all progress depends upon the unreasonable man."

How do the Brazilian death squads fit into all this? Reasonably enough, I think: they act deliberately to achieve a result the world achieves on a far grander scale despite itself. They hardly merit condemnation for that. And in a steadily more crowded world, there'll be all the more need for pest control men, for the neighbourhood grim reapers. We should be giving them medals.

A literary sensation took place in New York when a new editor was appointed at the New Yorker, one of the city's most venerable institutions. The weekly magazine – founded in 1925 – is unique in the United States: witty, urbane, intellectual, filled with dry cartoons and long articles by distinguished writers. Traditionalists feared the end of an era.

ALL CHANGE AT THE NEW YORKER?

DAVID WILLIS   NEW YORK   4 JULY 1992

*T*he New Yorker has been a symbol of excellence in America's most literary city since it was founded by an eccentric, moody but brilliant editor called Harold Ross in February 1925. It began as a product of the Jazz Age: irreverent, gossipy, biting. At first it struggled: after six months its circulation had sunk to a mere 2,700 copies a week. The editorial offices were shabby. One night Ross met the famous American humorist, Dorothy Parker, a regular contributor, and asked why she hadn't come to the office to write an article she'd promised that day. Recalled James Thurber, an equally famous writer, cartoonist and contributor: "Miss Parker turned upon him the eloquent magic of her dark and lovely eyes. 'Someone was using the pencil', she explained sorrowfully."

Gradually the magazine began to prosper. Ross, who edited it until his death in 1951, favoured the fine writing and sharp humour of essayists E.B. White, S.J. Perelman (who also wrote scripts for the Marx Brothers films), Woolcott Gibbs, George S. Kaufman and Robert Benchley, as well as Parker and Thurber. But the magazine also became known for its literary works by authors such as J.D. Salinger, John Cheever and James Baldwin, and for its profiles and analysis of national and international affairs, which often stretched to enormous length.

The last piece Ross himself commissioned, a study of the aftermath of the bombing of Hiroshima, by John Hershey, filled one entire issue.

Hundreds of articles and series later became books - including one of the pioneering works on the environment, *Silent Spring* by Rachel Carson, and *Eichmann in Jerusalem* by Hannah Arendt. Yet the atmosphere of its offices remained more university common-room than noisy newsroom. Someone once said the cracked leather sofas and decrepit desks looked like the branch office of a failing insurance company.

Staff writers were subjected to nothing as crass as a deadline. Once an idea was accepted, the writer was simply left to get on with it. William Shawn, milder than the acerbic Ross whom he succeeded, but almost as eccentric – he would never, for instance, ride in a lift – moved at his own pace. When the novelist, John Updike, turned in an article on the use of inverted commas, in 1961, Shawn paid him ... and published it in 1982 – twenty-one years, three months and one day later.

By 1985, when the magazine was bought by the publisher S.I. Newhouse and Mr Shawn was replaced by only the third editor in its history, Robert Gottleib, *The New Yorker's* reputation was towering. A veteran staff writer, Calvin Trillin, once said that if a fact could not be checked by a telephone call to France, someone would fly there to do it. But there was a suspicion that readers, especially younger readers, were finding the long articles too long. To critics, the relentless upper middle-class tone was becoming stuffy and stodgy. Gottleib made a minor change or two. But it's now clear that the publisher wants more. Mr Gottleib left unhappily.

The new editor, Tina Brown, has a reputation for being much more low-brow. She boosted the circulation of *Vanity Fair* by combining fashion and glamour with lively, controversial articles about personalities. Many now fear the worst. Others hope Miss Brown might just add a dash of the original gossipy irreverence of Harold Ross, without sacrificing his standards.

It was once said of Ross that he regarded perfection as his personal property, like his hat or his watch. But he also insisted that the magazine be funny. As well as its cartoons, it has always reprinted small items from the American press, misprinted or humorously odd. One item was a garbled account of a journey by a woman in Burbank, California in the local paper. It read: "Among the first to enter the plane was Mrs Clara Adams. Slowly her nose was turned around to face in a south-westerly direction and away from the hangar doors. Then, like some strange beast, she crawled along the grass."

THE MIDDLE EAST

The release of another British hostage – the former Battle of Britain pilot, Jackie Mann – was greeted with obvious delight and relief in the West. Soon, other captives were to follow, including the Archbishop of Canterbury's special envoy, Terry Waite. Amid the media euphoria, seasoned observers in the Middle East saw the whole affair as a maudlin and cynical exercise.

THE FARCES OF FREEDOM

TIM LLEWELLYN   DAMASCUS   28 SEPTEMBER 1991

T he ritual begins when word reaches Damascus from Beirut by devious means that the hostage is free, and that the kidnappers have handed him over to Syrian military intelligence. After they have looked him over at the former Beau Rivage Hotel on Beirut's waterfront, the dark tower that now houses the Syrian spooks – the men who really run Lebanon – the freed man is then subjected to a wild, two-hour ride over the mountains of Lebanon, and the Ante Lebanon, to Damascus.

There he is delivered to the Syrian Foreign Ministry, a building that combines the grandeur of a post-war Midlands town hall, and the comfort of a 1950s railway station waiting room. He is then in the hands of the Syrian officials and the Western ambassador concerned. After a quick check to make sure that the ex-hostage is presentable (and sane), he is led in to face the public – that is to say the cameras. This is his first contact with what might pass for the real world after his years of isolation, abuse, deprivation, torture, hopelessness, depression and despair.

Escorted by the diplomats and officials, he is stood or seated between them, in front of the press, like a prisoner at the bar, blinking into the glare of the lights and the buzz-click-buzz of the camera shutters, while the homilies are

145

read out. The Syrian minister thanks Syria for all it has done (whatever that might be), and makes hopeful noises; the Western diplomat does likewise, except that this week the British ambassador added to the fun by thanking the world's two great kidnapping and abduction nations – Iran and Israel – for all their help as well; presumably this was on the grounds that they are now giving it all up, for the time being anyway.

The prisoner at the bar (I mean the free man) is then allowed his few carefully prepared words under close supervision. Usually these are bland, happy and grateful; but at least this week the much-reduced figure of old Jackie Mann, although his voice had been bullied out of him by his captors, managed to convey to us that he was, rightfully and understandably, angry beyond articulation at the aimless evil to which he had been subjected.

But what no one seems to ask is, why is this all really necessary? For a start, other than running Lebanon now, what is Syria's role in all this? It is hard to believe that a country with as pervasive an inside knowledge of Lebanon, the Iranians, armed factions, criminals, drug smugglers, and all the various villains who have been loose in Lebanon these past sixteen years, did not know *precisely* where the hostages were. Let us be charitable and say the Syrians knew, but did nothing for fear of harming the captives in a gunfight. Did they pass on private assurances to the Western governments concerned? Were the relatives then privately advised that 'X' was okay, or that 'Y' needed this or that medicine?

There's no evidence to suggest any of this happened. And even if word did leak out, would the relatives or the press have been told? It seems that the Americans are already outraged that Jackie Mann has been allowed to tell the truth about his 865 days of purgatory. Perhaps Syria and Iran have put pressure on the kidnappers now that both countries want to be friends with the West again; and Syria, in its new and commanding role in Lebanon, is in a better position to exert such pressure. Certainly Syria could obstruct any release process if it so chose, which is worth bearing in mind. Is it a coincidence that no British hostage was freed until *after* Britain and Syria had renewed diplomatic relations earlier this year?

More obviously, Syria wants the kudos arising from a hostage release, however spurious, and it wants political control over the event. When my old friend, Charles Glass, the American writer and journalist, escaped his Lebanese kidnappers in August 1987, after being held for two months, he was brought to Damascus in the time-honoured manner; he had no choice. As Charles says: "When you're coming out of an experience like that, and you're in safe hands, you'll do anything, say anything, you're so grateful and so manipulable." When Charles arrived in Damascus an American diplomat told him he hadn't escaped at all; the Syrians had worked in their mysterious way and the kidnappers had allowed him to escape. So when his turn came to be prisoner at the bar he should thank the Syrians – and he did. What a coincidence, I thought at the time, that this was just when Syria and the United States were making strategic friends again after years of mutual distaste.

Hostages are a cottage industry for the Syrians, with everyone on the take: the hotels who house the hundreds of journalists and technicians and charge them double for their 'phone calls, calculating the room and 'phone bills at a completely artificial rate to the dollar; the thousands of dollars, both over and under the table, for allowing the media to use their satellites and facilities (a darkened air-conditioning duct in our case); the extra charges for expediting visas; the bribes at the airport for taking equipment in, taking it out, the bribes inside Syria for keeping it there. When this whole affair is over, there will be a terrible financial anti-climax in Syria, but hundreds if not thousands of much better padded bank accounts.

Jackie Mann was released at 8.20pm on Tuesday September 24th in West Beirut; he could have been safely back in the arms of the RAF within the hour, reunited with his wife a few moments later: the British base of Akrotiri on Cyprus is 30 minutes away by VC-10, or an hour by helicopter; England is just over four hours away. But it seems the last thing to be considered is the hostage's own comfort or convenience; there are many political and economic matters to be taken into account first.

A year after the start of the Gulf War, in Kuwait, the Iraqi occupation and the ensuing war were still a sombre memory. Our correspondent, Stephen Sackur, who witnessed the final expulsion of Iraqi troops from Kuwait, returned to find a country still ill at ease.

KUWAITIS – LIVING WITH TRAUMA

STEPHEN SACKUR   KUWAIT   16 JANUARY 1992

In the last couple of weeks strange things have been happening in the residential suburbs south of Kuwait City: streets have been cordoned off for hours on end, military helicopters have been heard buzzing overhead, and most alarming of all, columns of American Abrahams tanks have been seen heading for the city centre. For those of us who witnessed the final days of Operation Desert Storm, vivid memories have been revived. This time, however, the guns are firing blanks, the fight scenes are tightly choreographed, and at the end of the day the dead and injured dust themselves down and return to their homes.

A year on from the Gulf War, Kuwait City, as you might have guessed, has become a film set, in this case for an epic feature commissioned by the Kuwaiti government – to portray the heroism and glory of liberation. The making of the movie has received considerable attention in the local press, but not all Kuwaitis return from work to find tanks thundering past their homes: without pause for thought they rounded up their families, grabbed a few valuables, and headed with all possible speed for the Saudi border. Only after hours of reassurance from Kuwaiti guards at the frontier were they convinced that Saddam Hussein had not reinvaded their country.

The story, though comic, strikes a chord with many Kuwaitis; despite the oft-repeated commitments to Kuwait's security made in Washington and elsewhere, there's still a profound fear of Saddam Hussein at the heart of this society. Almost every Kuwaiti garage now boasts a four-wheel-drive vehicle capable of making the arduous desert crossing should Iraqi troops once again descend from the north. People take an intense interest in news from Baghdad, the local press reports in detail the latest evidence of atrocities committed against the Kurds and the Shias, and always the unspoken question hangs in the air: would he, could he, ever try again? "Don't be misled by all that you see around you," warned a Kuwaiti doctor friend of mine, when I remarked upon the apparent normality of life in Kuwait City. "Restoring the roads and the telephones, buying new cars and re-equipping our offices, that's the easy part," he said. "The real challenge lies in healing the psychological wounds. This is a deeply traumatised society."

To prove it he allowed me to sit in on a group therapy session he runs in a neighbourhood clinic. For a couple of hours, three women and a man talked about their experiences during the Iraqi occupation. One woman had lost her husband the day after the invasion – at the time she was two months pregnant. Another had seen her brother shot in the back of the head by Iraqi soldiers on the doorstep of the family home. The man did little talking, he was, he said, suffering from chronic depression after being severely beaten up last February. His glazed look and slow speech testified to the strength of the drugs upon which he now depends. The group generated a powerful sense of solidarity; two of the women cried quietly as they listened to the testimony of the third. But there wasn't simply a desire to relive the past, there was also a need to express continued feelings of unease in post-liberation Kuwait. "Those who weren't here throughout the occupation can't understand my feelings," one said, to general agreement. She described the anger she felt when bureaucrats pestered her to fill in forms and provide them with documentation to prove that her husband was dead.

The government here is loathe to acknowledge the psychological gap between the thirty per cent of Kuwaitis who spent seven months living under a brutal occupation, and a great majority who sought refuge abroad. Only now – almost a year after liberation – has a psychiatric centre been established to help those suffering from long term trauma. And while a film about Operation Desert Storm and the liberation of Kuwait is being made with government money, little public recognition has been given to those Kuwaitis and non-Kuwaitis who had, in the previous months, shown tremendous bravery in their passive and active resistance to the Iraqi occupying force.

This sense of a society ill at ease with itself pervades all aspects of life. In the political arena, promises made by the Emir and the Crown Prince about the early restoration of democracy have yet to be fulfilled. National Assembly elections are planned for October, but under the present rules less than ten per cent of the Kuwaiti population would be entitled to vote. Women are still allowed no part in the political process; this despite a general acknowledgement that women were in the forefront of the Kuwaiti resistance movement. "Sooner or later our leading men are going to have to realise things have changed," one powerful businesswoman told me. "Do they seriously think that after we've marched in front of Iraqi tanks, hidden guns in the folds of our dresses, we're going to settle back into the old ways as if nothing had happened?"

The Kuwaiti government has adopted as its post-war slogan, 'Kuwait for the Kuwaitis', in a desperate bid to foster national unity. With hundreds of thousands of non-Kuwaiti workers banished from the Emirate, Kuwaitis are indeed going to have to display a new sense of independence and self reliance in the coming months. Whether they will surely depends on the extent to which the Al-Sabah clan is prepared to redistribute political power. If the Emirate continues to be run like a relaxed family business, it will be no surprise if the excluded majority becomes increasingly restive. For the moment it will take more than a series of carefully crafted celluloid images to convince sceptical Kuwaitis that the lessons of the Gulf War have been learned.

The dramatic events in Algeria, where the Islamic Salvation Front had an apparently inevitable election victory snatched from its grasp at the beginning of 1992, cast a shadow across the whole of north Africa. Arab governments kept a low profile, but in Egypt the debate over the role of fundamentalist Islam was given a new edge.

THE PROFITS AND LOSS OF CENSORSHIP

BARNABY MASON   CAIRO   17 JANUARY 1992

Not long ago in southern Egypt some students were listening to a BBC tape as part of an English language class. The tape contained a song; at that point one young man ostentatiously took off his headphones in protest – music was against religion, he said. That's the puritanical view of the militant Islamic groups; it's at odds with the feelings of most Egyptians, who love music, weddings and parties. There is a tide still running towards a more Islamic style of dress and behaviour – more girl students wearing the full veil, for instance – though it's by no means overwhelming.

Another aspect is the attempt by one wing of the religious establishment to extend its control over what's published in Egypt. In December 1991 the verdict was given in the case of a little-known writer accused of blasphemy, Alaa Hamed. His novel *The Distance in a Man's Mind* contains a dream sequence depicting the Prophet Mohammed having sexual intercourse. The judge shocked the intelligentsia by imposing the maximum sentence of eight years in prison, not only on the writer, but also on the printer and on the distributor – Cairo's best-known bookseller, Al Haag Madbouli.

People who'd read the novel described it as very bad, not at all in the same league, artistically, as Salman Rushdie's *Satanic Verses* which is also banned here. But that wasn't really the point; and in the outcry that followed, many journalists and commentators pressed the Prime Minister not to ratify the sentence, as required in cases tried under the emergency laws. President Mubarak remarked that freedom of expression didn't mean you could attack religion. Apparently encouraged by this remark, and by the prospect of an Islamic fundamentalist government coming to power in Algeria, Egypt's highest religious authority, Al Azhar, went on the offensive at the Cairo Book Fair. A committee of Al Azhar's Islamic Research Centre ordered a halt to the sale and display of five books about Islam.

The author this time was a well-known exponent of liberal Islamic views, Dr Sa'eed Ashmawy, who also happens to be the head of the Supreme State Security Court. The committee later issued banning orders against three books by other writers; all had been in print for some time. Dr Ashmawy complained angrily that the decision put him at risk from extremist Islamic groups who might try to kill him; he challenged the Grand Sheikh of Al Azhar to appear with him on television and explain what was wrong with his books. But the religious authorities appeared to have gone too far: intervening behind the scenes, President Mubarak told Al Azhar that it had no right to ban books on its own; if it had objections to particular works it could only make recommendations to the legal authorities.

The government faces a permanent dilemma in deciding how to deal with the fundamentalists: whether to bring them into the system in the hope that they become part of it, or exclude them and crack down hard. One influential establishment figure told me it had been a great mistake to give the fundamentalists extensive time on radio and television. That just meant that public debate was conducted in religious terms, a debate they were bound to win. On the other hand, the authorities consistently refuse to legalise a religious party – the Muslim Brothers are tolerated at best – and recent events in Algeria will have convinced them that they're right. It's possible to argue that fundamentalist parties, convinced that they alone are carrying out the word of God, should be excluded from the democratic process; it's another matter to allow them to fight an election and then cancel the result.

Egyptian officials certainly heaved a sigh of relief when the prospect of such a government receded. They're already worried by the Iranian government's drive to increase its influence in the region, especially in Egypt's southern neighbour Sudan where fundamentalists are already dominant. Events in Algeria conjured up the spectre of Islamic governments to the West, the South and the East. At home the Egyptian authorities remain confident of their ability to contain the situation. And the fundamentalists are far from having things their own way. At the Cairo Book Fair, indeed, the unabashed publishers of Sa'eed Ashmawy were using loud speakers to attract customers to come and buy the books that Al Azhar had tried to ban.

In Israel, Yitzhak Shamir's government was facing a political crisis early in 1992. With two hard-line parties resigning in protest at the Arab-Israeli peace process, Israel's Prime Minister was deprived of his majority. The problem seemed to be with Israel's electoral system which uses a very pure form of proportional representation.

DISPROPORTIONATE REPRESENTATION

ALEX BRODIE   JERUSALEM   18 JANUARY 1992

In the matter of electoral reform, specifically proportional representation, Israel provides an excellent example of what not to do. The Israeli parliament, the Knesset, is elected by a system of pure proportional representation, which its apologists call complete democracy and its detractors call complete chaos. The detractors are growing in number as Israel's elected representatives persist in disgracing themselves. The sight of politicians openly clawing at the body politic for whatever they can get in return for their votes is a periodic drama; commentators cannot decide whether it's tragedy or farce; if it wasn't so sad it would be funny.

In recent weeks the Israeli voter has been subjected to a bravura performance by his chosen representatives – a vintage display of political cynicism. But the details later. First the system, which is the stage upon which the politicians are enabled to practice what members of parliament themselves have dubbed 'the morality of the whorehouse'. There are no constituencies. A member of the Knesset, an MK, is neither directly elected by, nor responsible to, the voters. The voter chooses not a person, but a party. The percentage of votes that party attracts decides how many seats it gets; the party itself decides who will fill the seats. Thus the MK answers to no one but the party or interest group.

And if he doesn't do what it tells him he could be dropped from the list at the next election.

In the one hundred and twenty seat Knesset, there are no less than twenty parties; only two of them are substantial; Labour with thirty-eight and Mr Shamir's Likud with thirty-seven seats. Of the rest, the biggest has five seats; the smallest, one; there are in fact six one-man parties. Under this system of pure proportional representation all you need to get a seat is some twenty thousand votes, one per cent. That threshold – which in Germany for instance is five per cent – has just been raised: but only to one and a half per cent. It was to be two and a half but, of course, the small parties bargained it down. They are able to exert influence out of all proportion to their support because the two big parties cannot build a majority government without them.

One of the recent performances which, by general acclaim, brought the Knesset into disrepute was the wheeling and dealing over an electoral reform bill to introduce the direct election of the Prime Minister. Its main aim was to clean up politics by reducing the power of the tiny parties to blackmail the government. But Mr Shamir enforced his party's discipline against it, and the bill to cut the power of the small parties could not be passed without the support of ... the small parties. It's now buried in committee. But the *tour de force* was the budget debate when, with breathtaking candour, the small parties in Mr Shamir's coalition set out the price of their votes. The Finance Minister, who had to shell out the money so that the budget could pass and the state could actually function, spoke of extortion.

A member of an ultra-orthodox religious party – a Machiavelli of political tactics when it comes to extracting money for religious schools – argued that the system was truly democratic, much more so than, for example, in Britain because every section of society has a say. A parliamentary correspondent, who despite more than twenty years covering the Knesset has still not lost his ability to be shocked, agreed that perhaps you could call it highly democratic; but he added that you need less democracy, and considerably more planning, to run a country.

Out of the horse-trading over the budget, two tiny parties, with a total of five members between them, were able significantly to increase the amount of money to be spent in the Occupied Territories on Jewish settlements, in defiance of the United States. Israel wants the Americans to guarantee a cheap loan for two billion dollars a year for five years, to help absorb the influx of Jews from the former Soviet Union. President Bush is holding it up because he wants a guarantee that the money will not be spent on, or liberate other money to be spent on, settlements in the Occupied Territories. Mr Bush, in common with much of the outside world, believes Jewish settlements on what the Palestinians consider their land, to be an obstacle to Middle East peace. Incidentally, those two billion dollars for this year, which the overt diversion of funds to settlements jeopardises, has already been included in the budget. If Israel doesn't get the loan, the already heavily taxed Israelis may have to pay considerably more, and the budget deficit will shoot up – all highly dangerous for an already ailing economy, according to the Governor of the Bank of Israel.

These are weighty matters. and that's without even mentioning the impact, psychological and otherwise, on the state of Israel if it fails to fulfil its *raison d'être*: Israel exists to provide a home for all Jews; its purpose is the gathering in of the exiles. The vast immigration from Russia has slowed down dramatically. Israel needs those loans to create jobs, and to build houses near the jobs, to keep the Russians coming.

That's quite a catalogue of possible consequences for a bit of political horse-trading by five members of parliament. The same five, incidentally, whose decision to resign in protest at the peace process will deprive Mr Shamir of his majority, possibly bring him down, and almost certainly provoke early elections.

Now can you see what a little fringe group can achieve with less than five per cent of the vote?

On Sunday February 16th, 1992, on a signal from inside south Lebanon, two Apache helicopters took off from their bases in northern Israel, and within minutes the Israeli gunners guided rockets into Sheikh Abbas Musawi's limousine, instantly incinerating him, his wife and his six-year-old son. The incident dampened any hopes for progress at the following week's round of bilateral Arab-Israeli peace talks in Washington.

BOYS FROM THE BADLANDS

TIM LLEWELLYN   NICOSIA   20 FEBRUARY 1992

Hezbollah, the Lebanese in general, and the Palestinians in Lebanon have had much experience of Israeli marauders overhead in the past twenty years. They tend to call it terrorism – state terrorism: bombs and air to ground rockets on densely populated Palestinian camps, towns and villages; artillery fire night and day; snatch raids on Lebanese youth. Four nearly fourteen years now these tactics have maintained Israeli control of a large swathe of south Lebanon – to protect, say the Israelis, their northern borders and population.

For the Israelis, everyone north of their border is a potential terrorist, and the rocket attacks and guerrilla raids of the seventies and eighties (largely ineffective though they were) explain Israel's vigilance. But Israel's military superiority, intelligence, air and artillery power, and its network of supporters and informers inside Lebanon have long made the struggle with the various guerrillas an unequal battle. And Sunday's epic display of aerial chutzpah was a reminder to the Arabs of their woeful vulnerability. Israel's illegal, and probably largely unnecessary, military occupation of chunks of south Lebanon, means that their battle with these Arab enemies can be conducted ten or fifteen miles from the border proper, instead of right on it. And as we know, the Israelis like their *cordons sanitaires*, the wider the better.

It is this effective Israeli control of Lebanese territory, with Israel's Lebanese proxies in the south Lebanon Army – Christians and Shi'ites alike – that the guerrillas are vainly fighting against; not, they say, for the right to launch raids into Israel proper. That they consider to be a Palestinian prerogative, if the Palestinians had not been emasculated in Lebanon by the Syrians, Lebanese and Israelis. This is not believed by the Israelis, who see south Lebanon as a chaotic, uncontrolled badland; a source of hatred and threat; a place where one shoots first, where there are no rules.

The people of south Lebanon, mainly Shi'ites, have always been low on everyone's list of priorities; at the end of the queue when it comes to grace or favour. In pre-Israeli days, the Palestinians regarded Shi'ites as fit only for boot-blacking and pot-cleaning, denizens of an inferior and inward-looking, martyr-obsessed brand of Islam. The politicians and fat-cats of Lebanon took the profits from the tobacco fields, citrus and apple and olive groves of the south, but gave little in return. When, in 1970, the arrival of the Palestinian guerrillas brought Israel's artillery on their heads, the state gave the Shi'ites little or no protection. Smart young men traditionally went to Beirut, or to the Gulf or to Europe, or in many cases further afield, where many made fortunes. They returned to their beloved south and built their *haciendas* on the rolling, stony hills; but, in the past twenty years, they have found their paradise turned into the battleground of various Shi'ite groups, Palestinians, Sunnis, Communists, Christians and Israelis.

The United Nations Interim Force, set up in 1978 after the first major Israeli invasion, has been allowed only to fulfil a part of its mandate to extend its control south to the Israeli border. Israel has consistently prevented this, in defiance of the Security Council, saying that the UN blue-helmets couldn't do the job. Well, that is certainly true; they can't as long as Israel and its Lebanese cohorts are in the way.

The continuing misery of the Shi'ites, from 1970 onwards – misery if they stayed, more misery if they moved (as so many tens of thousands did to the slums of south Beirut) was a magic sea in which the new Islamic activists could swim. First, there was the brilliant Lebanese Shi'ite cleric, Imam Musa Sadr, who rallied his people into the new Amal or Hope Party in the early years of the civil war. He disappeared, mysteriously, in 1978, intensifying his followers' pain. But soon came the more potent example of the Islamic Revolution of Ayatollah Khomeini, in 1979, and by 1981 the foot-soldiers of that Revolution, with their inspirational priests, were in amongst these underprivileged people, teaching, organising, arming and paying.

The most virulent strain of this new breed was Hezbollah, who I'd seen first in Teheran in the late seventies as thugs wielding knouts and cudgels, doing the Ayatollah's bidding against the leftists and liberals, whom the revolution was so soon, with Hezbollah's help, to crush. By the early eighties, the clubs had turned into guns, bombs, artillery, and the movement was strong enough to make much of South Lebanon unfit for the invading Israelis, after 1982, and decidedly unhealthy for the short- lived, inadequate multinational force.

But even though Hezbollah claims to serve Lebanese interests, and is Lebanese largely in membership, it is an arm of Iranian foreign policy, and that policy sees no future in trying for any accord with Israel. The Syrians have crushed the main indigenous Shi'ite party, Amal, a rival for membership with Hezbollah. Once again, it is the outsider who calls the shots in Lebanon, and the toughest outsider of them all, Israel, who shoots straighter than anyone.

Libya was locked in a stalemate with Britain and the United States at the beginning of 1992 over the blowing up of a Pan-Am jumbo-jet over Lockerbie in 1988. The Libyans refused to extradite the Libyans suspected of involvement in the bombing, thus running the risk of punitive sanctions being imposed. By way of a counter propaganda offensive, Western journalists were invited to look at the destruction wrought by American aircraft in 1986 on Colonel Gaddafi's residence.

GADDAFI'S BUNKER

MATT FREI   TRIPOLI   22 FEBRUARY 1992

W e were taken to see the house in which Colonel Gaddafi and his family slept on the night of the American bombing raid in 1986. A modest three story block, the residence inside Tripoli's heavily guarded Azariah barracks has been abandoned and turned into a bizarre shrine and museum. Anti-American slogans are scrawled across the walls and etched into the dust of the tables. Colonel Gaddafi himself appears on murals, paintings and photographs in numerous victorious poses. The Colonel's residence was bombed, but most of the destruction seems to have been caused by the museum's curators! A colleague of mine pointed out that the interior looked like an artificially distressed new-wave bar in Washington. Slabs of insulation and concrete dangled on cables from the ceiling like marionettes. Burned out US missiles, their index numbers still visible, stood around the reception room like embarrassed guests at a party. Pieces of shrapnel had been used as bookmarks in the large, green visitors' book. Outside the front entrance there was an eight foot statue of a golden fist crushing a model of an American fighter.

We were taken upstairs to the Gaddafi family bedrooms. The bed in which the Colonel slept, on the night of the bombing, was large, round and had electronic controls built into two bedside dashboards. Behind the stacked up pillows was a poster of a tropical beach with gushing waves. The bed, protected behind a glass barrier, was strewn with pieces of debris, concrete and shrapnel. The bathroom, with its round jacuzzi, was decorated with large blue polka dots; *Hello!* magazine would perhaps have described the style as 'early James Bond'. So far our tour had been bizarre, verging on the comical; but in the room that used to be the nursery it became grotesque. The walls were covered with a kind of photo frieze of Colonel Gaddafi's adopted baby daughter who was killed in the bombing. The first picture displayed the little girl surrounded by family and friends at a birthday party clutching a large cuddly toy; the toy, now dismembered, was on her empty bed. The last picture showed the same girl. She was dead. Her stomach was cut open in the autopsy, and what must have been a doctor's hand was holding up her liver, which had been partially singed – presumably during the bombing. It was a shocking sight, but the overall impression of the house-cum-shrine was one of heroism blended with self pity.

In its way, Gaddafi's residence is no less staged than, perhaps, Churchill's bunker in London. But as many Libyans now fear another military strike, this shrine has acquired a new poignancy; it is a poignancy that Colonel Gaddafi is busy exploiting. The Libyan government wishes to transmit a two-fold message: firstly, that it is being threatened, once again, by the overwhelming might of America and its allies; secondly, that Libya itself is behaving correctly by putting the two Lockerbie suspects under house arrest and investigation.

The Libyan High Court judge has a point when he complains that the Scottish Lord Advocate's Office has ignored his plea to send the accumulated evidence, so that he can begin filing charges against the two men. He is also correct in pointing out that Libya has no extradition treaty with anyone. None of this cuts any ice with Britain and the United States, who fundamentally distrust the Libyan judiciary for obvious reasons.

By charging the two Libyan Lockerbie suspects, and demanding their extradition, power politics have effectively been diluted with legal procedures. If Libya fails to comply with these demands, political pressure will be applied in the form of sanctions, which the UN is expected to endorse in a Security Council resolution at the end of the month. But apart from the desire to seek justice, is the current policy adopted by Britain and the United States a wise one? I have my doubts.

Libya has already transferred most of its financial assets in Europe to safe havens in the Gulf. An air embargo on commercial flights in and out of Libya would be a nuisance, but unless the borders with Tunisia and Egypt are closed Libyans will still be able to fly out of their country, and thousands of Western oil workers will still be able to fly in. In preparation for commercial sanctions, Libya has begun stockpiling goods. The ports in Benghazi and Tripoli are bustling with activity; moreover, the country has no more than four million people to feed. What about oil sanctions? If strictly imposed, they would harm Libya in the long term, but Western diplomats believe the country has enough financial reserves to survive for a year or two.

In the short term, oil and gas sanctions would, above all, harm European countries like Germany, which relies heavily on clean Libyan oil, and Spain which imports twenty-five per cent of its gas from Libya. Instead of destabilising Colonel Gaddafi, sanctions will merely cast him as the defiant underdog: they are unlikely to force him to extradite the two suspects.

There is another point: even if Colonel Gaddafi were to fall as the result of pressure exerted by the West, what or who would replace him? He has no obvious successor and he has successfully maintained the balance of power between Libya's rival clans. One senior western diplomat I spoke to said he was convinced that without Colonel Gaddafi, Libya would disintegrate into chaos and become fertile soil for Islamic fundamentalism. Algeria, Tunisia and Egypt may think that the Libyan leader is a maverick, but they admire his ability to suppress fundamentalism wherever it crops up in Libya.

Colonel Gaddafi is a survivor whose recipe for survival is based on a mixture of repression at home and rhetorical defiance in the face of external aggression. By putting more pressure on the Libyan leader now, Britain and the United States may actually be doing him a favour.

The American Secretary of State, James Baker, finally made America's position clear to Israel in February 1992: the ten billion dollars in loan guarantees it wanted from the United States were made conditional on there being a freeze on Jewish settlements in the Occupied Territories. Israel vehemently rejected the condition. But was is it so unreasonable to stop building in the interests of the peace process? For some, the answer was a resounding 'yes'.

LAND FOR PEACE

ALEX BRODIE   JERUSALEM   29 FEBRUARY 1992

Danny Hisme, a Yemenite Jew, lives with his English wife and six children in a tiny, gardenless apartment in the centre of the Arab city of Hebron. He never leaves home without a gun. If the children play out they do so under armed guard. He doesn't have to live there, he chooses to. He feels driven to settle where the Jewish patriarchs Abraham, Isaac and Jacob were reputed to have been buried nearly four thousand years ago.

There are some four hundred Jewish settlers among the thousands of Arabs in Hebron. "The reason we stay here as a minority among the Arabs," says Danny, "is the same reason Israel exists among all the Arab states – some sort of divine supervision." Danny's eleven year-old son has plastered the door of his bedroom, as boys do, with pin ups; however, they are not of pop stars or footballers, but of heavily bearded rabbis. There's one picture of Rabbi Levinger, the gun-toting spiritual leader of the Hebron settlers, and eight photographs of the late Rabbi Meir Kahane.

Levinger has been to jail for shooting dead a Palestinian Arab, and continues to open fire when he deems it necessary. Kahane founded the avowedly racist Kach movement. Danny was not concerned about his son's allegiances: he said all the settlers' kids of that age, and younger, were in the Kach youth movement. Its simple message appealed to them. " What do you think they'll understand better?" he said. "Being told to behave nicely, or being told to throw all the

163

Arabs out? When he's 14 or 15 he'll begin to understand what's wrong with Kach, but nothing I say now will change his views. The stones and knives of the Arabs are stronger than my explanations."

But I don't suppose he has tried too hard. There's great sympathy among the settlers for the message of Kach, which is all about the Jews' divine right to be here, their superiority to the Arab – strength and enforcement. Kach runs The Committee for Safety on Roads which mounts armed vigilante patrols in Arab areas to assert the right of the Jewish settler, sub-machine gun over his shoulder, to go anywhere.

In the hilltop settlement of Shiloh, Ira Rappaport was utterly matter of fact when he told me why he went to jail, more than a decade ago, for sixteen months. "We blew the legs off some Arab mayors. We set out to maim them." He thought it worthwhile in that it had stopped Arab resistance to mass Jewish settlement. Zvi Katsover, Mayor of the settlement of Kiryat Arba, is a member of Mr Shamir's ruling Likud Party, but he thinks it has gone soft. Unimpressed by the international outrage which greeted Israel's expulsion of twelve Palestinians, he argues that a thousand should be banished from their homes.

I could go on. I could report scores of such conversations to confirm the point I want to make: settlers' views are extreme, and are minority views. But what they have done – with a great deal of help from ideological allies in the Likud Party – is to make those views mainstream: the tail is wagging the dog. They have taken the majority concern of Israel's security from attack, and inextricably linked it with their own causes. Israelis who have the temerity to challenge the potent brew of ultra nationalism, religious zealotry, and holocaust invocation, are labelled self-hating Jews, traitors, or Arab allies.

Thus it is hardly possible now to separate the simple issue of a freeze on settlements from the ultimate fate of the nation. The Government Spokesman, Binyamin Netanyahu, asserted that Mr Baker's call for a halt to settlement building was an attempt to force Israel back to its 1967 borders, which was tantamount to dragging the Jews to the gates of Auschwitz!

Really ? . . ..

What Mr Baker is asking Israel to do is to abide by the spirit of the peace process which prescribes an interim settlement, and to stop building in the Territories so as not to prejudge their future status. But instead, more settlements are being built faster than ever before, precisely to preempt negotiation and make Israeli withdrawal impossible. Last year, in one year, Israel started building more than half as many settlers' homes as had been built in the previous twenty-odd years of occupation. That building boom was concurrent with Mr Baker's shuttle missions. His arrivals in Israel were greeted with the ostentatious planting of new settlements, intended pointedly to humiliate him. Settlers portrayed him as Hitler; George Bush was called an anti-semite. At the time, it was remarked that George Bush and James Baker abided by the maxim: 'don't get mad, get even.'

Virtually every settlement now has new homes, half built homes and caravans, many empty, incidentally, because the demand from ordinary Israelis, including Russian immigrants, is for homes in Israel proper – not there. More funds than the struggling Israeli economy can afford are being pumped into the settlements.

And now Israel wants the Americans to guarantee cheap loans to repair the damage, to help absorb the Russian immigrants, and to revitalise the economy. Settlement building was used as a weapon with which to bludgeon Mr Baker, and to mortally wound the peace process he is labouring for. But now the United States is using its economic leverage on Israel as never before. And Mr Shamir has to calculate carefully the cost of his unequivocal support for the settler minority.

Syria is often depicted as a sombre presence brooding over the knotted landscape of the Middle East, still the most uncompromising Arab adversary of Israel despite being engaged in peace talks. But the country also has another face: rich in beautiful and historic sites, particularly in the ancient city of Aleppo.

THE OTHER SYRIA

BARNABY MASON   DAMASCUS   4 APRIL 1992

The ruins of an enormous Byzantine church dating from the fifth century stand on a hilltop not far from the ancient city of Aleppo. After the severest winter for more than seventy years, the spring sun had brought the apricot trees into blossom and warmed a host of wild flowers: red and blue anemones, yellow vetch and pinky-white cyclamen. The church was dedicated to St Simeon Stylites, an especially ascetic monk who lived on top of a pillar for forty-two years – what's left of the pillar can still be seen, the focal point of the central octagon.

A wave of Christian devotion and mysticism swept this part of northern Syria in the fifth century; and besides many monasteries, you can see the well-preserved remains of three hundred villages of Roman and Byzantine times. When the Arab conquerors arrived in Syria two hundred years later, they took over much of the architectural style they found. The great Omayyad mosque in Damascus, built on the site of a cathedral, has green and gold mosaics unusually representational for Islamic art: they depict splendid buildings along a river shaded by elegantly waving trees.

In Aleppo the Byzantine cathedral was not demolished, it was simply turned into a Islamic place of learning. Some of the Corinthian capitals to the pillars, intricate foliage in golden stone, retain their carved crosses. At a little hotel on the Mediterranean coast, a young member of the local Greek Orthodox community waxes indignant about Syria's bad reputation in the West. "People are told it's a violent and dangerous place where they may be kidnapped," he says; "that's just false propaganda, like stories about the mistreatment of minorities." He points out that Christians are given two-and-a-half hours off on Sunday mornings to go to church. In the Damascus bazaar, a shopkeeper explains an amicable division of labour: the Muslims embroider the famous table-cloths, the Christians make the inlaid boxes and the Jews do the brass.

Ancient echoes of Muslim-Christian wars abound in the string of spectacular Crusader castles in the mountains above the coast. Potentially, they're another huge tourist attraction. The castle conquered by Salaheddin, Saladin in 1188 does get a thousand visitors a day on some weekends, most of them foreigners; but our taxi-driver didn't even know where it was.

Syrians are even less aware of the remote past. On a bus where we met an English expert on ancient religions, a young Syrian was astonished and delighted to learn that the world's first alphabet came from Syria, from the second millennium kingdom of Ugarit. Myths written down at that time are precursors of the stories of St George and the Dragon and Perseus and Andromeda.

Syria has echoes of the more recent past too: return to Aleppo, where the Baron Hotel seems frozen in time. A glass case displays a letter from T.E. Lawrence written "from this beautiful hotel" before the First World War; in a twist of modern politics, he notes receiving the thanks of the Turks "for settling the Kurdish-German dispute of last week." A 1930s poster in an upstairs corridor, beneath the brass chandeliers, proclaims "London-Baghdad in 7 days by Orient Express: Safety, Rapidity, Economy."

The proprietor of the Baron, Coco Mazloumian, an Armenian married to an Englishwoman, is in his eighties now. He reminisces in impeccably aristocratic English about the things he's seen: the brass band at the grand opening of the hotel, built by his father and uncle; the family's forced exile in Lebanon during the First World War to escape the massacre of Armenians by the Turks; a German archaeologist who wore a solar topee even when it was snowing: pioneering aviators like Amy Johnson and a procession of European royalty; Agatha Christie writing *Murder on the Orient Express* on the terrace; and the Household Cavalry holding mock fox-hunts, with bugle calls, up and down the stairs of the hotel during the Second World War.

Mr Mazloumian concedes that the Baron has seen better days. We're very happy with our government, he says – President Asad is an absolute marvel. But he complains about the economy; prices go up, while government controls have kept his room charges the same for five years. We can't keep pace with it, he says, so we have to let things go. But for outsiders, the air of gentle decay is part of the charm. One day, mass tourism or Middle East peace may turn the Baron Hotel into something unrecognisable; for the moment, we can enjoy those echoes of the past.

In early May 1992 a young man, thought to be an American tourist, ran amok in one of the holiest shrines in the Christian world, the Church of the Holy Sepulchre in Jerusalem, the place where Christ is thought to have been crucified. The incident only caused minor damage, but the affront was felt deeply among the city's Christians, and the area subsequently had to be reconsecrated.

THE JERUSALEM EFFECT

PAUL ADAMS   JERUSALEM   9 MAY 1992

It's not known why the unidentified man decided to attack the Greek Orthodox altar in the Church of the Holy Sepulchre, shattering oil lamps and a glass tabernacle and pulling a large cross from its stand. Some witnesses said he shouted: "Save the children of the world, don't worship idols", as he ran amok. When the police finally subdued him, he refused to cooperate and we still know nothing about him.

A female companion was only marginally more helpful, scribbling two words in Hebrew for the police, one of which was a word for God. The word got about that the two were Jewish tourists, probably from the United States. They're now under observation at Jerusalem's Kfar Shaul psychiatric hospital where, for the past thirteen years, a succession of disturbed foreign tourists has been treated, following similar, though usually less dramatic displays of eccentric behaviour in the Holy City.

Doctors call it the Jerusalem Syndrome. Some are obviously crazy to start with. Of the 200 tourists admitted every year, most have histories of mental illness, characterised by a variety of religious delusions. Some want to cleanse themselves, wearing white or simply throwing off their clothes in public. Some go further and take on Biblical personas. There are John the Baptists, Virgin

Marys, Abrahams and Davids. Recently the hospital treated a Canadian Samson: convinced of his superhuman strength, he managed to break down part of a wall and escape from the hospital. A nurse spotted him later on at the bus station and coaxed him back to Kfar Shaul, telling him it was God's will that he return.

But not everyone is mad to start with. Some of Kfar Shaul's inmates arrive in Jerusalem apparently sane and proceed to lose their minds in the course of a week or two in the city. Maybe it's the harsh, often blinding light, rebounding off the city's unyielding stones. Perhaps it's the relative thinness of the air at 3,000 feet. It might even be the hostile desert wind, the Khamsin, which blows sand, and who knows, perhaps the odd malevolent genie, from somewhere over in the desert wastes of the Arabian peninsula. Whatever it is, something about Jerusalem sets them off. They may be fine one minute, then disoriented, gibbering wrecks the next. Some may have come here looking for inner truth. Perhaps, as they gaze at the Holy Sepulchre, or the Wailing Wall, truth whispers to them and they find they really can't cope with it after all.

Few of those who end up in the psychiatric hospital at Kfar Shaul are likely to care much about the history of the place. Which is probably just as well, since Kfar Shaul is built on a hilltop that once was home to the Arab village of Deir Yassin, a quiet, tranquil place until the fighting which preceded the creation of the state of Israel in 1948. In April of that year, Jewish fighters of Menachem Begin's Irgun underground group massacred about 250 Palestinian villagers. To this day, the name of Deir Yassin reverberates in the brooding hearts of Palestinians. Jerusalem is full of unhappy ghosts, which doubtless contributes to the madness. Mysticism and history are all very well, but a more likely culprit for the Jerusalem Syndrome is surely the city's oppressive political and religious environment, in which every article of faith and conviction has its evil counterpart in fanaticism and hatred.

In a city which means so many things to so many people, the cacophony of differing beliefs is sometimes deafening. It's a Tower of Babel of political and spiritual languages; a place where the spirit of mutual understanding is a fragile flower, tangled in weeds of misunderstanding and suspicion. Is it any wonder that people here are forever doing things which really have very little to do with reason? A while ago, I stood on a balcony in the Church of the Holy Sepulchre, watching as hundreds of little old ladies from Greece went crazy at the sight of the holy fire, miraculously appearing from two portholes in the tomb itself. Perish the thought that the Greek Patriarch and Armenian Archimandrite inside had anything like a match about them.

Writers past and present have noted the disturbing effect Jerusalem seems to have on the people who live in or visit this city. Arthur Koestler called it the Jerusalem Sadness, a disease which he said was "due to the combined effect of the tragic, desolate beauty and inhuman atmosphere of the city". In the middle of the 19th century, Herman Melville found Jerusalem's rocky aspect too much to bear: "Stones to the right," he wrote, "and stones to the left ... stony tombs, stony hills and stony hearts." The Israeli poet, Yehuda Amichai, has a similar despairing refrain: "All these stones, all this sadness, all this light." More recently, the American novelist, Tom Robbins, summed it up with characteristic bluntness: "Jerusalem is not caught between a rock and a hard place," he wrote, "Jerusalem is a rock and a hard place."

Tim Llewellyn left his post of Middle East Correspondent having spent most of the past eighteen years reporting events in the Arab world. It was a period that saw the destruction of Beirut, the rise of the Ayatollahs in Iran and the defeat of Saddam Hussein's armies in the desert. In his final, special dispatch for From Our Own Correspondent, he reflected that – like most Middle East hands – he would no doubt return to the region – sooner or later.

GOODBYE TO ALL THAT

TIM LLEWELLYN   NICOSIA   2 JULY 1992

I t might be thought that I'm sad to be leaving. The Persian rugs have been rolled up; the Persian miniatures and Roberts prints are piled in a corner; the June sunlight, forcing its way through the wooden shutters, lights up an abandoned gallery, bare walls and tiled floors, and the stone staircase that winds up through the centre of the house has lost its hangings, its drapes and its pictures and looks, from below, as if it leads nowhere. Even the cat, with his fluffy white bib and bushy tail, knows something is up, he moans a lot: "Change and decay in all around I see," he may well be chanting. For him, rather than the indignities of England's quarantine custody and the realities of life in London, it will be another walled garden, more soft divans and a lifelong supply of lizards, crickets and small defenceless birds. A poignant but necessary parting.

So, it might be thought that I'm sad; but in many ways I leave with relief. My house, despite its age and Levantine attractions, is wide open to the elements, like an old Turkish *khan*: freezing in winter, a creaking, burning dust-bowl by mid-June. The old city of Nicosia, where I live in Arsinoe Street, is racked with noise all day and most of the night: drunks, rock and rollers, motor cycles and lorries without silencers, artisans who attack pieces of metal with other pieces of metal from dawn, through the siesta, to late at night.

In the fifteen years since I first visited Cyprus the affluence that has, ironically, followed on the heels of the Turkish invasion, has taught the Cypriots the pleasures of noise: fast, flashy cars and a predilection for honking the horn for no apparent reason. Despite their new-found wealth, or perhaps because of it, the Cypriots seem frustrated. All this money; all these *things*. Yet still they're stuck with the 'Cyprus Problem'.

The monotonous lack of progress on this question lives with us all, a few score yards from the green line that cuts through Nicosia: the Turkish flags in plain view; the muezzin's chant well within hearing. Most Cypriot politicians, Greek and Turkish, have so far seemed to prefer to score points than make meaningful concessions. The faces of the benighted diplomats and United Nations officials who deal with Cyprus look permanently drawn. At foreigners' dinner parties, the Cyprus Problem – the CP as it's called – is frequently banned as a topic.

The Greek Cypriots want, after 18 years, to go back to see their towns, villages, houses, and former businesses. The Turkish Cypriots are, largely, content to live in their part of the island, protected by the Turkish army, getting on with the simple but safe life, and wary about seeing Greek Cypriots returning – however briefly – to tread old stones and remember. If agreement is reached on some sort of reunification of Cyprus, and the pressure is on harder than ever at the moment, it will surely be so riddled with caveats and safeguards that the outcome will not be so different from today's divided island. I can imagine the anguish for members of both communities when they go back to their lost homes and the painful scenes that might erupt.

Cyprus *is* divided: but peaceful; and the Greek Cypriot community is one of the most prosperous in the whole Mediterranean. Why, you may ask, tamper with it all? Yet the urge for refugees and their descendants to regain, or at least have access to, what they lost is a genuine magnetic pull which, of course, politicians exploit.

People in this area – in Lebanon, in Cyprus, in the Middle East in general – are angry when their countries are partitioned, yet seem happier and more secure living in huddles with their co-religionists: the Maronite Lebanese in their mountains, the Druze Lebanese in theirs; the Muslim Turkish and Christian Greeks brutally sundered in 1974, but at least living calmly apart now.

In Lebanon, where Syria holds the lid down (just about) the most obviously lethal aspects of confessional factionalism have been suppressed but not solved; in Cyprus, where a United Nations peace-keeping force keeps the sides apart, the same applies. We know that the United Nations forces' political leaders – in Canada, Austria, Denmark and, to a point, Britain – would like to go home and thus force Cyprus to see collective sense. But is this wise? One keeps looking west to the Balkans. When I first arrived in the Middle East, people were talking of the Balkanisation of Lebanon; they talk now of the Lebanisation of the Balkans. The chronic nature, the circularity, of this region's dilemmas, become wearing after a time and, no, I'm not too sad to leave all this for a while.

But there is one crisis – at least one – that I leave behind with greater bewilderment than the troubles in Lebanon or Cyprus. There is an aspect of it, not much written about, which I was reminded of in Israel recently by a young Israeli, and it's reminiscent of that of Cypriots revisiting their old villages under new management. It is conceivable, though it cannot be said at this point to be likely, that under pressure from the United States and other world leaders, the Israelis and the Arabs will agree to carve out segments of the West Bank, with Gaza, which the Palestinians could call home, and which might be allowed to evolve at some stage into a mini state, tied closely to Jordan. *If* this happens, the Palestinian movement will have made some progress; calm should follow, albeit with rigorous security fixtures in place; and though the antagonists will not turn into fast friends, the region might have peace, with some justice restored to the Palestinians; perhaps by the end of the century ... *this* century I mean.

But what my Israeli friend is wondering about (and I wonder too) are the Palestinians and their descendants, maybe 3 million or more, who yearn for their homes and villages inside Israel proper – the Israel of 1948. Will West Bank statelets and a passport be enough for them?

My Israeli friend, like many others, is worried that a Palestinian state, or near-state, next door will add to growing Arab-inspired insecurity in what he sees as *his* land – where *he* was born 30 years ago. He is very aware, too, of increasing resentment, nationalism, and Islamic fervor among the 750 thousand Arab citizens of Israel, who feel more and more in touch with their disenfranchised and displaced Palestinian brethren. The fear amongst Israelis must be that the old idea of one state in all Palestine for Arabs and Jews is what many Arabs still ultimately want: and why shouldn't they?

Mr Rabin's new government may be the best the Arabs will find with which to reach a negotiated peace. I believe that is the case; but no one can imagine that what is envisaged at this tentative stage of peace negotiations is anything more than the shoving open of one door, beyond which stand many more, bigger, stronger, more fairly locked: Palestinian political rights, water, Jewish settlers, Israeli security, Jerusalem, and those exiled 3 million Palestinians who want to go *all* the way back.

For me, the people of the Levant and beyond will be hard to leave; so courteous and hospitable to foreigners, so hard on one another. The open street life, the familiarity; the Iraqi friend who's been forced to leave Baghdad with his family just to find work, but yearns to go back even under Saddam Hussein, whom he despises, as indeed do most Iraqis; the Arab expert who has served, single-handedly, as friend and *many* sources – 'Arab diplomat', 'Arab nationalist', 'oil analyst', 'exile', 'seasoned observer', and so on; the maddened expatriates who have sunk themselves so deep into the region, and often into cheap drink, that for them there is no escape; the evenings squatting on carpets in Teheran, swigging Armenian vodka and hearing the latest scandalous stories about the mullahs; the ineffable politeness of the Jordanians, the sour wit and black humour of the Syrians and the engaging charm of the Lebanese; the Palestinian exile who prowls the poker games of Nicosia, but is a hilarious source of insights, quotes and anecdotes – and racing tips. These will be missed, and perhaps, on a long grey Sunday afternoon in London, so will the noise and heat and dust of Nicosia's old town. Not for long, I imagine. Middle East hands are recidivists. They return to haunt the scenes of their youthful triumphs, disasters and excesses.

But for now, I'm relieved that someone else has to try to make sense of it all, in one and a half minutes, cuttable.

AFRICA

*In the autumn of 1991, Zaire felt the new wind of change bringing demands for
democracy to Africa. Zaire's President, Mobutu Sese Seko, was forced to appoint
a leading member of the opposition, Etienne Tshisekedi, as his new prime minister
following violence and looting on the streets of the capital, Kinshasa.*

AN OLD STORY OF
AFRICA

FERGAL KEANE   KINSHASA   3 OCTOBER 1991

The door opened and the muzzle of a rifle poked its way enquiringly
into the stuffy interior of the aircraft. Within seconds another gun followed, and after that a face hidden behind ludicrously large and menacing sunglasses. The face barked at us in French: "Who are you? What are you doing
here?" It was momentarily mollified by the offer of a cigarette but soon returned
to the interrogation. As the questions continued I noticed a long line of refugees
walking across the runway, guarded by several huge Belgian and French para-
troopers; they were clutching suitcases and plastic bags and small children, some
looking anxiously over their shoulders at the Zairean troops skulking around
our plane. It was a scene from an old newsreel circa 1960: terrified whites fleeing
the oncoming darkness and leaving behind everything that could not be carried.

After about two hours we begged our guards to let us go to the toilet. They
did so and we – all of us – regretted asking: the airport had been completely
ransacked in the mutiny and the toilets were now ankle deep in human waste;
in the stifling heat the odour was overpowering. On the way back I noticed
that all of the Zairean forces were wearing blue headsets but there were no
walkmans attached: the headsets had apparently been looted from aircraft stores
and, although useless without tape recorders, they were, apparently, a status
symbol of sorts. Eventually we were allowed out of the aircraft, largely thanks

to the resourcefulness of a Parisian colleague from Reuters who had given the Zaireans an impressive list of relatives serving with the French military. We were shown to a room where another group of surly guards took over, until a certain colonel Ndoma of the Presidential Guard arrived to say – to our great amazement – that we were welcome. An hour later we were sitting with the Information Minister, Monsieur Danza, under a huge portrait of President Mobutu. Monsieur Danza was a plump man with a clammy handshake and an oily sincerity; he held in his hand a cellular telephone, which in President Mobutu's new Zaire seemed to represent the very essence of civilisation and modern values.

There were quite a few such people in Kinshasa – men who sported expensive suits and gold chains – the inner circle that had grown prosperous under one of the most corrupt dictatorships the world had ever seen. Kinshasa was full, too, of nervous soldiers who for twenty dollars would willingly leave their posts to provide you with an escort through the dangerous night-time streets, past the skeletons of shops ravaged in the rioting, through roadblocks manned by other nervous soldiers. It was packed, as well, with hungry people, angry people who would surround you in the slums and castigate the European forces for preserving Mobutu's regime; whose children would stand on the roadside rubbing their stomachs and begging for food. "Mobutu is Lucifer!" the crowd at one crossroads shouted. Little wonder these people scavenged in the deserted shops: theirs was a looting borne of physical hunger and, in many cases, was simply following the long example of their overlords, who had plundered for years; except they had done it more often then not with pens and handshakes, dispatching vast sums into Swiss bank accounts and into foreign property holdings.

Out at the Presidential Palace – or should I say one of the presidential palaces – the dictator dined with the opposition on smoked salmon and champagne; down in the slums people struggled desperately to keep from starvation. It was an old story of Africa, but none the less sorry for that. Mobutu himself was charismatic in a deeply unsettling way, his head slowly turning to face me when I asked how he was feeling. "Obviously not a hundred percent. What did you expect?" he growled in reply. Everywhere he went in the conference centre a white aide followed, fluttering around him like a moth transfixed by light. The whole scene, the whole week, reminded me of V S Naipaul's magnificent evocation of the dictator and his cronies in his novel *A Bend in the River*:

"They didn't see, these young men, that there was anything there to build in their country. As far as they were concerned it was all there already; they only had to take; they believed that by being who they were they had earned the right to take; and the higher the officer, the greater the crooked-ness – if that word had any meaning."

As I conclude, the opposition are locked in conflict with Mobutu; the French and Belgians still patrol the streets; and the price of basic foodstuffs continues to rocket. Of the future one can only predict that, for the ordinary people of Zaire, it will be as hard and difficult as it has always been. A continuing struggle against impossible odds.

The Zimbabwean capital, Harare, was the venue for the Commonwealth Conference in October 1991. This was different from previous gatherings in that it was unmarked by the usual acrimony. The dismantling of apartheid in South Africa – for so many years the cause of such bitterness – had left the Commonwealth wondering about its sense of purpose.

WHITHER THE COMMOMWEALTH?

PAUL REYNOLDS   HARARE   24 OCTOBER 1991

I t went more or less as expected. Mrs Thatcher's absence, and the change in South Africa itself, defused the sanctions issue to everyone's satisfaction. The man who stole the show early on was Nelson Mandela: very cleverly he vetoed the presence in Harare of a South African government minister, and fellow black political leaders, so he had the floor to himself. Although he might have preferred sanctions to stay until the very end, the Commonwealth decided that they should be lifted in stages, and the ANC seemed content enough.

The British were neutralised: Mr Major himself had decided to tread softly on sanctions. So we were left with other issues, mainly that of the Commonwealth declaration about human rights and democracy. I suppose it is a start, though much of it was actually agreed in Singapore in 1971 – and that didn't have much impact. But the Commonwealth is casting around for a role, and since everyone else has gone democratic it was inevitable that the Commonwealth should do the same – or make noises in that direction. But will the declaration make much difference? It can at least do no harm and may encourage those brave people who do battle in their various countries for simple freedoms. On the other hand bad governments can simply ignore it.

Everyone is agreed, I think, that these 'CHOGMs' go on too long. Thankfully it's been agreed that it should be shorter in future, though they will keep the pleasant tradition that the delegates go off for a weekend retreat at some lush location – this time at the Victoria Falls, where else? It's called a retreat but it's a media event as well, and the leaders don't retreat from it: there were plenty of delegates looking at the falls one afternoon when the cameramen were there; there were none the next morning to see the glory of the falls by themselves.

One problem is that the meeting can lose touch with reality. A vast and boring communiqué is released touching on all kinds of world problems, over most of which the Commonwealth has no influence whatsoever. A colleague was honest enough to admit, the other day, that at the time he had written of the last CHOGM, in Malaysia, that if it would be remembered for anything, it would be remembered for the Langkawi Declaration. Quite.

But useful work is done. It saves immense amounts of time and travel for Mr Major to meet the Prime Minister of Belize, George Price, for example, to discuss the new Belize-Guatemala agreement. The Indian and Pakistani leaders also had their first meeting here. That took place, like others, in the huge Sheraton Conference Centre. This was built some years ago in the spirit of newly emergent Africa which valued large conferences of groups like the Non Aligned Movement. The most distasteful part of such meetings is that they encourage elements of 'them and us': them, the people, and us, the delegates. This is something the Commonwealth in its new spirit of democracy should tackle. There can be no citizen of Harare who, having heard them, was not fed up with the wailing Yamahas of the policemen accompanying motorcades for even the most modest Caribbean prime minister. As these cars whizzed by, the average Mr and Mrs Harare were waiting for hours at incredibly crowded bus stops, for incredibly decrepit buses, to take them back to their cramped homes on the very outskirts of the city.

One should not be unfair to Zimbabwe, it's a good symbol of how Commonwealth countries are changing. It even agreed, in the declaration, to the inclusion of formerly taboo phrases about such things as the importance of the market economy. For Robert Mugabe has abandoned his plans for a formal one-party state and has recently launched ESAP, the Economic Structural Adjustment Programme, which in real language means loosening the dead hand of the state over the economy. If Mugabe is about to move then the rest of Africa can as well. Zimbabwe certainly impresses for its lack of racial tension. Tribal feeling between Matabeleland and the Shonas is still touchy, but the whites who stayed on still enjoy life. At a charity cricket match in which various prime ministers took part briefly, a middle-aged white man said he had long ago accepted the changes. His two sons had stayed on and they had children of their own. His main problem was the ineptness of the civil service. But he was particularly pleased that the old Salisbury Sports Club, now the Harare Sports Club, would not be expropriated by the government. There had been talk of this soon after independence, but recently the government has assured members that their ground is safe. So the club remains: a fabulous piece of colonial exotica, white clubhouse with wicker chairs and elderly white ladies to sit in them, a green cricket pitch and blue marquees, a wonderful golf course nearby with jacaranda and bougainvillaea spilling out onto the fairways, and all within three kilometres of the city centre. Robert Mugabe may have dealt harshly with Matabeleland, and his economy may have been up an alley, but he has kept the place together.

I recall another unexpected moment in southern Africa on this visit. The Queen was at the Windhoek Show in Namibia, a vast country with a tiny population and independent for only eighteen months. The Windhoek Show is really for the white farmers, the blacks were there mainly to hold the cattle; but the Namibian prime minister turned up with the Queen and the white crowd dutifully applauded him. He waved back. A couple of years ago, he was at war with them; now they had accepted reality. Things do change; Africa may be changing; and maybe the Commonwealth has a role in helping that change.

Equatorial Guinea is one of the continent of Africa's smallest and most obscure countries. Andy Kershaw visited the capital, Malabo, early in 1992, where the discovery of oil was set to bring about a dramatic upturn in the country's economic fortunes.

THE BANANALESS REPUBLIC

ANDY KERSHAW   MALABO   2 JANUARY 1992

Y ou would call it a banana republic, if it still had any bananas. These days the old plantations are overgrown and the fruit is rotting on the tree. Yet before Equatorial Guinea gained independence from Spain in 1968, it was known as the Switzerland of Africa. Through its exports of coffee, timber, minerals and some of the best quality cocoa in the world, this tiny country, a speck of land between Cameroon and Gabon with its capital, Malabo, 300 kilometres away on an island in the Bight of Nigeria, was one of the richest countries on the continent. Today it ranks among the poorest and relies on foreign aid for seventy per cent of its income.

Much of the blame for Equatorial Guinea's economic decline and for its reputation as one of the most repressive and brutal regimes in Africa must rest with the previous president, Macias Nguema. Until he was overthrown and executed in a military coup in 1979, led by his nephew and current president, Obiang Nguema, Macias's savagery, paranoia and corruption rivalled that of Idi Amin of Uganda and Jean-Bedel Bokassa of the Central African Republic. "Everyone had a brother, father or cousin killed under Macias," I was told by one of the few Guineans prepared to speak of the country's horrific past. "My uncle was killed by men with hammers for criticising Macias." The legacy of the years of terror is still evident. On a recent visit to Malabo, Mrs Babangida,

183

wife of the Nigerian President, embarrassed her hosts at a luncheon when she asked: "Why does no-one in Equatorial Guinea smile?" A foreign diplomat in the capital gave me the explanation that nobody would give to Nigeria's first lady. "Everyone in this country over the age of 25 (old enough to remember the Macias years) is traumatised," he said. One third of Equatorial Guinea's population was wiped out or fled between 1968 and 1979. Killings on a large scale ended with Macias's execution. Even the army was sick of the massacres.

These days the authorities tend to be more selective and discreet as they steadily rack up what is still a notorious tally of human rights abuses. "People are being arrested for the wrong reasons," said the diplomat, "and political prisoners are kept in terrible conditions." "Does Obiang kill people?" I asked. "Think of it like this: this country has had the same government for the last 23 years. As head of the army, Obiang was Macias's main enforcer," came the reply.

One local youth who spoke to me at a pavement café, whenever the waiter wasn't hovering too near, regarded imprisonment as though it was just another routine difficulty in his day-to-day survival. He was smiling as he said to me: "Prison? It's like having a cold. We've all been to prison. Once I was arrested for a passport irregularity. Another time they wanted my brother, but he wasn't around so they got me."

On my arrival in Malabo, stepping off a coaster from Cameroon, I was treated immediately to the Equatorial Guinean authorities' enthusiasm for detention and corruption. My papers were in order, yet I was held by the police at the quayside for seven hours. The official with the proper stamp was not around, they said. And, no, none of them could say when he'd be back. Immigration procedures could have been concluded without the absent official and his stamp if I'd put my hand in my pocket, but reckoning the police would get bored with the game before I did, I waited outside their office. Still, my time at the waterfront wasn't wasted, and I was able to ponder on the possible use for a large quantity of heavy steel piping being unloaded from a Texan cargo boat. Two uniformed customs men went through my bags, supervised by a youth of ambiguous authority, dressed in denims and dark glasses. From their questions it was clear they were obsessed with my being a journalist. My camera seemed to mesmerise them. Until April of this year photography in Equatorial Guinea was banned. A marine from the navy's only gunboat sidled up and asked why I'd been there so long. I explained about the missing rubber stamp. "Scandalous!"

he said. As night fell they let me go but held onto my passport for another three days.

The capital I did eventually get to see – so small you can cover it on foot in ten minutes – was as picturesque and trim as Toytown or one of those idyllic, fictitious towns in a Spanish language textbook: (Lección Número Uno: Señor Nguema vive en la ciudad de Malabo ...) The streets are relatively empty of traffic, except for the odd taxi, ministerial Mercedes and the brand new four-wheel drive vehicles of the Spanish government agency, Co-operacion Espanol. And the colonial gingerbread buildings wouldn't look out of place in New Orleans. Malabo is the cleanest African capital I've visited, but this appearance of prosperity is deceptive: the embassy official later told me it was clean because people were too poor to throw anything away.

The only shabby building in town was my hotel. The Hotel Bahia has one of the most spectacular locations of any hotel I've seen: on a headland above the harbour, with views across the glassy bay to a chain of islets covered in thick tropical vegetation. It was on the terrace of the Bahia, in more glamorous times, that Frederick Forsyth was said to have written *The Dogs Of War*. But neither Forsyth, nor the Motoring Association of Switzerland – whose fading plaque for 'Recommended Hotels, 1957' was still attached to the entrance – would recognise the Bahia today. At some point it had been ransacked and now lies derelict and decaying, rather like its prematurely aging caretaker, Wisdom. Even the electric wiring had been ripped from the wall, leaving long gashes in the plaster. The pool was empty, the kitchens smashed and the bar was dry.

Rooms were available by the hour, according to Wisdom. It became clear what he meant when, one evening, I was unable to get into mine. It had been double-booked for an hour by the second secretary at the Nigerian embassy, who'd arrived in a new Mercedes accompanied by a European woman. Still, it was cheap and, despite the danger of discussions of a West African nature taking place on my bed as soon as I left the room, I stayed a week. "Who owns the Bahia?" I asked Wisdom one morning, wondering why its owner wasn't making more of its potential. "The owner is the President's son. He's in the United States taking flying lessons."

I ran into his father just a few minutes later. President Obiang was attending mass in the beautiful miniature cathedral. Strolling towards the square, I heard the banshee wail of sirens approaching from the palace, tearing apart the tranquillity of a Sunday morning. "What's happening?" I asked a policewoman. 'Mind your own business!" was her reply. The presidential convoy swung into the square – a black Mercedes and jeeps full of the mean-looking Moroccan presidential guard, provided by King Hassan and paid for by Spain. Obiang doesn't trust his own troops even though, like most of his ministers (including the illiterate Minister of Public Works) they're recruited from his home village. Although the Equatorial Guinean army is a constant presence on the streets, resentful soldiers strut around with unloaded AK47s. Only the Moroccans have bullets. "King Hassan has only got to make one 'phone call and Obiang is dead," said another foreign diplomat. "He's not paranoid, let's say he's justifiably worried about his own security. If there were another coup attempt he knows where it would come from."

It's unlikely to come from Equatorial Guinea's opposition in exile in Gabon and Madrid. Despite rumours of financial backing from France, the activists abroad lack credibility at home. As one dissident in Malabo put it: "They weren't here when they were killing us. We want them to come here and make a noise." Mindful, perhaps, of the opposition, the military simmering with humiliation, new democracies taking root elsewhere in Africa, and foreign aid being linked increasingly to political liberalisation, President Obiang organised a referendum last November to amend the 1982 constitution. The ballot was not secret – 98 per cent voted in favour of multi-party elections to be held some time in the future, although opposition parties are still banned for the time being. But the most significant amendment was that the President could not be prosecuted for any wrong doings 'before, during or after his term in office'.

If those sound like the words of a president preparing to stand down, a discovery several miles off the coast of Malabo last December may make him reconsider. As I walked back one night to the hotel, the sky above the north of the island blazed bright orange. A consortium of American companies has struck oil in Equatorial Guinea waters. Production of three to four thousand barrels a day is expected when the oil comes on-stream in February. It's not much by Middle East standards, but considering the country has a population of only 300,000, perhaps the official of an international finance agency didn't have his tongue too firmly in his cheek when he said the former Switzerland of Africa may be poised to be its new Kuwait.

At the end of its long, hot summer, South Africa was suffering the effects of what was described as its worst drought this century. Crops failed and thousands of cattle had to be slaughtered because there was no feed for them. And all of this coincided with a crucial by-election campaign, during which President de Klerk was hoping to convince his white Afrikaner constituency that his dismantling of apartheid was the only way forward for the country.

DRY WHITE SEASON

FERGAL KEANE   JOHANNESBURG   15 FEBRUARY 1992

It is just after sunrise here in the privileged avenues of north Johannesburg: in these impossibly dull suburbs, just about now, the water sprinklers are starting to shower the parched lawns with precious drops of moisture. It is a curiously beautiful hour of the morning: the birds are singing, the traffic has yet to rumble into action and the air is still cool. As I write, the voices of the other, real Africa are beginning to stir in houses along my road: they are the voices of maids, gardeners, security guards. It is one of the few hours of these drought days when movement is not calculated to bring the perspiration rushing to one's brow.

Not very far away, across the so-called Golden Highway that circles the city, out where the veld begins, the farmers and their labourers will be up and about, anxious to be at work on the land before the sun begins to heat the air and burn the skin: as they move through the fields of maize there will be a crunching sound underfoot; a brittle, scratching noise as the withering leaves of maize brush against the cloches of the workers; little clouds of dust rise and hang on the air and, ever more quickly, the temperature will start to rise, out of the sweet coolness and into the sticky regions of the mid morning. It has been the same every day for weeks upon end ... the dry white season evoked by the South African novelist, André Brink.

Drive in any direction from Johannesburg and you will encounter the effects of this torrid, unrelenting dryness: it has seized the land by the throat and is slowly draining its strength away, from the fields of the Orange Free State up into the ranchland of Southern Zimbabwe. In a cattle market in the Western Transvaal I saw truck after truck draw up, depositing animals that could no longer be fed; the farmers telling me it was the worst drought any of them could remember – a curse that would drive them to the unfamiliar and frightening cities, to compete for jobs with black people who had, for so long, been their servants. The manager of the hotel in Potchefstroom told me of how many farmers had given up the ghost; they sat in his bar all day, as their fields yielded to the sustained assault of the sun, and the debts piled up. "Whether they owe a hundred rand, or a hundred thousand, they don't seem to care," he told me. By the week's end there was an air of barely subdued panic.

Apart from the very real and sad human consequences, the drought has proved an important factor in the political sphere; the farmers – never the most liberal of South Africa's citizens – are blaming their woes on the government at a time when President de Klerk is fighting what is probably the most crucial by-election in South African political history. Little wonder, when he faced the voters of Potchefstroom during the week, that the President had to remind them that the government was not responsible for the drought or any other natural disaster: I am not sure they believed him; the Afrikaner *volk* have an instinctual faith in what they perceive to be warnings from the Almighty; the unholy drought falls into this category. The Conservative Party have been canvassing the farmers relentlessly in the past few weeks, offering them the promise of green pastures in a white homeland; it must be a tempting offer when you are gazing out on withering fields. The Nationalists, by contrast, have seemed almost apologetic in their campaigning, urging people to stick with them because there is simply no alternative. In terms of logic there can be little doubting the veracity of the Nationalists' argument: in no part of South Africa do whites form an absolute majority, so, any talk of a white fatherland is unrealistic in the extreme. But then these are extreme times and the CP's offer of a return to the simple certainties of apartheid finds ready acceptance in the drought stricken hinterland.

In March 1992 South Africa's white population gave an overwhelming endorsement to President de Klerk's reforms – paving the way for an end to white minority rule. The President won almost seventy per cent of the vote in the referendum, well ahead of expectations. It gave those covering the story pause for thought on a momentous day in South African history.

SOUTH AFRICA CROSSES THE RUBICON

FERGAL KEANE   CAPE TOWN   19 MARCH 1992

The day is clear and sunny and the waters of Table Bay are sparkling in the distance: from the jagged shapes of the Hottentots Holland Mountains, curving around the coast to the milky white sands of Blouberg Strand, there is an extraordinary calm. It could have been on a day such as this that Jan van Riebeeck's ships loomed on the horizon, edging in from the Atlantic, to cast their long shadow across the southern half of Africa. The poet John Masefield – writing of Columbus – called the ships of the explorers 'doom burdened caravels', recognising that what they carried with them was the beginning of a new order: the order of the white man. On the southern tip of Africa, as in the Americas, history was to roll across the plains, mountains and rivers, subjugating or annihilating anything which stood in the way. For the native peoples of South Africa it amounted to a catastrophe: as the white man drove back the horizon, the tribes of the Cape were either annihilated or forced into slavery; trekking further into the wilderness, the whites defeated black tribe after tribe. Defeat and humiliation became bywords.

For whites it was a pathway to unimagined privilege, but also to fear and

189

isolation: as the world moved forward they languished in the seventeenth century, despised and rejected; as they inflicted a code of racial supremacy on the black man, so the world inflicted its moral apartheid on them. They were of Africa yet had cut themselves off from it; they yearned for the fellowship of nations yet were shut out. That was until yesterday: in one great leap the whites came back to Africa, and to the world. It was not only FW de Klerk's triumph – it was a victory for ordinary people, because the choice to reject racism and embrace peaceful co-existence was a deeply personal one. Implicit in the 'yes' vote was a recognition of Anthony Trollope's wise dictum, that South Africa was a country of black people and always would be: no re-drawing of borders would ever change that fact. For any one of us to reject the certainties we have grown up with is difficult: it involves a measure of risk that most people would shy away from, and that is what makes yesterday's vote so remarkable. The people who voted 'yes' grew up with apartheid; leader after leader told them it was the only way in which to ensure the survival of the white race; racial separation marked every aspect of their lives – it was not something that could be taken or left.

In the light of that we should not be too surprised that just over thirty percent of whites felt unable to leave the past behind: they are not all raving racists, not all bitter enders, and certainly not all potential soldiers in Mr Terre Blanche's promised war of liberation. For the most part, I suspect, they are frightened people who have yet to begin the journey to realism. Now that the cause for which they campaigned has been well and truly lost it is difficult to believe that the right-wingers can sustain a concerted fight against the inevitable. Some will doubtless try to stain the future with blood – most though will, in some way or other, come to terms with the demands of survival, realising that a loss of political control does not necessarily mean losing a way of life. The more pragmatic in the ranks of the right will almost certainly come to the negotiating table, whatever the taunts of 'traitor' and 'sellout' that may come from the extremists.

A decade ago, when I first visited this country, there was a defensiveness and an arrogance about many whites that filled me with despair. After a while I learned to avoid arguments on the subject of apartheid – they invariably led nowhere. South Africa was a depressing place to be in: the heavy hand of the state was demolishing organised opposition, the border war was rumbling on and liberals were wringing their hands in despair. Back then, it would have been impossible to imagine a white president standing on the steps of Parliament and congratulating his people for voting an end to minority rule. And yet now that it has happened there is less a sense of surprise or amazement, than there is of relief. It is as if the South African nation breathed out a long sigh yesterday – and blew away the foul dust of history.

Dan Isaacs spent some time in Mozambique collecting material on the civil war between the FRELIMO government forces and the RENAMO rebels for the programme African Perspective. He visited a former BBC radio journalist Suleiman Cabir in the capital Maputo. Suleiman recommended that Dan should also visit his father who lives in Inhambane, 400 kilometres north of Maputo, an hour's flight up the coast.

TRUTH AND RUMOUR IN MOZAMBIQUE

DAN ISAACS   MAPUTO   28 MARCH 1992

Senhor Cabir is an old man – too old to move out of the front room of his house. By his side he has a stout stick which he bangs violently on the side of his chair to summon his house boy. I stayed in his house in the coastal town of Inhambane, as the guest of his son, Suleiman. Meals and conversations were punctuated by the sharp rat-a-tat-tat of wood on wood. Then a pause. Then a more insistent rat-a-tat-tat – followed by the slow obedient shuffle of the house boy, and a bad tempered shouted order – Senhor Cabir is extremely deaf.

Conversations with him were slow and repetitive. But little by little you become aware that Mr Cabir is choosing to hear more than he lets on. And more than that. He knows precisely what is happening throughout the town – who's going out of business, who's drinking himself to death, what the politicians are saying, and how the war is going in the district. You don't get that sort of information from the papers. And certainly not from the radio. Mr Cabir lives in the centre of town. And it's not by chance that he's chosen the front room of his house to spend his days. If you're passing his house – and it's difficult not to on a walk through the town – you drop in, pay or shout your respects and tell him the latest rumour doing the rounds. This is the news machine in full swing – rumour heard, discussed and passed on to the next pair of ears passing Senhor Cabir's front door.

I had wondered why getting to grips with Mozambican politics was like fighting your way into a devious maze. But Suleiman's father at work showed me the way in. Being the proud owner of a rumour, you don't let it go lightly. You work at it, chew it over, test it out within your circle of confidants, and draw in fresh strands of information. Mastering the goings-on in any part of the country, it's a question of becoming part of the circle – being an ear worth bending, which means having fresh strands to add to the tale.

Mr Cabir's son Suleiman is a freelance journalist. It's a strange profession in Mozambique. There's very little centralised information away from the government news agency and radio station. Very little critical discussion of major issues on the pages of the newspapers. There's a war going on, but it's extremely difficult to pin down hard, independent facts about who was killed and who did the killing. With roads and telephones links around the country destroyed and left unrepaired, communication from town to town outside the big cities such as Maputo and Beira is reduced to the traveller's tale. And you can't print travellers' tales as fact.

So what, as an independent journalist, do you do? Travel around the country yourself is an obvious answer. But count that out straight away. The only way to get around Mozambique is to fly. There are bandits, mines and blown up bridges out there. And flying is an extremely expensive luxury. It's O.K. for me, in Mozambique for a short while, expenses paid by the BBC – but count it out for a local journalist. If you want a one-dimensional picture of the country, there are always the papers, but on an average day there are at least three front page pictures of President Chissano squeezing foreign palms and smiling broadly. So that won't get you too far under the skin of Mozambican politics.

But take a lesson from Suleiman, working in the capital Maputo. Get into your car, with the vague aim of getting from A to B. Set off at a modest pace and scan passing cars and the pavement. When you spot someone you know, put your foot on the brake, and come to as theatrical a halt as possible. The more angry drivers there are behind you banging at their horns the better. This being your opening conversation of the day, it could lead you gently into some quiet old rumour that can be discussed and nurtured. Or you could strike really lucky and hit a brand new rumour right on the nose. This of course is the rarest of the two confrontations – but the one you'll be fishing for all day. So, back in the car you get – still with a vague destination in mind – drive off, eyes glued to the pavement. It's slow work being a motor-journalist in Maputo, but no slower, and not much different to sitting in your front room in Inhambane waiting for the town to come visiting.

Then, at the end of the long day, armed with rumours of coup plots, corrupt cabinet ministers and rebel skulduggery, you return home. Now, to earn your money, put pen to paper with that hot story. But remember nobody's going to believe a rumour.

Africa is often portrayed by the Western media as a problem area when it comes to poverty, food shortages and, even worse, famine. These stories are true enough of course, when it comes to disaster areas such Somalia or Mozambique, which are drastically affected by civil war and drought. But there's another side to Africa and its food.

DINING OUT IN ABIDJAN

MARK DOYLE   ABIDJAN   28 APRIL 1992

Tomatoes. The luscious taste of ripe, red, slightly soft, African tomatoes. It's a year or so since I was last in West Africa, and the part of me that is a journalist would like to report that my first impression on my return was, for example, of the spread of multi-party democracy on the continent, including, very haltingly, in this country, Ivory Coast. But I have to admit that the part of me that's an ordinary, eating human being was struck once again by the high quality of food available in West Africa to those people, and there are many of them, who live above the poverty line.

Tomatoes. The specimens I buy in London at the local supermarket are a suspiciously loud red in colour, with bullet-hard skin, and are, frankly, tasteless. In West Africa, by contrast, the food is refreshingly real. It was here that I, as a victim of the hyper-modern international food industry, learnt that oranges are not naturally orange but more yellow in colour. I also learnt that chicken bones are not supposed to melt in your mouth as in the American take-away restaurants, and that chicken flesh can indeed taste of chicken.

After about ten years of visiting West Africa I have come to the view that the average West African eats better and more healthily than the average European. There is, of course, malnutrition here among the very poor. But to make

195

a real comparison, what can you get to eat for the equivalent a dollar in London and what can you get in West Africa? In most of West Africa, a typical meal is a large helping of rice, or a local root crop, spiced up with some vegetables and a little meat or fish – the ideal nutritious mix. Give me that, any day, instead of a soggy hamburger, or a so-called cheese sandwich in bleached white bread.

For just a little more money, the average African has an embarrassment of riches – be it a bucketful of avocadoes from the market, a bowl full of fresh fish bought on the beach, or a joint of meat from the herders who roam the southern fringes of the Sahara desert. And for the African middle class, there's a rich variety of eating out establishments. In Abidjan, I was taken to a restaurant run by a Mauritanian called Babouiya. An extrovert individual, Babouiya doesn't bother with menus. He sits one down on a cushion, and proceeds to serve delicious couscous with mutton, chicken, and vegetables. In keeping with Abidjan's cosmopolitan image, the walls of Babouiya's place are plastered with posters of American pop and movie stars. One of the gay Mauritanian's favourite pictures, given pride of place next to the spluttering air conditioning unit, is of the American singing idol, Johnny Mathis.

Close to Babouiya's in Abidjan is a delightfully relaxed Ghanaian-run restaurant, where four of us ate masses of fish and chicken, cassava, potatoes and salad – all in delicious sauces – washed down with excellent local beer, for a total bill of less than fifteen dollars. Although that sum is still considerable for many Africans, the fact which might surprise some of you is that this restaurant was not full of expatriates but local people enjoying their own delicious, local cuisine.

Yes, food in West Africa, if you live just a little above the poverty line, is no problem. Here on the West African coast, much of the land is fertile, and the rain is usually abundant. For those who have not visited Africa, and who remember television pictures of starving babies, this gastronomic report may seem bizarre, even in bad taste. But the fact is that Africa has many facets, and one of them is a proud tradition of good eating that goes hand-in-hand with warm hospitality.

Before I leave here for London, I have promised myself a treat of my all-time favourite dish. It's from Senegal, and its called Chicken Yassa; that's real chicken, not the factory-farmed variety, braised and served on rice with a magical onion and lemon sauce. And when I do have to leave, I'm going to try to get a few kilos of those delicious tomatoes past the customs officers at Heathrow.

Like many countries in West Africa, Mali experienced the democratic process in 1992 when elections for a whole new administration culminated in a presidential poll at the end of April. International observers were invited by Mali to monitor the last stage of the electoral rounds.

VOTING IN TIMBUKTU

JANET ANDERSON   TIMBUKTU   13 MAY 1992

So there we were, three foreign observers in Timbuktu buying hats. We'd all realised at the same point that in the overpowering heat, if we were going to do our job properly, we would need some protection from the sun. The three of us – Jean, the former head of the Canadian Electoral Commission, Joe, who runs elections for Washington D.C. in the United States, and me – had been flown up to Timbuktu to observe Mali's multi-party presidential elections. Last year the twenty-three year-old dictatorship of Moussa Traore had been overthrown and Malians were having their first taste of democracy in a long time.

At first sight Timbuktu, the most northerly of Mali's major towns, stuck on the edge of the Sahara desert, is not prepossessing. It's hot, dry, dusty and full of mud-built buildings. There's one tarmac road to the centre of town. After that the sand takes over and you need a four-wheel drive. You can do the tourist attractions in less than an hour. But still, there's a fascination just in the name.

Nearly everybody has heard of Timbuktu – a semi-mythical place for children and adults alike, suggesting one of the most remote places on earth. Tales of caravans, of camels trekking through the desert with much-prized salt; of untold riches; of mosques; and a university more ancient than any in the Middle

East. But even in the great mosque of Djingereber the sand is piled high around the pillars, and there are more birds than people.

But we were there for the elections. And like most places in the world, the voting booths were in schools and community centres. But there were some special features in Mali: what they called itinerant voting booths on the backs of camels or in the backs of Landrovers which went from village to village to collect votes. Malians had been voting earlier in the year for a new constitution, a new parliament, new local councils, and the turnout was getting worse each time. But these itinerant voting booths were actually getting people to vote. Instead of the long, ten kilometre trek there and back, to vote for someone you'd probably never even seen, and miss a day's farming, the ballot box came to you.

So we travelled from village to village, over what seemed like non-existent tracks, monitoring the process. In one place the whole population turned out to say hello. In another we waited a full half hour just to see one voter. And there was no noticeable fraud – it was all calm and organised, we all agreed.

We ended up in a school slightly north of Timbuktu at the end of the day. Desks were brought outside for the count as the sun was beginning to set. Everybody sat on school benches in the sand. There was a break for evening prayer, and a hurricane lamp was lit. Then all the ballots were opened, counted and recounted. Each voter had to pick up nine ballots: one for each candidate, choose one and discard the rest. One joker had put nine of the same candidate inside his envelope, but of course his vote only counted once.

The result had just been confirmed when we realised that we had another appointment. A sheep had been slaughtered for us at the governor's residence and we were late for dinner. Sitting outside with the military commander of the area, we were pressed about our views on democracy. Unfortunately, a bit of cynicism must have slipped into our descriptions of vote-buying, vote-rigging, voter apathy and media manipulation in our own countries because our once-smiling host began to look quite worried.

But the 'phone didn't stop ringing all night, with results being 'phoned in to confirm what we'd already got – a sense of who would be Mali's next president. And as my colleague Joe said on the flight back, if they ran elections as well as that in the United States, he'd be a happy man.

*Cameroon played host to a gathering of the International Tropical Timber
Organisation in May 1992 – a body made up of the world's producers and consumers
of tropical hardwoods, whose depletion is the cause of so much concern among
environmentalists. Adam Raphael was in Yaoundé for the conference, but he learnt
some far more important lessons about conservation during a trip into the
rainforest.*

IN DANIEL'S DEN

ADAM RAPHAEL   YAOUNDE   23 MAY 1992

Tshere were several moments when I wanted to say, "Daniel, you go
on without me. I'll just stand here in the stream for a day or two."
The water was so cool, and the forest so hot, and my feet so sore.

I had gone to Cameroon to cover the twelfth session of the International
Tropical Timber Organisation in the capital, Yaoundé, a two-week long boring,
not to say turgid meeting at which little discernable progress was made towards
the goal of expanding the trade in timber, while conserving the world's rainfor-
ests. The 47 member countries are committed to Target 2000: that is, to allow
no tropical timber to enter international trade in the next century unless it
comes from sustainable forests. However, after nine years, neither the secretariat
nor the members have any idea of how to do it. The organisation meets twice
yearly in a kind of formalised square dance; producer nations to the left, consumers to the right – do-si-do and promenade, with the NGO's (the environmental non-governmental organisations) calling the figures. Everyone said the reason
so little was achieved was that the Earth Summit in Rio was in the offing.
The NGOs said Rio was an excuse, a smokescreen to cloak general indecision.
The producers know they can't just strip their forests, but they want the rich
consumers to pay for their restraint. The consumers want the producers to
learn from their own mistakes – even the British forests are disappearing faster

than those in Amazonia – and to show responsibility. In the end, say the NGOs, if no one acts we shall all be the losers.

At the end of the conference, a few of the delegates, and your correspondent, set off for Cameroon's own rainforest along the Nigerian border, the third wettest place in the world. We were invited to see at first hand what we had been discussing, in Korup National Park, a three-quarters of a million acre project in one of the oldest jungles in Africa; it was, perhaps, three hundred million years old, a survivor of ice ages, a refugium burgeoning with wildlife, hundreds of species of plants, butterflies, birds and other insects and animals.

There is a vine whose chemical complexity seems to control cancer cells, and a newly found liana which may defeat the Aids virus. There are elephants, colubus monkeys and baboons, drills, dyker, small antelopes and pests like the cutting grass rodents and small porcupines. There are also about a thousand people, living in six villages inside the park; thereby hangs my tale.

Man, according to Daniel, cannot live in harmony with animals. Daniel Aguns is the conservation education officer for the area. He comes from one of the villages, Erat, and he understands the villagers' need to hunt. They have killed twelve thousand animals in the past year, however, and numbers are falling. Hunting is forbidden in the park. The villagers are allowed to take game for the pot, but not for sale. They also farm but, the authorities told me, without a road to their remote villages, they can't get produce to market. What is more, the people want health centres, secondary schools, and other appurtenances of modern life. In short, they want to move out of the park. But an old newshound can smell a party line from a long way off: it was obvious who wanted the villagers to move. There was only one way to find out, and that was to go and ask the villagers.

So two days later, Daniel and I set off in a small boat, through the mangrove swamps, along tiny creeks, with the twisted mangrove roots eerily letting down into the water to make a small port; a three hour ride, followed by a three hour trek into the forest. We arrived at Akpesong, a tiny place where the river became unnavigable, where dozens of children played on a sandbar, and women washed clothes in the clear water. As we entered the village men rose silently from the shadows at every door and came to greet us, taking our hands in theirs, softly saying "welcome". We passed between the two rows of houses and by some fields with poor crops, and quickly into the forest.

Just then it began to rain; after all, it's not called rainforest for nothing. It was early afternoon and the jungle was dark with clouds above the high canopy; the path was narrow and twisting as it led through dense and verdant foliage. Through the drumming rain, birds called. In the distance I heard a monkey hoot. We walked for three hours.

As we approached Erat, we came upon a clearing, a place of utter desolation, where the villagers had felled trees over several acres, and the sun had quickly turned to the lush green leaves brown; some tree stumps had been burned. It was a scene that said more about conservation than all the posturing at the conference. Its bleakness was a rebuke to those who had done it. "But they need to grow crops if they cannot hunt," said Daniel. In the village, we were again gently welcomed, and then fed; curious children crowded the doorway to watch us eat tough, old chicken, rice and *garri*, the tapioca mush which people knead between their fingers into a ball, and then pop into their mouths. Then men came to talk, to confirm the need to move.

The economics of it are elementary. The only way to get produce to market is to 'head-load it', as they say. 20 kilos of game is worth much more than 20 kilos of cassava root, but it can't be legally sold. They used to smuggle it to Nigeria, but the Nigerian currency has crashed. If there were a road, they could farm for profit. They would leave for a new settlement with a road but the government, facing economic crisis, has not been able to build a road. Catch 22.

On the Equator, night falls in a few minutes. We drank fiery palm wine gin and went to bed. Next morning, we left the village at 6 am in a fine rain which turned quickly to downpour. My clothes, damp from the day before, were quickly soaked through, and began to chafe. We walked well for two hours until I noticed a blister and began to limp. The walk back – no boat this time – should have lasted five hours. We took seven, with me lingering in every stream. Had I known I should have worn other shoes; but had I known, said Daniel, was always Mr Late.

Nobody knows how much rainforest remains in Cameroon. Nigeria has almost none left. Cameroon now has a hundred logging firms, stripping its eastern hills. Korup must remain untouched. I very much hope the villagers get their road.

The Boipatong massacre, on June 17th 1992, broke any remaining threads of trust between the African National Congress and the South African government. The two sides then appeared to be locked in confrontation, as the ANC sponsored a campaign of mass action against the government. But there were those, more radical than the ANC, who believed any sort of compromise with South Africa's whites amounted to a betrayal. Tom Carver came face to face with supporters of the Pan Africanist Congress when he attended the burials of those killed in Boipatong.

IMAGES THAT NEVER FADE

TOM CARVER   BOIPATONG   2 JULY 1992

I have a notion, curious though it may seem, that memory is only truly created when the experience penetrates through the outer layers of our normal existence and becomes embedded, like a shard of glass, in the softer flesh of our feelings. On such occasions the visual images are liable to remain as sharp as the day they were recorded, unclouded by the passing of time. One of these images, for me, will be from Monday June 29th. It is of a boy, no more than sixteen, slight in build, wearing a blue baseball cap – on any other occasion a typical face from the townships. He is turning away having already hit me twice with a thick wooden club. In that moment, as he jumps over my body sprawled in the dust, I glimpse his face. He wears no expression, just a blank mirror of the violence that engulfs us.

The day they buried the dead of the Boipatong massacre was always going to be an emotional occasion. By 8.30 am the crowds were streaming into the township's dilapidated stadium. Many of the coffins were already there, propped up on plastic chairs, each one surrounded by the women of the family – grim figures wrapped in blankets, their eyes glazed with grief and the exhaustion of an all night vigil. A young priest walks slowly down the dreary line, trying to check the bodies. As he lifts the lids of each coffin, the sight of their teenage daughters, husbands and brothers causes many of the women to faint, crashing to the ground unconscious. The service lasted five hours – an intoxicating mix of the religion of forgiveness and the politics of revenge. By the time the cortège finally left the stadium for the short drive to the cemetery in Sharpeville, the warmth was already flowing out of the brief winter's day. Sharpeville cemetery is a bleak expanse of litter-strewn veld under a row of electric pylons. Many of the graves are marked only by a number plate and a bunch of plastic flowers. But in a country where there is so little respect for life, such a public wasteland hardly seems an inappropriate final resting place. As it awaited the arrival of the coffins, the huge crowd trampling the graves underfoot became increasingly restless.

Surrounded by their compatriots, youths started to show off their weapons. I saw several AK47s, a huge double-barrelled shotgun (no doubt stolen from a Free State farmer), and a frightening array of home made pistols. Several of the white journalists reported that threats were being whispered at them as they moved through the crowd; the most common was the slogan of the Pan Africanist Congress, 'one settler, one bullet'. Well aware that the mere sight of authority was liable to create an explosion in such a menacing atmosphere, the police limited themselves to monitoring the scene from the air by helicopter.

In their absence, the groups of youths, now running from one end of the graveyard to the other, started to look for alternative targets on which to vent their fury at the system. I was standing beside the empty graves when one of these mobs charged through. Though I was just ten feet away from other foreign correspondents, they were hidden by the mounds of earth that had been thrown up by the gravediggers. At that instant I was the only white face in the youths' path. They had no idea whether I was a journalist, a paid-up member of the ANC or a secret policeman. The only thing that mattered was that I was white. Out of the corner of my eye I saw the youth raise his club high above his head. For an instant I thought he was going to attack someone else, then I felt a crack as the club caught me squarely on the left temple. I went down sprawling against the mounds of earth. I could hear a women beside me screaming.

The youth raised his weapon again. This time I put up my left arm to protect myself and the blow caught me on the edge of my hand. I discovered later that it had been fractured, but at least it had saved my face. Then he was gone, unwilling to lose contact with the rest of his group which, thankfully, had kept on running. It was over so quickly it almost immediately assumed the proportions of a dream, only the pain in my hand and head told me it was real.

Though I know that it could have happened to any white, it was no coincidence that it happened in Sharpeville. The Vaal Triangle in which Sharpeville is situated, has always been one of the most brutal corners in this very brutal land. The character of the people here, both black and white – like the Gorbals in Glasgow or the Bronx in New York – has been moulded by the grim industrial landscape. The whites are among the poorest and most right-wing. The blacks have long supported the hardline Black Africa policies of the Pan Africanist Congress. It's often forgotten that the fatal Sharpeville massacre of 1960 was actually triggered by a PAC protest.

Though I sit here slowly and painfully typing with one hand – the fingers of my other hand swollen and discoloured like rancid sausages – and with a constant dull ache in my head, I do not feel bitterness for what has happened. How can I when, every day, blacks are enduring far worse miseries? At almost the same time as I was attacked, a man was being dragged out of his home in Boipatong by the same angry crowd and accused of being an Inkatha member. The people did not wait to hear his reply: first they shot him repeatedly then they necklaced him and then, in full view of his terrified family and news photographers, they axed and mutilated his body.

Those not living in this country often find it hard to comprehend how the ANC and the PAC can blame this sort of barbarism on the government. It's all too easy to see it as the savagery of blacks, the dark heart of Africa; but the conditions which have bred this have been created by the last forty years of white rule. It was the government which built the hostels in the middle of the townships, which filled then with Zulus, forcing them to live without their families; and it was the government which failed to dismantle this system despite agreeing to do so last year. Whilst it might not be possible to prove that the police are directly involved in the massacres, no one can doubt that up to now this fighting between blacks has benefitted the government. Divide and rule is the oldest and truest strategy of all.

I have been in violent situations before but never have I felt what it was like to be singled out for my race. The violence takes on a very different quality for it becomes loaded with a frightening hatred. Whatever I do, I cannot change the colour of my skin; but then, after all, that is what the black South Africans have suffered for forty years. In my darker moments I wonder, as we all do, whether it will ever be possible to unravel this mess by peaceful means.

ASIA AND THE PACIFIC

Friday 27th September is the anniversary of the day, in 1987, when the Tibetan capital, Lhasa, erupted in protest against Chinese rule in the region. Four days later, a protest demonstration turned into a bloody riot in which a number of people were killed. Since then there have been frequent outbursts of anti-Chinese unrest among the Tibetan population and for more than a year, from March 1989, Lhasa was under martial law and largely closed to foreign journalists.

SIMMERING DISCONTENT

SIMON LONG   LHASA   26 SEPTEMBER 1991

The holiest shrine of Tibetan Buddhism is the Jokhang temple in the centre of Lhasa. Around it runs the Barkhor, a lively circular route, lined with stalls selling clothes, trinkets, carpets, food, and religious paraphernalia, like incense, prayer beads and pictures of the Dalai Lama.

For most of the day the Barkhor is thronged with people walking, always as religion dictates in a clockwise direction. Some are pilgrims from more than a thousand miles away – wild-looking nomads, with long plaited hair, and shaggy sheepskin coats that flap against their ankles, while one arm is carried bare of the massive sleeves for coolness in the autumnal sunshine. This is a trip they make once a year, or more rarely. But there are regulars in the Barkhor too: there is the tall young man who seems to spend each and every day striding round; one, two, three big steps, then his hands raised briefly in prayer above his head, and a full length dive onto the dusty paving stones as he prostrates himself again and again. There are the two teenage nuns with cropped hair and long maroon robes, sitting every day in the same spot, softly chanting the scriptures as their begging bowls fill up. Some beggars are more aggressive, tiny, muddy-faced urchins who cling tenaciously onto your coat-tails until you have bought them off.

Then, in the Barkhor Square in front of the Jokhang, is the dog-lady. Her back against a flagpole, draped with scraps of cloth inscribed with prayers and scriptures, she sits cross-legged, quietly spinning a prayer wheel, a stick on top of which swivels a small cylinder containing a roll of scriptures: piety made easy for the illiterate. Something about her intent tranquillity attracts the dogs, hundreds of which roam Lhasa. Nocturnal beasts, to judge at least from the barking and baying that give the city an eerie air at night, they like to sleep in the day, and for a dozen or more, their favourite spot is at the dog lady's feet. But one day last week the dog lady was transformed: she was talking animatedly to a small crowd that had gathered around her; out of the stream of Tibetan, I kept hearing the Chinese word, *gongan* – police. Nobody would tell me what she was saying for fear of the plain-clothes police who are also among the Barkhor's regular loiterers.

The Square has seen the biggest and bloodiest of the confrontations in Lhasa in recent years between the security forces and Tibetan protestors, a number of whom lost their lives. Many more are now in prisons or labour camps for demanding independence. But China shows no sign of yielding an inch on its oft-repeated claim that Tibet is an inalienable part of China's sovereign territory, and will always remain so. Yet, remarkably, protests continue. Since May, when China organised a big propaganda effort to celebrate forty years of communist rule in Tibet, there have been at least twenty of them. Tiny affairs mostly, almost always staged by a handful of monks or nuns. They shout pro-independence slogans, or unfurl the banned Snow-Lion flag of an independent Tibet, or scatter leaflets and try to flee; usually, it appears, unsuccessfully.

The monks and nuns represent a religion that is the embodiment of Tibetan national identity. And after the incalculable damage wrought on Buddhism in Tibet by fanatical Maoist red guards in the sixties, it has also become the strongest symbol of what is seen as Chinese tyranny. Some of the monasteries have been rebuilt. They've become Tibet's main tourist attraction. But as one monk put it: "The monasteries used to be thought of as the best of schools. They were the treasure houses of a long, unique and complex cultural tradition. But now, the Chinese want to turn them into museums." If that is true, they haven't succeeded. Everywhere you go there's evidence of the power of the religion, from the constant requests for photographs of the Dalai Lama, to the prayer flags fluttering in the wind on the house tops and inaccessible mountain peaks.

Anniversaries these days are always tense times in Tibet, and security has been tightened in Lhasa in the last fortnight to forestall any attempt to commemorate the anti-Chinese protests four years ago. The likelihood must be that any demonstration would be short-lived, like its predecessors, and would bring harsh reprisals. But, somehow, the Tibetans will not give up. The Dalai Lama, reviled by China as a separatist, is still deeply revered and many Tibetans were aware of his recent more optimistic statements following the changes in the Soviet Union, and in particular the independence of the three Baltic States. Woken up each day in a Lhasa hotel by the shouts of Chinese soldiers drilling and practising martial arts, independence for the region seemed a dangerous illusion. But then, a few years or even weeks ago, many probably felt that way in Vilnius, Tallinn and Riga.

While the Communist Party had already lost power in western parts of the old Soviet Union, it remained in charge in most of the Muslim republics of central Asia. Opposition movements there had been comparatively weak, but in the mood was changing in the Tajik region.

TAJIKISTAN – THROWING OFF THE YOKE

TIM WHEWELL   DUSHANBE   3 OCTOBER 1991

The first time you see a cotton plant it's hard to believe that it is real. My neighbour's granddaughter took one look at the fluffy white balls on the stick I'd brought back to Moscow, and said contemptuously: "You've stuck them on!" I'd reacted almost the same way the day before as we tramped through a collective farm near the Afghan border.

But I suppose my disbelief was nothing compared with that of the other people in the field. The Tajik women, who'd picked cotton all their lives, but had never seen a man in a grey double-breasted suit, wading ankle deep through the mud with a large microphone held out before him. As I approached they started tittering and pointing, and they were reluctant to answer any questions – even after they'd covered most of their faces with their long red headscarves.

In retrospect though, I was perhaps lucky to talk to them at all: Khojikurbon Jomakhmadov, a forty-year-old welder who took me to the farm, never suggested I should meet his own wife, while the boiled mutton which we ate later in his courtyard was brought out by his male relatives who had plainly had not prepared it.

I met Khojikurbon the night before, when I took refuge from torrential rain

210

in a makeshift tent on the main square of Dushanbe. Under the plastic sheeting dozens of men in skull-caps and quilted kaftans were pressed tightly together. When I shoved my way in they broke off listening to the speeches, which continued despite the weather on the podium, and demanded to know where I was from. In reply to my question about how long they could afford to keep up the protest, Khojikurbon replied that they might not be earning wages, but they were earning freedom. In any case, on his collective farm workers sometimes earned as little as fifty roubles a month – about a fifth of the average Soviet wage – the equivalent of less than two American dollars. "We're slaves," Khojikurbon said. "We grow everything here, but the communists decide how much we can eat."

Tajikistan has the lowest standard of living of any Soviet republic, and it's also the place where I found the most violently expressed hatred of the ruling class. The protestors on the square weren't engaged in a national struggle like the Lithuanians or Armenians, but a social one. And that in a republic which, until recently, was so obedient that 95% of parliamentary deputies elected last year were communist bosses, collective farm chairmen, factory managers and institute directors. They won partly because of the eastern tradition of respect for those in authority but partly, I suspect, because of the unparalleled terror that Soviet power has inspired in central Asia. All over the country people say they've been freed from fear over the last few years, but in most republics they talk as though freedom was a natural state they've regained. The way Khojikurbon told me he prayed for Gorbachev – a gratitude I've rarely encountered before – made me realise he saw freedom as a precious gift he'd never even dreamed of.

Many of his father's family fled into Afghanistan at the end of the 1920s after nine years of guerrilla war against the communists. One uncle, who he said was captured, had a string tied round his neck with the other end attached to a galloping horse. Later, because they'd sheltered the guerrillas, all the inhabitants of his family's native village were expelled from their fertile valley and forced to build new homes in mosquito-infested marshland several miles away. Even in the more lenient seventies and eighties, unofficial mullahs, who came in the middle of the night to teach children the Koran, were often killed in unexplained road accidents.

Over the past year, however, the number of mosques in Tajikistan has risen from seventeen to a hundred and twenty-eight, with a further two thousand prayer houses. Khojikurbon believes that in ten or twenty years time, when people have, again, come to understand the principles of Islam, there should be new laws to cut off thieves' right hands, and to stone adulterers to death. That, he says, will be much purer – everyone would be equal and know where they stood, not like now when punishment depends on the criminal's connections and his ability to bribe.

Out in the cotton field, the women pickers also said they wanted an Islamic system, so they could stay at home and not do so much hard work. Was Khojikurbon prompting them? My Tajik's not good enough to say; but their eyes, the only bit of their face I could see, certainly looked sincere enough.

By awarding the Nobel Peace Prize to the Burmese Opposition leader, Aung San Suu Kyi, the committee focused international attention on a country renowned for its isolation and secrecy. Foreign journalists wishing to visit Burma are almost always refused visas, so many – including Humphrey Hawksley – have to resort to subterfuge.

BURMA'S LADY IN WAITING

HUMPHREY HAWKSLEY   RANGOON   24 OCTOBER 1991

A fter dinner in a Rangoon suburb (I can't say where it was, or with whom) my host asked: "Where do you want to be dropped?" I was staying at the Strand, the crumbling colonial hotel in the heart of the city. But I said: "Where do you suggest?" He spoke to his driver in Burmese. There was some discussion. "I've told him to let you out near the American Embassy," he said. It was 10.30 pm, half an hour before curfew. After a few days in Burma, the subterfuge comes naturally. Everyone does it. A John Le Carré spy novel becomes a text book – not so much to protect ourselves but anyone we might come into contact with.

In this case the Strand was crawling with military intelligence agents. If the driver had taken me there he might well have been arrested and interrogated about why he was playing chauffeur to a foreigner. We drove quickly through the broken down streets. Everyone was hurrying home. Figures moved here and there in the darkness. A woman and two children crouched over a stove in a road-side hut. Outside Aung San Suu Kyi's house two helmets bobbed up over the wall of the guard post as we passed. A dog ran across the empty road. A soldier searched a car at the petrol station next door.

The border between Thailand and Burma marks a line between the subcontinent and the Far East: not just because of colonial history, or the smells, the crowds, the clothes and the food; it is a boundary between a region which looks to the future, and one which is trapped in its past. Burma is controlled by an old man, General Ne Win, who rarely ventures out of his luxurious compound on the side of the Inya Lake. No-one knows the extent of his senility or paranoia, but his medieval whims have left their mark all over the country. It's a mess. The hospitals and schools are drained of talent. Their facilities are obsolete.

The people are told to be xenophobic; but really they're not, they're friendly. The currency notes include denominations of 45 and 90 – numbers suggested by Ne Win's astrologer to bring him luck. The only activities which are encouraged seem to be within the military and the building of pagodas. A missionary from the north spoke about people dying like fallen leaves from a tree because they couldn't get basic medicines. Yet the government is spending more than a billion US dollars on fighter aircraft, tanks, helicopters, mortars. In villages of shacks, malaria, diseased gutters and child malnutrition, the only construction will be a pagoda. There is a belief by the selfish and corrupt patriarchs that it will win them a fast track to Buddhist Nirvana. George Orwell, who served as a policeman in Burma, wrote of one of his Burmese characters: "He would devote his closing years to good works, which would pile up enough merit to outweigh the rest of his life. Probably his good works would take the form of building pagodas. Four pagodas, five, six, seven – the priests would tell him how many – with carved stonework, gilt umbrellas and little bells that tinkled in the wind." One of the newest pagodas in Rangoon is being built by Ne Win.

There are remnants of the vision, nurtured by many in Burma over the past few years, of creating a modern political society, fuelled by elections and international aid. The National League for Democracy still has offices open, a veneer set up by the government, given that some eighty of its MPs have been arrested. Others are in hiding or exile. Some Buddhist monks who rebelled in Mandalay can be found at sunset on the Mandalay Hills complaining about the abbots who have struck a deal with the dictatorship. But their fire has gone. Last year, they tied the inner tubes of their bicycles to tree trunks and used them as giant catapults to hurl rocks at soldiers. "Now," said one, "We're divided. We don't even know what we want."

In the country's post-war history, there have only been two people to have commanded the mass support of the Burmese. One is General Aung San, the leader of the independence movement; he was assassinated when he was thirty-two. The other is his daughter, Suu Kyi. She is under house arrest, with her maids, military intelligence agents and a piano for company. She hasn't been seen in public for more than two years. But intelligent, intellectual, forthright, she is the one person of whom the uneducated dictatorship is afraid. She knew from childhood where her destiny lay, and as much as one ever makes predictions in this job, I expect that one day – one, five, ten years hence, who knows – she will lead a democratic government in Burma.

After nearly thirteen years in exile, Cambodia's ruler, Prince Norodom Sihanouk, returned to his palace in the capital, Phnom Penh. During the 1970s he was held there as a virtual prisoner by the Khmer Rouge leader, Pol Pot. Hopes of bringing lasting peace to Cambodia rested on a peace accord signed in Paris in October 1991, but was it a little early to be optimistic?

THE RETURN OF THE PRINCE

PHILIP SHORT   PHNOM PENH   21 NOVEMBER 1991

Symbols count for more in the oriental scheme of things than in Western cultures. So when Prince Sihanouk returned here last week, he came aboard the same Chinese airliner that had been sent to fly him out in 1979, two days before Vietnamese troops occupied Phnom Penh. And his first official act was to hold a Buddhist prayer-ceremony before the silver pagoda of his ancestors, in a courtyard of the royal palace, beneath coconut palms and white frangipani blossom, thereby publicly reuniting the two great supports that buttress the Khmer identity – the monarchy and the Buddhist faith.

Dancers in sumptuous costumes of blue and gold, orange and purple, with heavy silver ankle rings, monkey masks, and gilded pagoda head-dresses, performed the sinuous, stately movements of the Ramayana. The Prince reclined – half kneeling, half lying, on a golden cushion – while Prime Minister Hun Sen and other leaders of the Vietnamese-backed government, together with their wives and children, officials and retainers, knelt a few yards behind. Incense was lit; offerings were made of rice and fruit and roasted boars' heads; and monks in orange robes chanted the sutras. The atmosphere was a mixture of religious devotion and a family picnic; yet even here, in this Ruritanian setting, the memory of the 'dark years', as Cambodians call the period of Khmer Rouge rule, was not entirely absent: the opening prayer was intoned by a dignified old man, wearing a white tunic and maroon sarong, who is a distant relation of Prince Sihanouk – and also happens to be the elder brother of Pol Pot.

Some people say you can read all the gruesome statistics about Cambodia – one in eight of the population killed, or even one in three, the doctors, the architects, the teachers who were exterminated – but it only really sinks in when, day after day, everyone you meet here talks about their father, their husband, their wife or child who died. I met one young woman who described how, as a girl of six, when Phnom Penh was evacuated by Khmer Rouge troops and its people made to walk to the provinces, her uncle, her aunt and their ten children were all executed. Later her sister died of hunger, and when Pol Pot fell she returned to Phnom Penh to learn that her father had also died. The young man who looks after the telephone at my hotel here – a complex of dilapidated cottages beside the Mekong river – lost everyone he had, and from the age of twelve was brought up in an orphanage.

And to the psychological trauma of those years of madness must be added the physical ruin of the country. Phnom Penh is still a city of great charm and faded colonial grandeur – but decay and neglect have so deteriorated its fabric that almost every building needs to be gutted and rebuilt. Pigs and chickens grub and scratch for food on the pavements, and small naked children play on the streets. And what's true of the capital is far more so in the provinces. Drive down to Kep on the southern coast – (if you have the time that is, the roads are so bad a local official asked in amazement why I hadn't come by helicopter) and you find a riviera resort peopled only by ghosts. For about three miles, along a winding corniche, luxurious villas look out over the sea; but they have no windows, the doors hang off their hinges; here a roof has fallen, there a wall; the jungle is reclaiming them. In what must once have been a garden, I suddenly came across an elephant munching leaves.

It's because virtually everything else in Cambodia is in ruins that the monarchy – for to his people Prince Sihanouk is still the king he once was – is the only institution on which to build. The immense practical problems – moving half a million refugees, clearing mines, demobilising rival armies, organising a government and preparing elections will be hard enough – but with a minimum of goodwill it should be possible, provided the rest of the world doesn't lose interest, which is a real danger. But future stability depends less on that than on reconciling the Khmer people with themselves; and regardless of Khmer Rouge intentions, which no one at this stage knows with any certainty, that is a problem of an altogether different scale and intensity.

What's needed is an alchemist, a man to juggle with symbols and refashion fate, rather than a leader in the Western sense. It may be that the task is beyond human hands. But Prince Sihanouk is certainly the best hope Cambodia has.

When they came to power, the Chinese Communists attempted to stamp out traditional folklore and replace it with what they called 'scientific socialist values'. In doing this they failed to reckon with the enduring pull of qigong – or the art of breathing. As unemployment climbs in China, many people are turning to qigong as a form of consolation and self-help.

QIGONG – THE ART OF BREATHING

CARRIE GRACIE   PEKING   3 JANUARY 1992

"Stand on your tiptoes and sway – that way you protect yourself from heart disease."

The speaker was Li Fengchun, a white-haired pensioner in a blue cotton jacket, cap and slippers. The scene was Tiantan Park in south Peking on a wintry morning, the ground hard with frost and a weak sun struggling through the mist. Ghostly shapes circled, some jerking and convulsing, some waltzing languidly with imaginary partners, and others simply falling prostrate on the yellowed grass. These are China's *qigong* faithful. They now number about seventy million and in cities like Peking, inhabit almost every park and patch of open ground. The basic belief is that by disciplining the flow of air through the body, it is possible to cure and fend off disease. But *qigong*, like every other faith, has spawned a host of exotic forms.

Some were on display in Tiantan. A tiny old lady in her seventies was lying motionless on her back on a pile of leaves. And a large man with a slack stare slumped listlessly against a tree. "He's retarded," said a middle-aged woman, as she pirouetted over to stop me breaking his trance. "That tree is helping to cure him," she explained. "We push him down here in his wheelchair every day and 'the power' flows into him from that tree." The old lady on the pile of leaves looked up. "This is really very cosy and comfortable," she confided. "People who don't understand think it's cold to lie on the ground, but if you understand it's not cold at all because you get the power."

Meanwhile, Li Fengchun was still dancing on his tiptoes, flailing his arms, and lolling his head from side to side. "You simply can't do too much of this," he advised. "Just rub your face like this, and your temples, and your chest. It's really very good for your circulation," and he began wrenching his stomach in circular motions. "Of course you can't really teach people how to do it," he said when I asked for further instruction. "You must just obey your nature. It must be spontaneous," he went on, performing a particularly flamboyant spin.

It's this spontaneity which worries the Chinese government. In the past it was suspicious of all kinds of *qigong*, but now it approves in principle – after all, *qigong* is a particularly Chinese form of medicine, and some of China's octogenarian leaders are themselves thought to have regular *qigong* therapy. But what the government objects to is *qigong* as a form of religious faith, especially when it's accompanied by mass participation. So it has clamped down on mass *qigong* rallies in sports stadiums and opened clinics for those whose *qigong* obsession has resulted in psychiatric problems. But it's hard to control a national passion, and Qing Youbang, the director of the state administration of traditional medicine, has the defensive air of a man struggling to uphold his authority.

"All clinics which offer *qigong* therapy must be approved by inspectors from my office," he insists. But he couldn't deny that his approved *qigong* masters are far outnumbered by the unofficial kind, many of them claiming miraculous talents to see through people, light up electric bulbs with their *qi*, smash bricks off balance on sharpened spikes. "These people have destroyed the image of *qigong* masters because they only cheat people," said Mr Qing. "*Qigong* must be scientific, and we must ensure that practitioners maintain professional standards." He admits that this is hard to achieve in the Chinese countryside where education is limited, health care primitive and the pull of miracle-workers correspondingly great. "We are issuing pamphlets," he says rather helplessly. "If we rectify these people, there will be no problem. *Qigong* must not be treated as a mystical art."

But whatever the edicts of the state, the faith, in all its forms, goes on spreading. And watching the devotees embracing their trees and clutching the cold earth in Tiantan Park, I have to admit that they all look rather well on it.

On St Valentine's Day in Britain, Cupid gets a little extra help from the card manufacturers. But the Japanese have a more unusual way of declaring their undying love.

SAY IT WITH CHOCOLATES

DAVID POWERS   TOKYO   15 FEBRUARY 1992

I've always found that cultural differences make advertising hoardings a fascinating, although sometimes confusing study of a nation's character. A particular case in point is a pair of posters that have hit me in the eye every morning over the past couple of weeks, as I spill out onto the platform of Shibuya station with thousands of other commuters. The one on the left is a huge close-up of a young man, who appears to be in considerable agony as he gnaws at his wrist. On the right is an equally large close up of a young woman, her face buried in her hands, and also apparently in a state of anguish. In the corner of each poster is the single word 'Godiva' and a tiny chocolate.

Newcomers to Japan might be forgiven for puzzling at what all this means. Surely the advertiser can't be suggesting – eat one of our chocolates and you'll end up as wretched as these two. No, it's simply that years of clever marketing have taught the Japanese to react with an automatic Pavlovian response to February 14th, Saint Valentine's Day. Just say Valentine to any Japanese and the first thing that will come into their head is chocolates – and lots of them. The young couple on the posters are meant to be saying, I'm so much in love with him or her that nothing but these chocolates will do. If only it were true.

Admittedly, Japan's younger generation have become less reticent than their parents about displaying their emotions in public, but kissing on the street is still virtually unheard of, and many young people still prefer to leave the choice of a marriage partner to their parents or family. So when a young woman goes out to buy her Valentine's Day chocolates – and it's only the women who do so – she doesn't buy for the man in her life, but for the *men* in her life. Although boyfriends do normally get a special box of chocolates, the average Japanese woman buys no fewer than ten boxes; one each for all the men in her office or workplace.

This practice, known as *giri-choko* or duty chocolates, is unashamedly exploited by the chocolate manufacturers, who sell some forty per cent of their annual output in the first two months of the year. The Japanese may not shop early for Christmas – they don't have to anyway with all the department stores open on Christmas Day – but they're certainly urged to shop early for Valentine's Day. One big department store began its sales campaign a whole month ago, and for the past two weeks stalls have sprouted up everywhere selling nothing but Valentine's chocolates. But trust the Japanese, once they've latched onto one good marketing wheeze, to dream up another.

Japanese etiquette demands that when you receive a present, you have to give one back in return, after a suitable period. So what better way to say thank you for your Valentine's Day chocolates, even if they were given only out of a sense of duty, than by giving chocolates in return? Now, in a country where most people don't really have a sweet tooth, this could have turned into a marketing disaster, with a lot of men simply recycling the chocolates they received, and just making sure they didn't give the same box back to the person they got them from. So the Japanese chocolate manufacturers invented White Day. This falls on March 14th, when all the men are expected to go out and buy not just any chocolates, but white chocolates. And Japanese men have all fallen for it, which of course has set other enterprising manufacturers wondering how they can get in on the act. One idea that caused quite a stir last year was a gift that looked like a single white rose, but when it was unpacked it turned out to be a rather skimpy pair of briefs.

Now, as I've already said, most Japanese people prefer not to show their emotions in public, but that doesn't mean they don't show them in private. And the implication behind giving a fake rose is a none-too-subtle invitation to one of the thousands of love hotels that can be found in every corner of the country. Given the matter of fact attitude that most Japanese have towards sex, such establishments don't have the grubby image they do in other parts of the world. But then, that's a different story.

After the former Soviet Central Asian republics became independent states, they
received a visit in February from the U.S. Secretary of State, James Baker, who
made a whirlwind tour of the new states. Hugh Prysor-Jones also visited Uzbekistan's
capital, Tashkent, for BBC Television, and found it strangely unaffected by
independence.

UZBEKISTAN'S MAFIA MENTALITY

HUGH PRYSOR-JONES   TASHKENT   26 FEBRUARY 1992

I t was raining hard, cold rain in Tashkent that afternoon so the blood on
the steps of the Writers' Union Building looked oddly pink. Great pools
of it, slopped over a comb, a handkerchief and dozens of shiny 15 kopeck coins
– the metro fare in this sprawling city.

Uzbekistan has been technically independent since January but the rouble
is still the currency and Tashkent, still dominated by the biggest statue of Lenin
in the world, looks like any grim Russian town two days train journey to
the north. Independence has brought a little more colour to Uzbekistan. The
red flag on what they still call the 'Presidential apparat' has been replaced with
the new national emblem of blue, white and green, with stars and an Islamic
crescent. But it has also brought political uncertainty and violence.

A few days before I'd arrived in the Uzbek capital, there'd been a lot of
blood spilt. Student protests against price rises had been followed by an attack
on the student hostels by the militia. At least half a dozen people had been
killed, some by gunfire, others by being thrown out of windows. The blood
I saw that Wednesday afternoon didn't belong to a student, it belonged to a
journalist, Abdurashid Sharif. He worked for the Moscow-based Interfax agency.
He'd reported the riots and their violent aftermath, despite anonymous warnings

223

to stop. Five minutes before I got to the Writers' Union, three men with short haircuts and lengths of steel pipe caught up with Mr Sharif and put him into the reanimation unit of Tashkent's Hospital Number 15. When I rang the next day, he was not expected to live.

Violence bubbles just beneath the surface of Uzbekistan. In the old days, when the republic grew cotton at the expense of everything else, a sophisticated system of official corruption bled off billions of roubles to pay off politicians in Moscow. And the freelance gangsters took their share, too. Central Asia is the mafia's home base. The mafia run the place. After a while you begin to notice what this means. In the lobby of a restaurant in the city, the attendant paused from cleaning his revolver to take my coat. Expensive cars sit parked outside shabby apartment blocks. Every important man you meet has his security chief on hand. And everyone accuses everyone else of being run by the godfathers. Loyal communists use the shadow of organised crime to denounce the submerged private business sector, of which they disapprove.

The political opposition turns the accusations round. According to them, crime syndicates control the sale of Uzbek cotton and run many state industrial and distribution networks. Whatever the truth, there's no mistaking the fear. One young businessman I spoke to wouldn't discuss the mafia, making signs to indicate he thought my hotel room was bugged. I asked him in writing to spell out for me the names of the two leading godfathers and he started to write a name – but then hastily scratched it out and, visibly frightened, refused to do anything more. Students are braver. They named the godfathers as Salim and Garfur, hand in glove with the leading lights in the party and no longer afraid of the KGB. The students have now been banished from the capital, their colleges closed indefinitely. They laughed when I asked what difference independence had made. Economic reforms were making life impossible for the poor while the old habits of repression and corruption continued.

But times are about to get harder for the politicians, too. Uzbekistan's ruler, Dr Islam Karimov, has just performed the delicate political feat of transforming himself from First Secretary of the Communist Party of the Uzbek Soviet Socialist Republic into the first elected president of the brand new state of Uzbekistan. That was the easy bit. Now he has to transform the staggering economy and bring in multi-party politics. So far, he's done quite well in keeping change at bay. Only one opposition group has managed to get itself registered as a political party. It has nine seats in a 500 seat parliament dominated by the People's

Democratic Party – which is, as you've guessed, the Communists under new management. Businessmen are in despair. The state still levies punitive taxes and onerous licensing procedures make legal enterprise hazardous. And journalists are having difficulty too. But then Uzbek people are tough – descended from the Mongols and the Turks.

I finally met Abdurashid Sharif three weeks after I'd first seen his blood all over the pavement. He said no to lunch, he'd lost most of his teeth and couldn't eat. He had a bandage round his head like the victim of some demented dentist and great scars and depressions in his head where the men with the steel pipes had done their work. He blamed the rapidly expanding Tashkent KGB. When I asked him what was the difference between the old Soviet KGB and the new independent Uzbek one, he looked at me as though I'd said something stupid. "The only thing they've changed is their name," he explained patiently, "like the government."

*The people of the Far East – with its runaway economic growth – have earned
a reputation for hard work, pragmatism and a talent for making money. But is
it only due to skill? Humphrey Hawksley in Hong Kong examined the oddities
of astrology and geomancy, regarded as essential to every successful business, even
for the smooth running of the BBC office there.*

ROCKY THE GEOMANCER

HUMPHREY HAWKSLEY   HONG KONG   12 MARCH 1992

From the windows of the BBC Asia Bureau in Hong Kong you look
out north-west. Immediately below are the headquarters of the British
Forces, *H.M.S. Tamar*, with its helicopters flying in and out, and visiting war-ships
from Australia, Canada and the United States. Further along is the Star Ferry
terminal, half-hidden at the foot of huge buildings, then the bright red hydrofoils
cutting through the water on their way to Portuguese enclave of Macau; the
container ships and the tramp steamers of the Far East are anchored here and
there in the harbour. Beyond are the rugged and green hills of the Kowloon
Peninsula and, far in the distance, are the chimneys of a power station on Tsing
Yi Island.

The chimneys are the problem. The other evening, I was about to go home
when Becky Tseng, our office manager, said: "You must wait a minute." "Why?"
"The Feng Shui man is coming." That's the geomancer; a mix of astrologer,
Chinese fortune teller, problem solver – the man who tells you how to deck
out the office, ward off the demons, keep the staff healthy and – particularly
important in Hong Kong – how to make money.

Our geomancer is Sung Sui Kwong. He's slick. Call him Rocky, he says.
Rocky swept into the office dressed in a dark suit, with a mobile phone, pager,

calligraphy kit, and in his leather briefcase, a sort of compass with an astrological time-chart and lots of other complicated markings. Rocky took note of all our birthdays and set about working out the clashes and alliances between the five elements – fire, water, earth, metal and wood – swirling around the office.

The tiny radio studio was in an appalling position; burnt up, so to speak, by the smoke and fire coming from that power station so far away. Traffic from the main road below cut through the office destroying the harmony. And the door faced an unfortunate direction, letting bad luck flow into the bureau. In Feng Shui terms the whole thing was a mess. But Rocky said he could fix it. Seven coins under the carpet by the door. Two miniature stone lions on Becky's desk. Eight tortoises on the windowsills to ward off the fire from the power station; stone, not wood, which would burn. A picture of mountains and water to envelope and drown any bad luck, and an octagonal gold clock as a general shield against all demons. There were a few other things. The television correspondent, Brian Barron, his cameraman, Eric Thirer, and Becky all had problems with wood because of their birthdays. Rocky's solution was wall-to-wall green carpeting to represent a forest. They settled for green foot mats under their desks instead. My problem was with metal. Rocky suggested I get a gold watch and a medallion.

If you ask exactly what Feng Shui is, you'll get half a dozen different answers. It translates literally as wind, water and concerns the harmonious movement of energy. Good Feng Shui has become synonymous with good luck. And it's important. The Bank of China has become a symbol of Peking's powerful shadow over Hong Kong. It's the tallest building in the territory and dominates the sky-line. But whether because of its political association or its shape, it's believed to give off bad Feng Shui. It soars skywards like a dagger and its angular edges are sharp. The geomancers say they should be smooth. China knew that. Perhaps the communist giant just wanted to prove its muscle.

Anyway, the colonial government quickly responded. Three trees of a soft and harmonious character have been planted in the gardens of Government House. A spokeswoman confirmed they were to balance the sharp edges of the Bank of China. There are reports that the Chairman of that other bastion of colonialism, the Hong Kong and Shanghai Bank, has put a mirror in his office for the same reason. The Bank also called in a Feng Shui advisor when it was designing its new building in the eighties. He told them to change the direction of the escalators so they weren't pointing down towards the harbour.

"That means all our wealth would have been flowing into the water," said a spokesman. The bank's profits, incidentally, grew by more than eighty per cent last year.

Feng Shui – whether you believe in it or not – can't be ignored. If, say, the Hong Kong Bank was known to have bad Feng Shui, its depositors would put their money elsewhere. Developers find their buildings difficult to let, if word gets around that the geomancers aren't happy. When Hong Kong's democracy leader, Martin Lee, came to our radio studio to be interviewed by the *Today* programme, the first thing he said as soon as he came off air was: "terrible Feng Shui in here."

And perhaps the most touching story is that of the dragon from the hills of Kowloon (Kowloon means nine dragons). The myth says that one of them liked to swoop down south across Hong Kong island every morning to take a dip in the sea at Repulse Bay. Which was fine when only the elderly, elegant, low rise Repulse Bay Hotel stood in his way. He could jump over it. Then a huge and high development of luxury flats began amid all the apprehension of bad Feng Shui. So the architect designed a huge gap for the dragon to fly through, right in the middle of the block.

The apartments sold for millions: the architect won an award.

In March 1992 about 120 students and other peace activists set sail from Darwin in northern Australia for the Indonesian-administered island of East Timor. They hoped to lay wreaths in memory of civilians killed by Indonesian troops towards the end of 1991, but Indonesian warships forced the boat's crew to turn back to Australia. Red Harrison sailed with the protestors and sent this description of life on board.

PEACE MISSION AFLOAT

RED HARRISON   SYDNEY   18 MARCH 1992

No-one suggested that this might be a luxury cruise – not with Indonesia's threats of armed confrontation on the high seas – but the signs were promising. The organisers collected one-and-a-half million dollars for the expedition and went shopping in Darwin, with a Portuguese immigrant who owned a grocery store, spending forty thousand dollars on food and other supplies. Darwin would be a fine place to go shopping now because everything in that grocery store must be fresh. All the old and hard-to-sell groceries were cleaned out and went aboard the ship. No-one realised that until volunteer cooks among the students served the first meal.

But long before that, the high ambitions of this venture were dampened by more pedestrian concerns. Just as we pulled away from the wharf, a noisy rolling thunderstorm crackled overhead. Darwin welcomes storms at this time of year because, for a few minutes, lashings of warm tropical rain make the ferocious heat almost bearable. On board however, we were horrified to see rain streaming through the light fittings in the ceiling of the main cabin. And while we scrambled to salvage soaking bags and radios and television cameras – all the computerised paraphernalia of the modern media – we prayed that the bottom of the ship was more secure. Then we discovered that the lavatories didn't work.

Our cargo of students, about ninety of them, came from all over the world: Portugal, Britain, Germany, Sweden, Japan, China, Canada – more than twenty countries – and I assure you that calling for a plumber in these circumstances sounds just as frenetic in any language. Happily, that problem was rectified quickly. Dinner, that first night at sea, came from some vigorous exercise in the galley with can-openers. So, unhappily, did almost every other meal. There was a greyish something that might have been meat once and onions that must have perished long ago from lack of sunlight. But there was bread and fresh fruit and absolutely no shortage of Portuguese sardines. Tinned, of course.

It took some hours to settle down to discover that for most people aboard there was nowhere to sleep. The big saloon was crammed with comfortable armchairs, but – did I mention that the air-conditioning wasn't working properly? And never did? Outside, the deck slippery with rain, seemed only slightly cooler. A few distinguished passengers, such as the former President of Portugal, General Antonio Eanes, and a few elderly reporters such as myself were allocated cabins normally occupied by the crew. But first the crew had to be evicted. Unwillingly. It was after one o'clock in the morning when I was escorted down into the bowels, to a tiny cabin which offered instant heat exhaustion and suffocation. And, I warned myself, this was just about the level a torpedo might strike. I went for a shower, but only the hot tap worked, so I climbed wearily back to the deck and stayed there.

We'd been advised that if we wanted a nightcap we should bring supplies. Some brought whisky, but there was no soda. Some brought gin and found there was no tonic. But hundreds of cans of beer and soft drinks were offered free. It was a pity, really, that the failings of the refrigeration system meant they had to be drunk hot.

Fortunately the sea remained calm and most spent the long days dozing after restless nights, or scanning the horizon for aircraft or ships. Lifeboat drill broke the monotony. Drill with drinks, we called it. Down in the hot saloon we clutched our hot drinks and watched a crewman demonstrate how to put on a lifejacket. No-one suggested actually going to a lifeboat station, though it was obvious many of the passengers had never been on a ship in their lives.

For all this, they were a pretty cheerful, exhilarated crowd until an Indonesian warship, after shadowing us through the night, closed in after dawn and ordered our captain to turn back. We could see Timor clearly. We could also see Indonesian sailors manning machine-guns. Then the so-called peace mission became very tense, very pensive. Only on the way back to Australia did some protest that the ship should have pressed on – at least until the Indonesians fired a shot across the bows. Fortunately restraint and self-control governed both sides in this little chapter of East Timor's long, infinitely sad story.

In the sense that it undoubtedly helped keep international attention focused on the killings in Timor, the voyage was far from being failure. But I still wonder where all the money came from, and whether the students would have come to Australia had someone not paid their fares. And I still wonder about the new stamp in my passport. It says: Did Not Depart Australia.

You have to be desperate to make yourself a refugee in Bangladesh. It's one of the world's poorest countries, and still recovering from 1991's devastating cyclone. So when the Rohingya people of Burma's Arakan state started leaving their homes and heading for the border, it was clear that this was their last resort.

BROTHERLY LOVE IN BANGLADESH

LINDSEY HILSUM   COX'S BAZAAR   18 MARCH 1992

A trocity stories have a horrible sameness the world over, and the details lose their resonance in the recounting. What shocked me was that these people were so poor, so bewildered, and they recited without emotion, as if it were a shopping list, a catalogue of despair. Thousands of men seized by the military for forced labour, mass abductions of women kept in army camps and repeatedly raped. The woman who told me that she only learnt what had happened to her husband when she discovered his body – eyes gouged out, one arm and his penis cut off – abandoned in the jungle.

The Rohingyas are conservative Muslims. For the women, many of whom live in a special section of the refugee camps, called Widows' Corner, the nightmare will be with them always. Some are pregnant with children conceived through rape. Their choice is to have the child, or use traditional roots and leaves to abort. Septic abortions are not only common in such situations, but often fatal. The teenage girls will probably never marry now, because no man will want them. One health worker explained to me that everyone hates the women who have been raped.

Newly established refugee camps are often chaotic places, where people scrabble and fight for scarce resources. But these camps are strangely quiet. The people seem subdued, cowed. Most of them are malnourished and sick. Few of the children under seven have vaccination scars – a sign that health services have deteriorated or been withdrawn.

Arakan is the poorest and most remote state in Burma, and it seems clear that the Burmese government has deliberately left it under-developed and deprived. But why has the Burmese government turned against these illiterate rice-farmers, poor people who pose no threat? The two rebel movements in the area are negligible – small bands of men, trying to fight the Burmese army with Second World War rifles handed down from their fathers.

The answer has its roots deep in history. The Rohingyas were first persecuted in 1784, when the Buddhist Burmans occupied the Muslim Kingdom of Arakan. Over the years there have been periodic purges and you can find Rohingyas scattered around the world. According to one historical article I read, in Burma there's a proverb: if you see a snake and an Arakanese, kill the Arakanese first. The last major onslaught was in 1978, when some two hundred thousand Rohingyas were driven into Bangladesh. They returned when the two countries signed an accord. I think it will be different this time. One of the few occasions when one of the refugees showed emotion, was when I asked an old woman if she would return. She sobbed as she said: "I would rather drink poison or drown myself in the Bay of Bengal than go back to Burma."

The State Law and Order Restoration Council, the SLORC, which rules Burma, is impenetrable, closed to outsiders. That in itself gives a clue to its policy. As the SLORC turns in on itself, isolated internationally, loathed by its own citizens, those on the margins are regarded as outsiders. The Rohingyas are Muslims, while the SLORC is Buddhist. The Rohingyas are therefore *kalas* – foreigners. The SLORC claims there is no such people as the Rohingyas, they're just Bangladeshis living illegally in Burma. So it is exploiting long-standing divisions between Arakan's Buddhist population, known as the Moghs, and the Muslim Rohingyas.

Refugees told me how the SLORC is encouraging the Moghs to desecrate mosques and *madrasas*, Islamic schools. The Moghs have been given licence to take Rohingya paddy fields. When the refugees speak of their tormentors, they say the Moghs cause them as much misery as the army. For the refugees, the priority is to be safe. But conditions in Bangladesh are worsening. As long as the Rohingyas were coming across the river at a rate of five hundred or so a day, Bangladesh could cope. But recently the influx has reached five thousand or more each day.

The refugee camps are overcrowded, the government and aid agencies are desperately digging tube wells and latrines to provide sanitation and stop the spread of disease. But they can't keep up, and thousands of Rohingyas are massing at the side of the road which leads from the border to the town of Cox's Bazaar. They're cutting down the forest to clear land, and burning valuable Burma teak for cooking fires. They're willing to take on any menial job for virtually no money, so they're undermining the local economy.

What struck me about this tragedy was the response of the Bangladeshi people in the border area. It was here that the 1991 cyclone hit hardest, and many have been unable to rebuild their houses properly or recover their livelihoods. But I didn't hear anyone protest about the newcomers. Some Bangladeshis I spoke to said, "well, they're Muslims so they're our brothers and we have to accept them." Others said, "they're human beings and they're being persecuted so of course we have to help them." People in Cox's Bazaar have formed a group to help the Rohingyas, and Bangladeshi non-governmental organisations have sent staff to work in the camps. Most of the doctors and health workers I met were Bangladeshis, working long hours in difficult conditions for very little reward.

The government is trying to establish larger camps and attract more international aid to take the burden off the local community. But resources are scarce and it's inevitable that the day-to-day development needs of the area will suffer. The monsoon is coming, with its yearly toll of collapsed houses and sick children. It will be terrible for the refugees, but it will be bad for ordinary Bangladeshis too. As I left the country, I thought about the extraordinary truth that it's always those who have the least who give the most.

In Britain a bus decked out in BBC logos, carrying radio celebrities in a meet-the-audience promotional exercise is no longer an uncommon sight. But on Pakistan's North-West Frontier, such an exercise is a novelty, as Gordon Adam, head of the BBC's Pashto Service, discovered when he travelled through some of Pakistan's most remote regions.

ON THE NORTH-WEST FRONTIER

GORDON ADAM   PESHAWAR   28 MARCH 1992

Broadcasting in Pashto, the language of the Pashtuns or Pathans of Afghanistan and the North-West Frontier, is a mixed blessing. On the one hand, you are performing a public service function in the highest traditions of the BBC – most of our audience have no other source of impartial news and comment about world and regional affairs, and they are devoted listeners, particularly because this region seems to be in permanent news-worthy crisis. On the other hand, they live in a particularly difficult area in terms of access: most of Afghanistan is off-limits because of war, and Pakistan has only a tenuous grip of the tribal area where our most loyal Pakistani listeners live.

Mounting a road-show – or Pashto Service Caravan as we preferred to call it – was therefore an enterprise not lacking in risks. The Pakistan government was nervous about our route, and banned us from entering the more remote areas at the last minute. We were saved from what could have been much greater danger on the supposedly safer route by a group of listeners, who hearing a broadcast about our change of plan, came to our hotel at six o'clock in the morning to warn us that our new route was being plagued by attacks from dacoits or bandits from Sindh province.

So another change of plan: but then genuine misfortune struck. Late at night, the bus failed to take an unmarked right-angle bend, toppled off the road and rolled over twice. No serious injuries but a wrecked vehicle, and a driver in jail. Twenty-four hours later, thanks to talented Afghan mechanics, the bus was on the road – just; and the driver was out of jail, thanks to an Afghan refugee living in Britain. Unknown to us, his brother had been killed in the fighting in southern Afghanistan, and he was travelling to his home via Pakistan when he came across our crashed bus and learned our driver had been arrested. With great presence of mind, he sought me out in my hotel and told me the news. After lengthy discussions with the military and the civil police – the driver had chosen to crash uncomfortably near a big ammunition dump which raised questions about his motive in the eyes of the authorities – he was released.

The crash turned out to be a bit of a blessing. The wide publicity in the BBC Urdu and Pashto services assured us of a sympathetic and curious gathering wherever we went over the next ten days. The Afghan mechanics armed with hammers and welding kit had managed to bash the bus into shape and, complete with plastic windscreen, we finished our hectic schedule in a battered state but without further mechanical problems.

In several places, people lined the streets in welcome, and up to seven or eight hundred people jostled around our woebegone bus to have a chance to share in the discussion of our programmes. The police were remarkably tolerant – we were moved on only once, and that was just a couple of hundred yards. The enthusiasm of the listeners at being confronted with broadcasters in real life was remarkable: at last they could put faces put to the voices whom they hear daily at seven in the morning or quarter to nine at night. There was genuine astonishment that we should have made the effort to come all this way to canvass their views about our broadcasts.

They weren't slow in coming forward with criticisms - alleged pro-western bias in reporting the Gulf War was a common complaint. But what struck me was the extent to which these audiences, schooled in an aural tradition of learning, were able to recall the detail of our educational broadcasts. For instance, the Afghan boy who recited off pat a verse from one of our sketches warning about the dangers of unexploded mines, and even mimicked the distinctive voice of the broadcaster who delivers the warning. And then there was the young man who told us he had given up smoking heroin after listening to our series of short plays on this theme, but had taken up hashish instead.

Not everyone was so enthusiastic: just as the tour was ending, an angry,

236

bearded man jumped on board the bus, shouting that we had affronted Islam by allowing a woman – my colleague Safia Haleem – to address the crowd of men. In this society, no women came to the bus to enter the debate, Safia had to seek them out in their homes. It was no use entering into a religious debate about whether or not such an action was condemned in the Koran, the crowd was instantly divided between those who took the man's side and those who believed we should be allowed to hold our meeting.

The next day – the last day of the trip – we spied a van with a mounted loudspeaker warning people of the dangers of listening to foreign journalists and their alien ideas. It was the right time to end a tour which had otherwise been marked by the generous hospitality for which the Pashtun people are justly famous.

India's ruling Congress Party held its first conference since the assassination of Rajiv Gandhi, in April 1992. Although his successor lacks charisma, and the magic bestowed by the Nehru name, he emerged from the conference as the undisputed leader of Congress, which is still India's only national party.

LIFE AFTER RAJIV

MARK TULLY   DELHI   23 APRIL 1992

Hindu pilgrimages are big business in India, and nowhere does better than the temple of Lord Venkateshwara at Tirupati. While cathedral chapters in Britain find themselves involved in endless controversies over admission charges, selling their treasures and other fund-raising activities, the brahmins of Tirupati have only one worry – what to do with all the money they collect. No Hindu objects to paying for a very brief *darshan*, or sight, of the gleaming black idol of Lord Venkateshwara. What is more, those who believe that the Lord has shown them a favour bear their gold and jewellery, and of course currency notes, into the *hundis*, or collection bags, dotted around the temple. The brahmins sometimes even find pistols in the *hundis* – perhaps offered to Lord Venkateshwara in thanks for a murder successfully completed, who knows?

Over the last few years Hinduism has become a major political issue and there was always the risk, by holding its first party congress in such a sacred town, that Narasimha Rao would be accused of going for the Hindu vote which, in theory at least, the secular Congress Party strongly disapproves of. But he wasn't. It was simply accepted that he had chosen Tirupati because it was in his home state of Andhra Pradesh.

Narasimha Rao has somehow developed a reputation for being above, what are known in India as 'dirty politics'. In Tirupati Narasimha Rao was at his most decent, conveying the impression of an amiable father-figure who wouldn't stoop to the level of his colleagues. He sat peacefully on the dais, listening to delegates commenting, quite often critically, on his government and his policies: behind the scenes senior party members were trying to wheel and deal their way on to the all-important Congress Working Committee, which had to be appointed before the conference was over.

Those who were doubtful about winning a place in an election to the committee tried to arrange for consensus: the party treasurer became so eloquent in his advocacy of consensus that he burst into tears. When there was a deadlock Narasimha Rao said he couldn't stop the election, thus further enhancing his reputation for decency, by refusing to take advantage of the deadlock to follow the precedent, set by Indira and Rajiv Gandhi, to nominate all the members of the committee. He didn't even bother to let it be known whom he would like to be elected, and allowed his own son to be badly defeated, which is unheard of in modern Indian politics.

The election sorted out the ranking below Narasimha Rao; Arjun Singh, one of the most astute members of the cabinet, emerged as the second most important person in the party, beating his main rival into fourth place. But victory really went to the Prime Minister. When the results were announced, Arjun Singh's supporters leapt up shouting: "What sort of leader does the country need?" But before they could get onto the second line of the slogan, "Arjun Singh, Arjun Singh", the usually far from spritely minister was on his feet, pushing his supporters back into their chairs. He knew that even the slightest hint of opposition to Narasimha Rao would run counter to the spirit of the conference.

After the elections were over, Narasimha Rao retired to the temple on the hill to have his *darshan* of Lord Venkateshwara. I don't know what he put in the *hundi*, perhaps some of the money he'd saved by not, himself, taking part in expensive campaigning to get his own men elected to the Congress Working Committee? He certainly had a lot to be grateful for. With his leadership endorsed by the party conference, Narasimha Rao will now want to concentrate his energies on the serious problems facing the government. But Indian politics are never as simple as that: when Indira Gandhi was at the height of her power, allegations of corruption knocked her off course and the same happened to her son, Rajiv.

There's so far absolutely no indication that Narasimha Rao will fall into that trap. His main threat comes from the economy. He has put his full weight behind the liberalisation, demanded by the I.M.F. as the price for rescuing India from bankruptcy. But the I.M.F.'s structural adjustments are painful processes, and India is already beginning to realise that. Narasimha Rao's economic reforms have never been popular with a large section of the Congress Party who think they're antagonising the poor, and thus threatening their chances of re-election. Arjun Singh is in charge of education, so he has been able to ensure he is not associated too closely with the economic reforms. If he feels they are becoming unpopular enough to threaten Narasimha Rao's position, he might well allow his supporters to shout the second line of that slogan – to campaign for him as the nation's leader.

In mid-May 1992 fighting broke out in the autonomous Azeri republic of Nakhichevan, a thin strip of land sandwiched between the borders of Azerbaijan, Armenia, Turkey and Iran. The Azeris living in Nakhichevan accused neighbouring Armenia of launching an unprovoked attack but the Armenians denied this.

TO NAKHICHEVAN AND BACK

JONATHAN RUGMAN   NAKHICHEVAN   20 MAY 1992

"**Y**ou can't cross the bridge to Nakhichevan" said the man in the Turkish Foreign Ministry. "It's not officially open yet, it's impossible." For a journalist this is like putting a red rag in front of a bull – there was now no choice; I *had* to cross the bridge to Nakhichevan. The Russian embassy gave me a visa with a few hours' notice. The Soviet Union may have collapsed, but the Russians were in holiday mood and not about to be obstructive.

After a long bus ride through the dusty grey towns and villages of eastern Turkey, the next potential obstacle was the governor of the border region. He could give me an official looking piece of paper which would at least get me on to the road leading to the bridge, although Turkish soldiers might well turn me back.

The best way of getting official pieces of paper in Turkey is by sitting opposite the wide wooden desk of the right official, drinking and smoking cigarettes and above all pretending not to be in a hurry. "Do you know the Dirty Duck pub in Stratford?" asked the border governor sitting at a wide wooden desk as we drank tea and smoked cigarettes. The governor had spent a year in England learning English; but the experiment had not been entirely successful. I was asked to read him a letter from his landlady in Margate, who wrote about how much she missed his wife's kebabs. The governor could not have been more pleased. We parted the best of friends and the official piece of paper was mine.

Once Turkish soldiers had radioed to base and decided that I was not a British spy I was on the Nakhichevani border bridge itself. It crosses a fast-flowing river and has the magical peaks of Mount Ararat as a backdrop. But the man in Ankara had warned me that the bridge was not finished yet, and it throbbed to the noise of cement-mixing lorries, one of which drove me across.

Lieutenant Ivanov was waiting. With only a year-old copy of *Time* magazine to keep him company, and the border officially closed, Lieutenant Ivanov has very little to do in the disused railway carriage which acts as his office. But Ivanov is a social asset to the Nakhichevani border, a dashing officer from Moscow who should be sweeping around the ballroom of some 19th-century Russian novel rather than protecting the edges of an empire which no longer exists. The Lieutenant does at least possess the unique power to work in the Azeri enclave but visits his dentist across the border in Armenia. We got on, and he let me in.

A lorry-ride later and I was in Nakhichevan's capital, an elegant town of parks, tree-lined avenues and a high number of people in possession of golden teeth. With the shops so empty and the people so poor, the number of golden teeth in Nakhichevan was a mystery to me which I did not solve, although I did notice that sugar-filled tea is very popular. The other question which bothered me was why the president of the Nakhichevani parliament had eight pink and blue telephones on his desk. When more than two telephones were ringing at once the president didn't know what to do. Telephones are easy to come by, but hands to hold receivers and ears to listen with are in short supply.

Then with my work finished, back to the unfinished bridge. The cement mixers were busy at work, and I was stuck without a lift for the drive into Turkey. Salvation comes in the most unexpected ways. A convention of Turkish wrestling referees had decided that it would be interesting to take a look at the bridge. The only problem with the ride they offered me was that a fight broke out along the way. One wrestling referee told another wrestling referee that he was the most important person on the minibus because he had served as an officer in the Turkish army. The other wrestling referee said he was more important because he was driving the minibus.

The issue was not resolved, and so, with my companions growing more angry and red-faced by the minute, I made the long journey home.

*In 1992 the award-winning science writer, Arthur C. Clarke, celebrated his 75th
birthday in the place he's long made his adopted home, Sri Lanka. To coincide
with his birthday, his latest book "How The World Was One - Beyond The Global
Village" has recently been published. Christopher Morris paid him a visit.*

THE COSMOS FROM
COLOMBO

CHRISTOPHER MORRIS   COLOMBO   30 MAY 1992

I
f you ever want to find Arthur C. Clarke at about five o'clock in the afternoon
you have to head for the Otters Sports Club in Colombo. He plays table
tennis there every day. Seventy-five this year, he describes himself as an addict,
and, as the commentators might say, he can still play a bit. With monsoon
rains thundering down outside, this correspondent was humiliatingly defeated,
as youth was once again bamboozled by experience. When he's not playing
table tennis, Arthur Clarke still leads an astonishingly active life. Recently he
went back to one of his other great loves - diving - as he explored a wreck
one hundred feet below the surface of the ocean a few miles off the Sri Lankan
coast.

His house in Colombo used to be the residence of the city's Archbishop,
and it's just about big enough to contain a lifetime's acquisitions. A typically
futuristic extension has been built at the front of the house. Arthur Clarke
sits inside, surrounded by books, computers, television screens and even old-
fashioned piles of the letters which arrive every day from all corners of the
world. He has also been spending a great deal of time recently on a new hobby.
He's become a gardener - and unlike for most of us that doesn't mean pottering
about in the back garden pruning the roses. True to form, Arthur Clarke is
busy landscaping the planet Mars. With the aid of an addictive and highly complex

243

computer programme which can produce images almost as sharp as a photograph, he demonstrates how he has covered the sides of Olympus Mone – at about six hundred miles wide the largest volcano in the solar system – with lakes, pine trees and even cacti. A book entitled *A Garden on Mars* is just one of many projects planned for next year.

As for his latest book, *How the World was One*, it traces the history of telecommunications, from the laying of the first transatlantic submarine telegraph cable to satellites and beyond. Its basic premise is that the information revolution now taking place will have far more influence on the course of human history than the industrial revolution which we read about at school. Arthur Clarke describes the book as his magnum opus, or "the book which will finally make me famous". Of course most people would suggest that Dr Clarke is somewhat famous already. Science fiction books such as *2001 – A Space Odessey* and *Childhood's End* have brought him a world-wide audience. But about half of the seventy or so books he has had published during his lifetime have been works of non-fiction. And in 1945 it was Arthur C. Clarke who wrote the first scientific paper to predict the enormous potential of communication satellites. "The wartime censors okayed this article in a suspiciously short period of time," he says. "They probably thought it was so crazy that there was no danger of giving anything away to the enemy."

Now the wheel seems to have come full circle. Arthur Clarke admits he did not predict the speed of technological advances, especially the invention of the transistor. By the 1990s satellite technology had helped change the political complexion of the world. "The Second Russian Revolution couldn't have happened," he argues, "without fax machines and satellite TV showing what was happening in Moscow during the attempted coup." The conclusion is that repressive regimes around the world can no longer guard their borders against the information explosion.

On a personal level Arthur Clarke looks set to continue contributing to the communications revolution for some time to come. He says communication has always been in the blood of the Clarke family. His parents both worked for the Post Office, and apparently courted by Morse code.

Already such wonders seem hopelessly old-fashioned. Arthur Clarke himself says we will all soon be wearing telephone watches around our wrists. Towards the end of *How The World Was One* there is a chapter called *As Far As The Eye Can See*, in which Arthur Clarke indulges in his favourite pastime – speculating about the future. What price teletransportation of solid matter, including human beings? For the moment *Star Trek* and 'Beam me up Scotty' remain in the fantasy realm. But Arthur C. Clarke will continue to dream. In his own words "Science fiction is the only genuine consciousness expanding drug."

While the finger is often pointed at developing countries for causing so much pollution, one way to reduce it is to recycle. Our Delhi Correspondent, Mark Tully, reflected at the start of the Earth Summit in mid-1992 that, in this respect at least, India was leading the world.

ANY OLD RUBBISH

MARK TULLY   DELHI   30 MAY 1992

Many years ago I received a pained letter from an Indian who had bought some peanuts. Unfortunately the peanuts had been sold to him in a paper cone, made from a letter a listener had sent to the BBC. My correspondent wrote: "You are always asking for listeners to write in. Now I know why I never get a reply."

There was no denying that, in those days, when listeners' letters were dealt with in the Delhi office we did sell them as waste, but I was under the impression that we replied to them first! The staff were most upset when I told them to destroy old letters; waste paper is considered a legitimate and valuable perk in Indian offices. An Indian newspaper editor, bemoaning a fall in circulation, blamed it on the proprietor's decision to reduce the size of the paper. He said: "The bigger the paper the more it will sell, because it has a better resale value to the *Kabari* wallah."

The *Kabari* wallah, or waste merchant, is the lynchpin of the recycling industry and, appropriately enough, he is a cyclist himself, biking around residential and office areas shouting "*Kabari* wallah *Kabari* wallah" to attract business. He is the equivalent of the old rag and bone man in Britain, but is far less choosy about what he will take.

When the *Kabari* wallah has filled his sack, and the carrier on the back of his bike can take no more newspapers, he rides to Old Delhi where the Turkman Gate, built by the Mogul emperors, is the centre of the *Kabari* bazaar. Its narrow alleys are lined with small *godowns* or sheds, the proprietors sitting in the doorway weighing waste paper, cloth or whatever else it may be, in old fashioned scales suspended from the ceilings. Much of the reprocessing also starts in Turkman Gate. Outside one shed men strip cables for their copper wire, inside a darkened room young boys cut and fold paper to be used for those cones in which peanuts are sold, or for some other form of packaging. There are specialists in retreading tyres. Those that are so bald and cut that they are even beyond the tyre wallah's skill to repair are sold for the handcarts which are the most common form of transporting goods in Turkman Gate. There are also skilled mechanics renovating shock absorbers, dynamos, and other motor parts. They proudly boast that nearly half the parts sold in Delhi are recycled, many of them neatly packed to look as though they are genuine spares.

Bottle wallahs assess the value of each empty they buy. It matters whether they are Moghul Monarch, Officers Choice, Bagpiper Gold, Diplomat, or any other of the countless brands of Indian whisky, because each distiller pays a different price for empties. In Delhi there is a specialised market in genuine, good condition scotch whiskey bottles sold by diplomats' servants. They go to the bootleggers who run the black market in scotch. Very few can afford to pay the official price and, if you deal on the black, you may well find yourself with a crate of scotch bottles filled with indian whiskey. I challenge anyone to detect that before they have either tasted or at least smelt the contents.

Even plastic – that scourge of environmentalists – has a market in Turkman Gate. it's packed up in sacks and sent to factories where, apparently, it can be recycled. But there is a problem: most *Kabari* is easily recycled and the local supply usually meets the local demand. With plastic that's not so. It does not find ready buyers in the smaller towns with no plastic manufacturers near them. The Himalayan hill station of Mussourie was drowning in the plastic left behind by the visitors who fled there from the summer heat of the plains. Some local worthies persuaded four hundred and fifty children from the boarding schools, which are a feature of every hill station, to come to the rescue. Their collection of plastic bags weighed over one hundred kilos.

India would not have a plastic problem if it treasured its traditional methods of packaging which are all biodegradable. A recent railway minister did, rightly, insist that caterers went back to the little clay cups tea should be served in. After use they are thrown out of the window to return rapidly to the clay whence they came. His successors have allowed plastic cups to make a come back. Travellers, seeing the small boys scavenging for the cups that have been deposited on the tracks, should remember that they may get the same cup again on their next journey. That ought surely to be an encouragement for the return of clay. But, unfortunately, as so often happens, the developing world catches onto our habits just as we are beginning to realise how bad they are. There should be no demand for plastic shopping bags when jute is desperately searching for markets. There should be no market for artificially flavoured potato crisps in plastic bags when freshly cooked spicy potato tikkas, served on leaves, are available in almost every bazaar, but crisps are catching on fast. Even that most Indian of all Indian habits – chewing pan – a hard nut wrapped in a pan leaf smeared with lime, is going the plastic way. If you want a take away pan it will still be packed in a dried leaf which preserves the moisture, but nowadays the posher pan wallahs will then put the package in a plastic bag which, of course, guarantees that the pan does *not* stay fresh. Pan wallahs tell me their customers don't think they are getting their money's worth without a plastic bag.

But then perhaps India will solve its plastic problem in a very Indian way. Maybe, as the demand grows, the *Kabari* wallahs will find an ever spreading market for second hand plastic to meet that very demand. Personally I think it would be better if the demand didn't grow: give me tea in a clay cup, potato tikkas, and fresh, moist pan any time.

In the South Pacific, the republic of Fiji held its first parliamentary elections in
May 1992, since the government was overthrown in a military coup in May 1987.
The elections were conducted on racial grounds – Fijians had to vote for Fijians,
and ethnic Indians could vote only for candidates from their own community.
General Sitiveni Rabuka, the coup leader, was sworn in as the country's new Prime
Minister. But he later astonished voters by promising to reform the constitution,
and so undermine the central purpose of the coup.

ROOM SERVICE IN FIJI

RED HARRISON   SUVA   5 JUNE 1992

For all the exaggerated rubbish written about the South Pacific islands, Fiji does have a sweet illusion of paradise. Some of that was lost for me, during the coup five years ago, when the army developed a singularly effective way of waking any visiting journalist whose unwelcome reports of the new political apartheid could be heard on short-wave radio. About four o'clock in the morning, soldiers wearing balaclavas and carrying powerful automatic weapons would creep into the hotel room and stand silently around the bed. One soldier would then shake one of the sleeper's big toes. I can guarantee the sight of those masked faces and their pointed rifles banished sleep instantly. There are no journalists in the cells today, hardly a soldier to be seen on the streets and room service comes with a smile. And so, I have to say, does General Sitiveni Rabuka, who invited me to drink *kava* with some of his friends.

Kava – Fijians call it *yaqona* – is made from pulverised tree roots and drunk in elaborate ritual from a half coconut shell. It is not ambrosia. It looks like dishwater but actually tastes much worse. But *yaqona* is the social cement that bonds Fijian society, so deeply woven for centuries into the fabric of culture that it is impossible to imagine doing business, making friends, settling arguments or social contracts without it.

Squatting around the *kava* bowl, I discovered some reasons why, for all his grassroots support, many educated Fijians still question General Rabuka's fitness to be Prime Minister. Back in May 1987, when he arrested the newly elected coalition government and installed himself at the head of a military administration, the General was only a colonel – just a humble soldier, he said, doing his duty for Fijian race, salvation, and culture. His aim, which still has enormous support, was to ensure that never again would ethnic Indians dominate government as they did in the deposed coalition. Fijians were jealous of Indian commercial power and frightened about where this new political power might lead. They regarded Indians as a greedy, mean, tricky, over-ambitious lot who had to be forced into subservience for their own good.

With the declaration of a republic and a new constitution guaranteeing Fijian supremacy, it might have seemed that the General achieved his aim. But five years of adulation as the hero of the coup has taught Rabuka how to change his mind – and to keep changing it. He told me, for example, how he wanted desperately as prime minister to lead Fiji out of the economic pit created by the coup. Then he declared he'd be happy to be a mere backbencher, or be nothing at all and simply go back to his village and vegetate.

There's no chance of that – yet. General Rabuka's party is called *Soqosoqo ni Vakavulewa ni Taukei* and it means The Organisation of Indigenous Rulers, which is another way of saying: no room for Indians. But within hours of winning the election, General Rabuka turned back the clock and contradicted himself again. In return for parliamentary support, because he doesn't have an absolute majority, he promised to reform the constitution, to remove its racist clauses and give Fiji a document of which no-one need be ashamed.

This is not what his party wants. More astonishingly, it is the Labour Party and the Federation Party, both dominated by Indians, which have agreed to support him in parliament. These are the same parties which formed the government he deposed by force five years ago. What, we might ask, was the point of that military coup? Prime Minister Rabuka's promise is arousing intense and open hostility among his own people and more than one has suggested he should have gone to the London School of Economics for a few years to get some academic qualifications and experience in running a government. Many more are suggesting that the Great Council of Chiefs, the traditional indigenous authority in Fiji, might, within just a few months, give him all the time he needs to do that. Those who handed Rabuka his own taste of paradise still have the power to take it away.

The
From Our Own Correspondent
Series

Also Available:

Volume One (1989–90) detailing the collapse of communism in Eastern Europe £8.95

Volume Two (1990–91) with a special emphasis on the Gulf War £10.95

Available from good bookshops, or directly from:

BEBC Distribution
Unit 15 Newton Business Park
Parkstone, Poole Dorset BH12 3LL
freephone 0800 262260
freefax   0800 262266